D0857147

World Monetary Disorder

edited by
Patrick M. Boarman
David G. Tuerck

Sponsored by the Center
for International Business
of the School of Business
and Management, Pepperdine
University, Los Angeles
and Malibu, California

The Praeger Special Studies program—
utilizing the most modern and efficient book
production techniques and a selective
worldwide distribution network—makes
available to the academic, government, and
business communities significant, timely
research in U.S. and international economic, social, and political development.

World Monetary Disorder

National Policies vs. International Imperatives

PRAEGER SPECIAL STUDIES IN INTERNATIONAL BUSINESS, FINANCE, AND TRADE

Praeger Publishers   New York   Washington   London

Library of Congress Cataloging in Publication Data
Main entry under title:

World monetary disorder.

(Praeger special studies in international business,
finance, and trade)
Includes bibliographical references.
1. International finance--Addresses, essays, lectures.
2. Currency question--Addresses, essays, lectures.
3. Foreign exchange problem--Addresses, essays, lectures.
4. Monetary policy--Addresses, essays, lectures.
I. Boarman, Patrick M. II. Tuerck, David G.
III. Center for International Business.
HG3881.W63   332.4'5   75-8401
ISBN 0-275-00580-1

PRAEGER PUBLISHERS
111 Fourth Avenue, New York, N.Y. 10003, U.S.A.

Published in the United States of America in 1976
by Praeger Publishers, Inc.

Printed in the United States of America

PREFACE

The 20 papers that comprise this book were presented originally
at an international monetary conference held in May 1974, at Malibu,
California, under the sponsorship of the Center for International Business, Pepperdine University. The authors have subsequently reviewed
the papers, and updated them where necessary, in the light of more
recent developments on the international monetary front.

The title selected for this collection, World Monetary Disorder,
represents the title of the conference that inspired the papers. Though
at least one contributor objected to it as unduly negative, we believe
it fairly describes both the content of the book and the situation that
has come to pass since the Bretton Woods system, founded on gold
and fixed exchange rates, collapsed (or was caused to collapse) in
1971. Uncertainty is the hallmark of the present international monetary regime. This is true whether one has in view the exchange rate
system of the future (Will we have fixed or floating rates?), the role
of Special Drawing Rights, the future role of gold, the new demands of
the Third World on the monetary institutions of the developed countries, the escalation of oil prices and the resultant flow of monetary
reserves to oil-producing states, the impact of multinational business
on traditional monetary arrangements, or the nature and purposes of
the International Monetary Fund itself.

The persistence of the present monetary interregnum is patently
full of dangers for all countries, developed and less-developed alike,
and the urgency of the need to find an appropriate solution (or solutions)
is the red thread running through all the papers in this book. The
subtitle of the book, and of the conference—National Policies and International Imperatives—puts in relief a primary cause of the current
monetary impasse and, indeed, of the disintegration of the Bretton
Woods system itself. Nations continue to pursue economic and monetary policies at home that are primarily nationalistic in orientation in
a world made ever more interdependent by an exponentially advancing
technology. International agreements on the need to limit the production and use of nuclear weapons are obtainable, if with difficulty. But
the giving up of national self-determination in economic matters would
appear to be considered tantamount to the abandonment of an indisputa-
ble imperative in the current lexicon of enlightened statecraft. Nevertheless, cooperation in monetary matters, as Paul A. Volcker remarks
in one of the lead-off papers, is the precious commodity without which
any reform projects are likely to come to naught.

Even if that cooperation could be counted on in the months and years to come, a variety of major obstacles, both theoretical and practical, will have to be overcome by the architects of a new international monetary system. This book draws on the skills and wisdom of an outstanding group of experts from the academy, government, and the business community to identify the obstacles, erect the signposts, and hopefully bring the final goal into view on the road back from disorder to order.

CONTENTS

LIST OF TABLES

LIST OF FIGURES

1

WORLD MONETARY DISORDER

Patrick M. Boarman

For some time it has been apparent that the international monetary system is anything but a "system." The term implies a set of standards or objectives and a common discipline to which the major nations, at least, adhere. In fact, the behavioral rule for nations that predominates today is "do your own thing," economically, monetarily, and fiscally. Our problem today is that we have a world without a world monetary system.

THE BRETTON WOODS SYSTEM

Under the old Bretton Woods system, which expired in 1971, there was at least some recognition and acceptance of the idea that an orderly world monetary system requires a process of adjustment, and preferably a continuous one, in which the participating nations modify their internal policies to the degree needed to achieve external equilibrium over the long run. The International Monetary Fund (IMF) was established as an instrument for bridging, in the short run, the inevitable failure of some countries to achieve equilibrium. And specific arrangements were put in place aimed at inducing such countries to move to overcome their short-run imbalances. This was the regime of stable rates, which were judged to be desirable on a variety of grounds, and which, in any case, were perceived to be a logical outcome of a system that placed a high priority on national adjustment to international imperatives.

Even before the demise of Bretton Woods in 1971 the ethic underlying it had been seriously compromised, not least because of the fateful role of key currency enjoyed by the dollar, whereby the United States was enabled to run its domestic economy—the largest in the world—as if the international economy did not exist.

Now that Bretton Woods is down the drain, the concept of adjustment appears to command even less interest than it did when the system prevailed. Indeed, the opposite idea—that the requirements of the international economy should always be subordinated to strictly national economic interests—has taken on a life of its own, notably in some highly respected academic circles. Gottfried Haberler has described the phenomenon, and his acceptance of it, succinctly: "No country," he notes, "is willing anymore to accept a deflation (i.e., a reduction in its price level or in money national income)."[1] He could have added that, conversely, many countries are willing to accept inflation in greater or less degree.

To the mercantilists of 300 years ago all of this would have very much the flavor of deja vu. The world of 1975, however, is vastly more complex and vastly more interdependent than the world of 1675. Revolutionary changes in the technology of communications and transportation have brought virtually all segments of the world economy into intimate juxtaposition with the other segments. In the economic global village of today the impact of purely national economic events is transmitted, through the balance of trade, the balance of payments, and the international money markets, with ever greater efficiency; the freer the flow of goods and money internationally, the more effective the transmission process.

The de facto internationalization of trade and investment on a grand scale, symbolized, for instance, in the proliferation of multinational enterprises around the globe, combined with an ever more intransigent insistence on national autonomy in domestic economic matters, is guaranteed to produce and, in fact, has produced profound structural disequilibrium in the world economy. The monetary shock waves of the oil crisis have introduced major new distortions into the system that have tended to obscure the preexisting imbalances. Overlaid on the old adjustment problem is the new one—staggering in its dimensions—between the oil-producing and oil-consuming countries. But the root problem, the disequilibrium that attends the pursuit of national or regional economic autonomy, is the same in both instances.

It is the problem that, for example, on a smaller scale, the European Economic Community has had to face up to, and upon the existence of which the Community's gropings for a greater measure of monetary integration have been predicated. It has become clear, to members of the Community at least, that contemporary attempts to immunize the domestic economy—in respect to money flows, prices, wages, interest rates, social policies, and so on—from external events is a major perversity that renders any meaningful approach to an integrated international economy most difficult, if not impossible, to attain. In effect, nations cannot have it both ways: They cannot want to participate in an optimum way in international trade and investment

and at the same time do what they want at home. For this is precisely
what yields chronic international disequilibrium.

CONSEQUENCES OF FLOATING RATES

If the concomitant of international equilibrium is stability of exchange rates, the logical accompaniment of disequilibrium is instability of rates. The generalized system of floating that has been in effect
since March 1973 is the reflection of the current deep structural diver-
gences in the world economy and of the acceptance of this situation as
a more or less permanent one. Thus, the Committee of Twenty of the
IMF, charged originally with devising reforms that would lead to stable
but adjustable parities, has, at its most recent meetings virtually
abandoned that objective, in addition to several other items on its
agenda.

The Committee of Twenty has, in effect, declared a monetary
interregnum, whereby the concern will no longer be even the establishment of rules for floating but merely the establishment of some general
guidelines. The dilution of terminology here reflects less a desire to
avoid the misuse of floating for selfish national advantage than a pervasive uncertainty about the future trend of exchange rates and of the
international economy in general. The following question arises at
this juncture: Is floating—pure or managed—itself a system that, in
the end, will overcome disequilibrium (as maintained in an impressive
body of opinion), or is it simply an expedient that will carry us for a
while until the real disequilibria become totally unmanageable?

It is certain that uncertainty is the word that best describes the
current situation, which led us to conclude that the phenomenon to be
analyzed is world monetary disorder. The costs of uncertainty and
disorder have been and continue to be high, in spite of the frequent as-
sertions of how well the monetary system and the trading system have
reacted to floating exchange rates. Ray Vicker, writing from London,
provided these grim indications of a time of troubles:

> In Zurich, Switzerland, Union Bank of Switzerland,
> the biggest bank in the country, recently suffered a
> massive foreign exchange loss due to bad deals in the
> money market. The amount was never disclosed but
> it may have been in the tens of millions of dollars.
> In New York, the Franklin National Bank is seek-
> ing to sort out the implications of a foreign exchange
> loss which might total as much as $37 million.
> Here in London, bankers uneasily report that the
> Eurodollar market is concentrating in the short-term

field. Hardly anybody wants to buy a bond when nobody knows what the dollar, the French franc, the
Italian lira, the pound sterling or the Japanese yen
will be worth ten or fifteen years from now. . . .

Obviously, there is no other way to handle international exchanges, today, than through floating
rates. But the manner in which some banks are being burned when trying to provide customers with
forward coverage shows that risks are considerably
greater than with fixed rates. And the bad experiences, which have been broadcast around the world,
emphasize not just to affected banks, but to all lenders that caution is in order. The combination of
soaring interest rates plus greater caution by bankers in their foreign exchange dealings doesn't bode
well for international commerce. When few people
want to take any more risks than they have to, you
get stagnation.[2]

An executive of the same Union Bank of Switzerland that was
plucked in the foreign exchange market added: "Perhaps trade won't
be affected right away. We may see confidence deteriorating in currencies. This may lead to economic difficulties in many countries.
Only then will trade be affected adversely."[3] And in the article quoted
above Vicker concludes:

The truth is nobody really knows where the world is
heading today, politically, economically, or financially. There never has been a time when so many
imponderables hung over markets and over those
elements which control actions of markets. So
there are no real havens anywhere, no matter how
men might seek for them.[4]

MONETARY "ESCAPE MECHANISMS"

The present disorders of the world monetary system have surfaced precisely during the period in which inflation in every country
is reaching an intensity unprecedented in recent history. Is the coincidence in time of the two phenomena, inflation and the collapse of
the world money structure, merely coincidental, or are the two or-
ganically related? Is not the acceptance of the postulate that defla-
tions will not be tolerated but that inflations will be tolerated part and
parcel of the world money muddle? On every side, in fact, the evi-

dence piles up that the virulence and amplitude of inflation that is being propagated internationally is likely to be much greater under a
world monetary system that enables inflating countries to escape the
domestic and international consequences of their lack of self-discipline than under one that severely limits resort to escape mechanisms.
The principal escape mechanism for the past 25 years, one that served
primarily to relieve the United States of the need to adhere to monetary
discipline, was the key currency role of the dollar. This, in effect,
permitted the United States to finance its external deficits by simply
printing more money rather than by yielding up real goods and services.
It conferred upon us the marvelous secret of having "deficits without
tears," in Jacques Rueff's unforgettable phrase. And it was the buildup of the enormous dollar overhang abroad, which the use of this escape mechanism entailed, that in the end brought about the collapse of
the Bretton Woods system in 1971.

Another escape mechanism, much more in vogue a few years
ago than at present, was the manufacture of international liquidity,
then judged to be in short supply. It was a device that appeared particularly attractive to those inflating countries not enjoying the preroga-
tives of a key currency. The plausible rationale offered in support of
this device was that if world liquidity did not expand pari passu with
the expansion of world trade, such trade would shrink, possibly to
catastrophic levels. The idea survives in an important way in the concept of Special Drawing Rights (SDRs), which are reserve assets
created ex nihilo for the express purpose of enabling deficit countries
to cover their deficits.

The truth is, of course, that there is no necessary relationship
between the expansion of world trade and the expansion of world monetary reserves. The purpose of reserves is not to finance trade itself
but rather the inevitable net differences between the value of a country's total imports and its total exports. To put it another way, balance of payments surpluses and deficits (or excess or deficiencies of
international liquidity) arise in specific countries as the product of
their individual policies and not in the world at large. No "world
state" exists of which it could be said that it is short of "world liquidity." Rather, it is each country's own balance-of-payments position
that determines its need for liquidity; it is not the position of the
world as a whole. This being so, the pernicious outcome of a general
creation of additional international liquidity, as, for instance, in the
form of SDRs or other instruments, is seen to lie in the fact that the
deficit countries—the only ones who would be wanting such credits—
would in effect be able to obtain carte blanche for further deficits.
It would be the creditor countries, the ultimate suppliers of the credits, who would be required to bear the burdens of the continuous import of inflation to which such a perpetuum mobile would give rise.

There is no question that the widespread acceptance of the liquidity shortage thesis, with the resultant resorting to liquidity-creating techniques as an escape mechanism, has contributed in a major way to spreading inflation through the system. Indeed, it is the increasing awareness of the inflation-generating potential of such devices as SDRs that has caused attention to be shifted to yet another mechanism for escaping the need for national self-discipline: namely, floating rates of exchange.

Yet I would like to offer the following hypotheses for discussion. First, since floating does not mean we can forget about the international consequences of our domestic actions, it is not an escape mechanism. Second, floating has not worked as well since March 1973 as has been claimed. Third, it is an engine of international inflation.

The classic defense of flexible rates of exchange was made many years ago by Milton Friedman. His argument was powerful and rested in part on the general applicability of the law of supply and demand. If one accepts that law, so the premise runs, then one ought not to exempt foreign exchange from it. The difficulty with this point, then and now, is that foreign exchange, foreign currency, is not just any commodity. If it is to be a store of value—a prime function of sound money—then one of its attributes should be stability of value. Since, in effect, international money is the set of relationships that exists among the different major currencies at a given time, stability of international money means stability of the network of existing exchange rates.

VIRTUES OF STABLE RATES

In reality, the desire to have exchange-rate flexibility is the desire to "do your own thing," whatever it might be, at home and not to have to suffer the international consequences thereof. In that respect, advocates of flexibility are very close to advocates of more international liquidity: Both groups aim at avoiding the international results of domestic actions, and both are to that extent nationalistic —or, more technically, closed-economy advocates. In essence, under a system of stable rates there may be some hope of bringing inflation under control, given a desire to do so, but that hope all but disappears in a context of floating rates, for reasons that are both psychological and narrowly technical.

While the role of the dollar as key currency was the Achilles' heel of the Bretton Woods system in that it allowed the United States to export dollars instead of goods and services or gold to cover its payments deficits, a key currency is not inherently necessary to a well-functioning system of stable rates. Witness the old gold standard.

It is fallacious to ascribe to a system of stable rates of exchange per se the inflationary bias of a system of stable rates coupled with the use of a key currency (the so-called gold-exchange standard). But even with respect to the Bretton Woods variant of a stable-rates system, one could not speak of a uniform or universal inflationary trend. In the United States, for instance, throughout the late 1950s and early 1960s prices were unusually stable, partly in response to decisive steps taken in both the Eisenhower and Kennedy administrations to cope with the acute surges in the U.S. balance-of-payments deficits in those years and with the associated loss of U.S. gold reserves.

In addition, the losses of reserves by the deficit countries and accompanying accumulation of reserves by the surplus countries were subjects of protracted discussion and concern at the time. Such losses, as in the case of the United States just cited, seem to have triggered a number of actions in the affected countries aimed at removing, at least in part, the source of the disequilibrium. A prime case in point would be, for example, the economic and financial reforms, coupled with devaluation of the franc, undertaken in France at the beginning of the de Gaulle presidency in the late 1950s.

The point is that a loss of reserves is a highly visible, easily understood symptom of international disequilibrium that seems to have been frequently effective in inducing compensatory actions, especially in the deficit countries. After all, when a country ran out of reserves under the old system, it had had it: It had either to stop inflating or to renounce imports, or it had to resort to a combination of both.

While the same constraint does not apply to surplus countries, the player who is accumulating all the chips in the international trade game will also be concerned that the game may abruptly end (as other countries conserve foreign exchange by imposing restrictions on imports) or, alternatively, that he may end up with all the chips and have nothing to consume. It should be added that since the movement of reserves in or out was generally gradual rather than sudden (exception being made for situations of pending changes in currency parities or other major disturbances), it allowed time for making considered judgments about the strategy to be followed in coping with the imbalance. In short, the system of stable rates served, however imperfectly, as a mechanism for the limiting, interruption, and on occasion even the effective containing of the international spread of inflation.

INTERNATIONALIZATION OF INFLATION

Consider now the system of floating rates and how it relates to the new world of two-digit inflation. In the last few years—that is, since the flexible-rate system (with interruptions) has been in operation—price levels in the major industrial countries have not only risen much faster than ever before; they have also tended increasingly to move in tandem with one another, and, to that degree, to reinforce each other's upward movements. And the reinforcement of such inflationary impulses, as they migrate from one country to another, is occurring with an intensity hitherto unknown.

This is to be observed especially in the case of the industrialized countries. Whereas, as noted earlier, there were marked differences in price trends in these countries in the first half of the 1960s, since the beginning of the 1970s their inflations have been moving in virtually parallel fashion. This phenomenon might be traceable to deliberate synchronization of the business cycles of these countries. However, no such conscious supersynchronization has yet been attempted on any significant scale. Rather, I would argue that it is the propagation of inflation from country to country that has played a major role in the process and that the speed and efficiency of such propagation has been aided by the flexible-rate system. Even more, the current coincidence of cyclical peaks in the major industrialized countries, far from remaining the statistical rarity as it was in the past, may itself turn out to reflect the completeness and the rapidity with which inflationary impulses are transmitted from one country to another.

In sum, the increasing internationalization of the inflation process may be attributable in significant degree to the system of floating rates. Floating rates seem to communicate inflationary impulses more quickly and to lower incentives to combatting inflation more certainly than is the case under stable rates. How does the process work? First, where a country is undergoing a more rapid inflation than in other countries, its currency will tend to depreciate in value externally. The process may continue even over a protracted period; its effects are diffused rather than localized. There is no visible end to the capacity to import, as in the case of a loss of reserves. It is clear that depreciation will tend to aggravate inflation in the depreciating country, in part because it raises the cost of imports. And even if, as in the case of the United States, the share of imports in total consumption may be small, the effects of devaluation may be significant, given the fact that, because domestically produced goods can be sold for higher prices overseas, U.S. consumers must pay for them in order to prevent them from being exported.

While devaluation or depreciation as a means of coping with a trade imbalance is less painful than deflation, especially if deflation should produce unemployment, it will almost certainly intensify or initiate a process of inflation. Moreover, since the inflation induced by a depreciating currency is simply a continuation of the same process—i.e., inflation—that produced the depreciation in the first place, it tends to continue. There is little incentive for the authorities to

take remedial action, since there is no perceived possibility of loss
in the sense of a disruption of discontinuance of ongoing behavior,
such as a sudden rise in unemployment, and no need to impose quantitative restrictions on imports.

On the other hand, in the case of a country with an appreciating
currency the organized and articulate business interests, seeing their
competitiveness in international markets being eroded, will tend to
resist further appreciation. In short, the process of appreciation,
which is normally antiinflationary for the appreciating country, will
tend not to be carried as far as depreciation, resulting in a net increase of inflation in the system. It may be noted, as well, that countries, such as Germany or Switzerland, whose currencies have risen
sharply under floating, should be able to enjoy lower prices because a
unit of their currency will buy more goods from abroad. But given
the quasi-monopolistic positions acquired by many industries in these
countries (and elsewhere), it is probably true that price cuts in a
country whose exchange rates rise will not be as pronounced as price
increases in those countries where currency values have dropped.
Again, there is a net gain for inflationary forces in the international
system as a whole. I am supported in this analysis by the Bank for
International Settlements (Basel), which has found that, in general,
increased exchange-rate flexibility tends to have an inflationary bias.

Also, there is the general momentum of a process in which more
and more of the psychological and technical barriers to the spread of
inflation have crumbled, and in which the authorities simply reconcile
themselves to lower standards of performance in the fight against inflation. The very escape mechanisms to which I have been referring—
SDRs and exchange-rate flexibility—are the outgrowths of a universal
faltering of the will to resist inflation. For instance, those who spend
their time constructing such devices tell us that the SDR, which hitherto
had a gold guarantee, is henceforth to be defined as the average value
of a unit of a basketful of currencies, each one of which is subject to
floating in greater or lesser degree. A system of floating rates an-
chored to an SDR that itself is floating is surely not calculated to stem
the international inflationary spiral. On the contrary, the concept is
an integral part of the whole philosophical and moral ambience in which
inflation of the sort we are experiencing today becomes possible.

The resorting to rate flexibility grows out of the same moral
bankruptcy. Here, too, the marginal morality of the most inflation-
prone nation tends to become the prevailing morality of the world community. For once the idea of defending stable rates is abandoned,
there is little incentive for deficit countries to defend any particular
rate any more. That is, there is a reduction in the incentives to
take any positive action to counter the inflationary forces that are
pushing the rate down. On the other hand, the forces tending to push

a rate of exchange up in the surplus country are likely to be interfered
with at some point as exporters struggle to retain markets. As
noted, this failure of the appreciating currency to rise to its true "market level" means that some additional inflation will be imported into
the surplus country, thereby still further relieving the deficit country
of the need to deal effectively with its own inflation.

In the final analysis, whether we are talking about a fixed-rate
system or a floating system, inflation can be successfully dealt with
only if all major nations together cooperate to do so. Such cooperation would include, at a minimum, an agreement to restrain national
inflations within some specified rate per year, to strive continuously
for long-term equilibrium in external trade and payments relations,
and to take the steps, on a national basis, required to achieve these
results. The burden of my argument is that it simply appears to be
much easier to accomplish these things under a stable-rate system
than under flexible rates.

THE GOLD QUESTION

Finally, there is the gold question. I agree with Milton Gilbert
of the Bank for International Settlements, that the general level of
discussion on gold is about the lowest of all the subjects being considered. The reason for this, he observed:

> It starts with the conclusions and never bothers with
> any analysis. There is not one analytical paper on
> the functions of gold in the monetary system that has
> been produced by the Group of Ten or by the Commit-
> tee of Twenty. You may all have your ideas about why
> this is so, but I think the reason is that the United
> States found gold convertibility to be an embarrass-
> ment; it was obliged to raise the official price twice
> when it had said it would not do so, and hence it con-
> cludes that gold is just an inconvenience. It should
> be phased, out, as the saying goes.[5]

It is my belief that gold is needed and will continue to be needed
as an adjunct to any return to the convertibility of the dollar, which
in turn is a precondition to a return to any form of stable-rate system.
It will also continue to be needed as a means of helping to reestablish
the confidence of the public. As Janos Fekete, deputy president of the
National Bank of Hungary, said recently, "[There] are about three
hundred economists in the world who are against gold, but unfortunately there are about three billion inhabitants of the world who believe

in gold. Now, the problem is how the three hundred economists can
convince the other three billion. Maybe it is possible, but it would
certainly take a long time."[6]

In reviewing the working of the old gold standard (1875-1914),
I find that its remarkably effective functioning had to be attributed not
so much to gold movements per se, though that was an invaluable part
of the whole mechanism, but to the acceptance by each of the participating countries of the need for some degree of internal discipline—
in respect to wages, inflation, interest rates, and so forth—as the
essential condition for the maintenance of external equilibrium. That
is the ingredient that was egregiously lacking in the gold-exchange
standard of the 1920s and 1930s, the Bretton Woods system, and, a
fortiori, since August 15, 1971. We do not think there is any international monetary mechanism that can be devised that has any chance of
surviving as long as the central problem, the need to harmonize, in
some degree, the internal economic structures of the different nations
with one another, is not faced up to.

If the national self-discipline to which I have referred were in
fact observed by all the major trading nations, balances of payments
would tend to come into rough equilibrium over the long term, and
such imbalances as doubtless will occur in the short term could be
easily handled by existing reserve holdings and international borrowing facilities. Moreover, if balances of payments were to move more
nearly in tandem, gold could quite easily resume its erstwhile function.

Suffice it to say that while economists of the chair continue to
attack people's scrambling for the yellow metal as irrational, they
reveal their own irrationality in ignoring, or trying to ignore that
major constant in human behavior: people's liking for gold. Historically and today, the preference for gold is a preference for a money
of last resort that provides security from and independence of the
follies of national governments. It is the means by which people say
to governments, "You cannot go on giving me pieces of paper that I
don't trust, can't use, and don't want."

In response to the point that there is not enough gold to go around
to meet the needs of world trade, the answers are simple. First,
neither gold nor any other constituent of international monetary reserves is used to finance trade. Trade in every country is financed
by ordinary commercial credit. Gold and other reserves are used
exclusively to finance balance-of-payments deficits (or were so used
until recently); only those in chronic deficit can complain about a
shortage of gold or other reserves. Second, whether gold is judged
plentiful or scarce is mainly a function of its price. There will always be plenty of gold to serve the needs of the international monetary
system, if only its official price is adjusted upward sufficiently. If
the present dollar price of gold ($42.44) were tripled or quadrupled

(and we are not concerned with the benefiting of the South Africans or the Soviets therefrom), there would be no shortage. But for such a step to have long-run beneficial results it would, of course, have to be accompanied by a new commitment, on the part of the major nations at least, to a code of internal fiscal, monetary, and economic behavior that would be compatible with long-run international equilibrium. Gilbert puts the matter succinctly when he asks:

> What would happen if the United States changed its anti-gold attitude and announced that starting tomorrow it would begin to build up its gold reserves by acquiring gold in the market with the objective of an eventual return to convertibility? I am sure the public would not question the sheer financial strength of the United States to carry out such a program; that being so, there would be an immediate improvement of the dollar in exchange markets; there would be a reversal of the previous flights from the dollar and a return to a more normal position of leads and lags of payments; and incidentally, the discussions about the reform of the system would begin to take on a more realistic character. [7]

These are some of the great questions to which solid answers will have to be made if the world is again to enjoy the benefits of a world monetary system.

NOTES

1. Gottfried Haberler, "Two Essays on the Future of the International Order," American Enterprise Institute, reprint no. 21, February 1974, p. 9.
2. Ray Vicker, "Grim Day for Money Changers," Wall Street Journal, May 21, 1974.
3. Ibid.
4. Vicker, op. cit., p. 2.
5. Milton Gilbert, "International Monetary Reform," paper presented at a Monetary Symposium of the South African Institute of Directors, Johannesburg, October 2, 1973, p. 7.
6. Janos Fekete; compare Milton Gilbert, op. cit.
7. Gilbert, op. cit., p. 9.

2

THE UNITED STATES AND INTERNATIONAL MONETARY REFORM
Paul A. Volcker

When we talk about monetary reform, we are talking about achieving a reconciliation between national imperatives, policies, requirements, and objectives and the needs of other countries, their own imperatives and requirements—what is generally termed the "interests" of the international community.

A COOPERATIVE ORDER

We do have conflicts in this process, and we do have a need for cooperation. I think the creative act, of course, is to make out of the potential for conflict a cooperative order that can enable an individual country to further support its domestic objectives, such as growth and a high standard of living, and at the same time mutually interact with others in supporting their goals.

If that sounds a little ingenuous (and sometimes it does seem that way), it should be remembered that the whole theory of free and liberal trade is based on the simple notion that what is good for one country in the economic area can be reconciled with what is good for countries in general and that there is a road not simply toward the gain of one made at the expense of another but to the gain of all together.

I will turn from theorizing, however, because the world is rapidly approaching a benchmark: not the completion of monetary reform but a bench mark on the road in that direction, in the form of the discussions of the Committee of Twenty. The fact is that these discussions were caught somewhat in midstream by two sweeping economic events: the oil crisis and world inflation. The first has no close parallel in international financial or economic history, characterized

13

as it is by vast amounts of money moving through world markets to
countries that, in a financial sense, have not loomed large before,
with great new problems inherent in the situation. It was not clear
how this situation could or should be handled within the framework of
a reformed monetary system. Even more important in terms of shock
impact than the oil situation has been the emergence of worldwide inflation. With domestic monetary systems disturbed to the extent that
they have been by rising prices, and with all the instability and uncertainties associated therewith, it is difficult to have a strongly organized
international monetary system. An international monetary system
links domestic monetary systems, and if the domestic monetary systems are themselves in an unstable condition, it is very difficult to
have a stable international monetary system.

Because of these factors, I think there is a consensus very widely
shared among governments that for the time being the kind of flexible
arrangements that are now in place are going to have to persist for
awhile. There are certain advantages in these arrangements during
this period of considerable uncertainty and fluctuations in domestic
and international markets. If floating exchange rates are particularly
suited to coping with anything, they certainly are suited to coping with
this kind of uncertainty.

WHERE ARE WE HEADED?

Against this background, it is time to pause and take stock of
where we want to go and how we want to get there. First, a new system will develop in a more evolutionary way, perhaps, than was contemplated when the reform process started several years ago. It is
difficult to quarrel with that as a possible approach, but it obviously
is not a fully satisfactory situation. It has met with two different and
opposite responses around the world by those who are to some degree
frustrated by the reform effort. I will state these views in extreme
form and caricature them a bit, because I do think that they articulate
real issues.

There is a group that says in effect that all these reform discussions have not achieved anything: Bretton Woods has broken up;
we have made no progress in putting anything concrete in its place;
monetary reform is a failure. We ought to bury this reform exercise
politely, wait awhile, and start over again. This view is quite widely
held, perhaps particularly in some European circles; I label it the
"European banking view," just to give its flavor, recognizing my
label as a vast oversimplification. It is a view widely held by those
who equate monetary reform with a rather rigidly fixed exchange-rate
system, convertibility, and par values set and held firmly in place.
Lacking those, a country has no reform.

There is an opposite view that is considerably more smug. This school says that the monetary-reform effort has been irrelevant, because the problem has basically been solved. We should and do have floating rates, so, regardless of what officials and others have been talking about interminably, events have turned out just fine. We have reform without knowing it, and a good reform, despite the best (or the worst!) efforts of the central bankers and finance ministers to arrange a different system. I call that view, just to give a little of its flavor, the "American academic view," because it is rather widely held in U.S. academic circles. But, again, that label is, of course, a simplification.

Now the one thing the two views have in common is the assumption that the organized reform method is rather beyond the point, either futile or damaging. We think that both of these views are rather fundamentally wrong. They both lead to a dead end and to difficulties. The first is really a counsel of despair, that if a country does not have a particular kind of system that fits one vision of the future, it has nothing. The danger is that this attitude easily leads to incentives for a country's not cooperating in the context of what it has, for not making the best of what it has, for not recognizing the fundamental need, whatever the formal characteristics of the system, to cooperate closely to make the system work. The second school, although it is more hopeful and optimistic in its view, would lead to the same kind of difficulty. It ignores the fact that, economically, there are fragmenting tendencies in the world, not only in the monetary system but also in other elements of the world economy, to say nothing of political issues. It would ignore the elements of disorder in the present situation and the fact that, in a general framework of floating and flexibility, flexibility can be abused. It forgets that we need to be working toward rules of conduct that help assure a more cooperative and more cohesive system than we now have.

AN INTERDEPENDENT WORLD

We cannot escape the fact that we live in an interdependent world. That fact will hold for any kind of an international monetary system we can design. To take just one example, proponents of floating rates have sometimes argued that one of the advantages of floating rates is that they enable a particular country to insulate itself from external influences—say, in the monetary policy area. However, I find merely that the basic interdependence takes a different form. If one country has easy money and another high interest rates, under a floating-rates system the first country does not lose reserves, so there is not the kind of a crisis, or potential crisis, characterized by a reserve loss, but there is a depreciation of its exchange rate.

For a variety of reasons, most people do not want to see the exchange rate of their currency depreciate sharply. For one thing, it will have an inflationary impact at home. There have been times in the recent past when the depreciation of the dollar in the exchange markets was at least as strong an influence on policy makers, in terms of shaping their general economic policies and monetary policies, as international movements of funds had been under the old system. And if we can contemplate situations in which one country may be happy with a depreciating exchange rate, we have to consider whether its trading partners are also willing to live with the situation.

So, first, it is an illusion to think that an international monetary system can be devised that will insulate one country, making cooperation unnecessary, avoiding the necessity of integrating the policies of that country to some extent with the situation in the rest of the world.

Second, we need rules, guidelines, codes of conduct, permitting or prohibiting actions that countries may take in particular situations, to the end that they do not get in each other's way. How is there, in a practical way, cooperation when countries are interdependent?

The rules obviously need to make economic sense; that is why we argue about the amount of flexibility that exchange rates should have, about objective indicators, about the amount of liquidity that is right for the world, about what to do about gold, and about what to do about SDRs and all the rest. These are all technical questions that have to be resolved in a way that makes economic sense, respects the way markets operate, permits and promotes a flow of trade and capital that is as free as possible, and so on.

In addition, it should be emphasized that the rules have to make political sense. The rule maker is dealing with international institutions, with a variety of countries, with international life and behavior. To the various governments the rules must seem fair, evenhanded, and equitable, giving no country undue advantage. Sensitivity to this political dimension may become more important, not less, as we move ahead. The United States is not as dominant as it once was. The political self-consciousness of other countries is increasing as their economic strength increases. The European community, collectively, is now strong and viable as an economy that is almost equal to the United States. We see, in many ways, that this growing economic strength is finding political expression. One can say the same thing about Japan. The voice of the developing countries is increasing in strength. All of this needs to be respected in a reasonable monetary agreement, for such an agreement is also political.

Finally, as a corollary of the two requirements, that monetary rules be economically and politically sensible, the system must be understandable to the citizenry. There must be some sense of national commitment to the rules if they are going to be any good at all.

UNDERSTANDABLE RULES

Perhaps the hardest objective to achieve is to keep the rules reasonably simple and understandable. It is so easy to elaborate one complex scheme after another that fits an idea of the ideal international monetary system. If somebody raises a problem, one is tempted to add another little refinement here or there to take care of it. It is very easy to forget the need for simplicity and understandability.

Given these criteria, I do think that a fair amount of progress, intellectual and substantive, has been made since that day in August 1971 when we suspended gold convertibility and, in effect, said the Bretton Woods system was finished. We do not have the new system, with all the t's crossed and i's dotted, to put in its place. But the record of the meetings of the Committee of Twenty will show that we have made quite a lot of progress. It will show that in that terribly difficult area that goes in the jargon under the label of the "adjustment process" we have employed a sensible approach—experimenting with a blend of so-called assessment and objective indicators—to summarize in just a few code words the complex discussions that have taken place through the years. There is also a consensus for a more flexible use of exchange rates in the international system—a consensus that certainly does not extend to maintaining a fully floating system permanently. There is also a recognition that, in the liquidity area, we want to move toward emphasis on a new international reserve unit, the SDR, as modified and adopted. We want to move away from dependence on gold and dependence on national reserve currencies.

Any of those points can be questioned, but they do represent a wide and, I think, rather deeply felt consensus among the governments participating in the creation of a new monetary system. This does not imply that many questions have not remained open, particularly in the detailed implementation of the concepts mentioned. We will, however, be able to put forward a reasonable vision of the manner in which the system should evolve. Moreover, it is too much to expect that the framework I have described will be filled out in all detail in the near future. But there is a willingness to experiment together, using some of the technical devices that have been put forward, and also a willingness to recognize that they should be adapted, changed, and evolved in the light of experience. It is important that there is some sense of an agreed vision, subject to evolution and adaptation, of the broad directions in which we want to move. And I think that that possibility exists.

Backing that up, there is a series of immediate steps that can be taken to help manage the present situation and move it toward the vision to which I have referred. Steps need to be taken to redefine the SDR, to adapt it to the current floating situation, and to put that instrument practically on its feet. It is important that the so-called International Monetary Fund (IMF) oil facility, a kind of back-up facility for recycling some of these vast flows of oil money, continue operating.

In the present uncertain situation, with strong pressures and great uncertainties weighing on the minds of officials in many countries responsible for balance-of-payments and trade positions, it is important that the countries of the Western world reaffirm their resolve not to take selective and restrictive trade measures for balance-of-payments purposes. We can and should strengthen the hand of the IMF in this area.

Most important, given the current situation, I expect that governments will agree upon some general guidelines for floating (rules of good behavior in the management of a floating rate system) to help assure that one country's intervening in the exchange markets (or taking other action to affect its exchange rate) acts in ways that are compatible with the interests of other countries.

STRENGTHENING THE IMF

Finally, there should be an institutional step taken (and sometimes institutional steps turn out to be more important than any of the detailed policies adopted at a particular time) to reinforce the central position of the IMF in managing the monetary system. The idea is to bring within the IMF, as a permanent body, a council of ministers charged both with keeping the reform exercise moving and with keeping the current situation, as it develops, under close review.

The object here, quite frankly, is to bring a little more international political clout to the IMF and in turn to have international concerns reflected intimately and directly in the councils of national governments. And this will happen simply as a result of ministers merely being at a meeting and sitting together discussing common problems. We must force governments to sit together, at reasonably frequent intervals, so that they can discuss problems around a meeting table, arrive at some consensus about a course of action, and do it at a sufficiently high level of responsibility, so that when the official goes back to his capital there is some chance that there will be follow-through on the agreed action. This can be an important institutional innovation in maintaining and strengthening the position of the IMF.

Whether the objectives expressed here will actually be achieved is going to depend, in the end, not upon what economists say, or upon what the resolutions say, or upon what amendments to the IMF articles say, but upon what people actually think, how strongly they support the objectives, and how they behave over time. We need a certain amount of faith, in the sense of a political commitment by the governments in the Western world that they want to act together, that they will not individually act in an isolationist way, that they recognize that there is a broader community that must be served. We need a little hope that internal economic pressures and domestic political turmoil are not going to turn nations inward, that, to take one important example, the United States can resolve its political problems domestically and abroad to the extent that such constructive initiatives as its trade legislation and international trade negotiations can go forward (for this is a subject that is closely related to the monetary problem).

Not least, in the light of the development problems around the world, we need in a quite literal sense to retain a sense of charity. Certainly, for instance, the International Development Association (IDA) legislation passed by the U.S. Congress in 1974 is an essential part of the effort toward a constructive world order.

I have not discussed the oil problem in any detail. Briefly, the most severe repercussions of that problem will be on a group of developing countries that have no way of paying the increased oil bill without being faced, literally, with starvation and the arresting of their development programs for many years. Progress in response to the crisis has in a sense been slowest, although the first priority is in meeting this particular need. The day is long since past when we could consider the problems of the developing countries as out of the mainstream, to be dealt with separately from the chief problems of the world economy.

Finally, we need a better sense of price stability in all of our domestic markets, including the United States, if monetary reform, among many objectives, is to be a reality. Whatever the mechanics of the system, whether we try to go in one extreme direction toward fixity or in another direction toward floating rates, we are going to have disorder if we have inflation of the magnitude that characterizes the countries of the Western world today. It would be outside the scope of this chapter to deal in detail with the problem of inflation. Insufficient attention has been given to the problem in the past, however. We have been inclined, whenever the hard choices arise, to take the risks on the side of a little more inflation. That attitude is rather widespread in the U.S. community and in foreign communities. But it is becoming clear that that kind of thinking will ultimately result in deep disillusionment. The kind of inflation that we now have, if prolonged, will have effects on U.S. economic institutions, and certainly on financial institutions, that will not merely involve a simple tradeoff between a little more inflation and a little less unemployment. We will wind up with both, and in more severe form than if the problem is handled in a more timely fashion.

I recognize that the prospects for slowing inflation are improving. I do not pretend that it is an easy problem: Clearly, we run the risk of major disturbances, including recession, in the process of bringing inflation under control. It should be emphasized again, in conclusion, that our success internationally (or the lack of it) in the monetary area is going to be determined by the success of our joint attack on inflation and recession, domestically and abroad, more than by any other actions.

3

WORLDWIDE INFLATION:
A MONETARIST VIEW
David I. Meiselman

Although it is widely believed that stable prices are the norm, the annals of price history do not appear to have recorded a single era of stable prices. In her "Secular Price Change in Historical Perspective," a survey examining available price data of the last two and a half millennia, Anna Schwartz concluded: "Episodes of rising prices have alternated with episodes of declining prices, apparently for as long as money has been used as a medium of exchange."[1]

Focusing on just the past several generations, prices have risen in most countries most of the time since the Great Depression of the 1930s, which followed the worldwide deflation of the late 1920s and early 1930s, which in turn followed the sharp inflation during and after World War I, the earlier gradual inflation from 1896 to 1914, and a still earlier deflation that (in the United States) started shortly after the end of the Civil War. Widespread, persistent, and variable inflation has been a characteristic of the world economy since the end of World War II, itself a period of severe inflation. Not only has there been no important deflation in the postwar generation on the scale typically experienced from time to time within the past century, but prices have risen in every country whose price level statistics are reported by the International Monetary Fund (IMF) in its International Financial Statistics. Since 1965 worldwide inflation has tended to accelerate, especially in advanced industrial countries, such as the United States and Japan.

Reprinted with permission from The Phenomenon of Worldwide Inflation, published 1975 by the American Enterprise Institute for Public Policy Research, Washington, D.C.

In country after country continuing inflation has been an intractable problem for more than a generation. In the non-Communist world, inflation may well have been the main economic factor undermining democratic government and political stability, weakening free markets, arbitrarily impairing private and public contracts, capriciously conferring windfall gains and losses, and enlarging the variety and scope of mischievous and inappropriate government controls that have failed both to curb rising prices and deal with their causes and to alleviate their major consequences.

An old and noble tradition in economics assigns to money the central role in the analysis and determination of the level of prices, especially secular changes in prices. From at least Adam Smith, Hume, Ricardo, James Mill, and John Stuart Mill to Irving Fisher, Alfred Marshall, Pigou, and the younger John Maynard Keynes inflation and deflation have been viewed as monetary phenomena. But more important than the imposing authority of this bibliographical name dropping is the fact that the dependable secular relationship between money and prices is the most tested and verified proposition in all of economics, covering a wider range of economic experience in time, place, and circumstances than any other, and with essentially the same results. As Schwartz noted: "Long-run price changes consistently parallel the monetary changes, with one exception for England in the sixteenth century."[2] In the four centuries since the coronation of Queen Elizabeth I, there is no important episode of inflation or deflation that has been studied that contradicts the general proposition that changes in the price level stem primarily from changes in the nominal stock of money per unit of output. These are some of the bases for the hypothesis that the current era of inflation is primarily a monetary phenomenon. Part of this study will examine some of the evidence necessary to test this proposition.

For at least the past two centuries, inflation and deflation have occurred in many countries at approximately the same time.[3] The empirical association across countries appears to have been even closer in more recent years, suggesting that the source of price-level shifts is common to many or all countries and that there is some mechanism linking them together.

The second purpose of this chapter is to examine the propagation of worldwide inflation in recent years and its relationship to monetary phenomena. It will be shown that worldwide inflation has been closely associated with the rapid worldwide increase in money made possible by the Bretton Woods system and the IMF and its associated fixed exchange-rate system, which turned into an engine of worldwide inflation by encouraging worldwide monetary expansion. As in earlier periods, the system of fixed exchange rates has been a crucial part of the mechanism for worldwide dispersal of excess money among

countries, including those with seemingly independent monetary authorities. This system is the major reason why today's inflation has been
worldwide rather than restricted to particular countries. We will
conclude that the worldwide abandonment in the first quarter of 1973
of fixed rates and of heavy central-bank intervention holds potential
for an early slowdown in world inflation because large numbers of
important countries are now able to pursue essentially independent
and less expansionary monetary policies. They did so in the second
half of 1973 (the end of the period covered by this study), once they
were no longer tied to the fixed-rate system. Thus, we may well
have already passed a watershed of major significance.

Under the system of floating rates, no longer will it be necessary
to inflate in order to forestall or prevent exchange appreciation, and
no longer will it be necessary to borrow newly created foreign-exchange reserves in order to forestall or prevent devaluation. Moreover, the average increase in money of the nine major Organization
for Economic Cooperation and Development (OECD) countries other
than the United States (Japan, Germany, France, United Kingdom,
Italy, Netherlands, Belgium, Canada, and Switzerland) has markedly
slowed from an annual rate of 25.9 percent in the fourth quarter of
1972 to 5.1 percent in the fourth quarter of 1973. This occurred on
the heels of a 55.8 percent increase in money during the three years
1971-73. Over the same period, for the United States the average
increase of the narrow measure of money, M_1, slowed from an annual
rate of 7.3 percent in the fourth quarter of 1972 to an annual rate of
4.0 percent in the fourth quarter of 1973. Essentially, the entire
slowdown in the extremely high rates of monetary expansion took
place in the months of July through October 1973.*

Data for 1974 on money outside the United States are not yet
available. For the United States, with the exception of the four-month
period between July 1973 and October 1973, M_1 has been increasing at
annual rates in approximately the 7 to 8 percent range. From October
1973 through April 1974 the U.S. stock of money has been rising at a
rate of about 7.5 percent for the M_1 measure of money and 10 percent
for the M_2 measure. Thus, it is not yet clear that the Federal Reserve
System has basically altered its highly expansionary policy that, since
1971, has caused both the narrow M_1 and the broad M_2 measures of
money to rise at the fastest rates since World War II. Given this,
my note of potential optimism about world inflation may have to be
qualified to exclude the United States, at least for the near term and

----

*This period of no growth in U.S. money appears to have been
related to several increases in reserve requirements for demand deposits and large certificates of deposit at approximately the same time.

until more information about Federal Reserve performance as distinguished from statements of intent becomes available.

The sharp reduction in monetary growth outside the United States also holds the danger of economic slowdowns in the short run. If recessions do materialize, the future path of worldwide inflation will then depend on the response of world monetary authorities. If they overreact and resume high rates of monetary growth, then the potential for slowing inflation afforded by the breakup of the fixed-rate system will have been wasted.

But that is running ahead of the story.

WHY IS THIS AN ERA OF INFLATION?

In earlier times the stock of money was often composed of precious metals, and the nominal value of goods measured in terms of a fixed amount of gold or silver largely depended on the relative quantities of goods and of precious metals, that is, money. Then, secular inflation and deflation usually stemmed from changes in the volume of coinage resulting from mining or from plunder, as well as from the debasement and restoration of existing metal coins.

More recently, money has typically come to be made up of paper money and bank deposits largely controlled directly by a country's monetary authorities through alterations in the volume of high-powered or base money they create, essentially the sum of currency in the hands of the public plus the reserves of the banking system. Monetary authorities may also issue, or print, high-powered money to intervene in particular markets—for example, to trade in gold or to fix its price, or to trade in foreign exchange. This is why countries with currencies linked to fixed prices for securities, fixed prices for gold, or fixed prices for foreign exchange generally lose an important degree of control over their money supplies in the sense that central-bank intervention is necessary to maintain these pegged prices. Under a system of fixed exchange rates, intervention in the gold and foreign exchange markets helps to explain the worldwide dispersion and synchronization of monetary change, as central banks intervene to alter the monetary base or the money stock in order to maintain fixed nominal prices of gold and of foreign exchange in the face of balance-of-payments disequilibria.

Economists in the monetarist tradition who have analyzed earlier eras of inflation and deflation have generally included an analysis of corresponding changes in monetary relationships, especially with respect to the money-supply process. For example, the creeping inflation in the 1896-1914 period has been widely attributed to an acceleration of monetary growth related to an increase in the flow of newly mined gold resulting from improved gold-mining techniques. Similarly, there have been special factors in the current era of inflation, many of them related to fundamental changes in money-supply processes around the world.

These changes have strengthened incentives to increase money at the same time that past constraints on monetary growth have been progressively weakened and removed. First, we have seen the systematic weakening and then the elimination of the gold constraint on monetary creation. Whatever the other merits of the adoption of the two-tier gold system in 1968 and the closing of the gold window in 1971, it is hard to believe that the acceleration of inflation in 1973 and 1974 would have been possible had these steps not been taken, because they permitted the United States to run extremely large deficits in 1971, 1972, and 1973. In turn, the deficits were an important source of the sharp increase in monetary reserves throughout the world that fueled the inflationary surge of 1973 and 1974.

Second, the Bretton Woods system itself turned into an engine of worldwide inflation for at least several reasons. One, the IMF effectively added directly to the world supply of international reserves and to the world's monetary base by SDRs and by other means. Two, because the IMF was available to bail out deficit countries, a permanent reduction in the demand for reserves resulted, thereby permitting more inflation per reserve dollar or per ounce of gold by deficit countries. The extension of credit to deficit countries delayed the deflationary actions they would otherwise have been required to take to maintain their fixed rates without at the same time requiring any parallel or offsetting action by surplus countries. The IMF system thereby weakened the balance-of-payments constraints on inflation and biased the general outcome.

Third, the Bretton Woods system of fixed rates meant that individual countries wishing to pursue stable price-level objectives were unable to do so because they essentially had to import the higher prices from abroad, both because the nominal prices of internationally traded goods expressed in their own currencies would rise and because the surplus countries would not be able to restrict the increase in their own money resulting from the deficits of inflating countries. Infrequent changing of parities helped to alleviate this situation but did not effectively curb the bias or sop up the excess money. As Haberler and others have demonstrated, given the apparent worldwide tendency for nominal wage rates to be rigid downward, plus a worldwide commitment to full employment, there is a necessary implication that deflation has been effectively ruled out as a means for achieving balance-of-payments equilibrium. Thus, balance-of-payments adjustment under fixed or semifixed rates requires the inflation of surplus countries.

In this context, and with the added impact of the spread of the modern technology of central banking, it is little wonder that contemporary governments, given their inherent myopia, find it difficult to resist pressures to inflate or to weigh correctly the costs of longer-run inflationary consequences resulting from a wide range of tax, subsidy, and full-employment programs financed by or depending on the distortions of monetary creation. These sources of the worldwide inflationary bias of public policies are also strengthened by the apparent tendency in many markets for output and employment responses to monetary change in the short run to precede price responses, so that monetary expansion may initially lead to the good results of increased output before the later bad results of higher prices. On the other hand, monetary restriction may correspondingly lead to the bad results of reduced output and employment before the good results of moderating inflation. Given widespread commitment to full employment, these lags bias monetary policy toward inflation.

THE SECULAR ASSOCIATION OF MONEY AND PRICES: CLOSED AND OPEN ECONOMIES

The secular association between inflation and increases in the stock of money per unit of output follows from stability in the marginal rate of substitution of money (in real terms) and goods—which is to say that the public wishes to hold a stable fraction of income in the form of cash. This is another way of stating the stability of income velocity in the income variant of the quantity equation:

$$MV = Y \tag{1}$$

or in real terms:

$$MV \left(\frac{1}{P} \right) = \frac{Y}{P} \tag{2}$$

where Y = the nominal value of current output of goods and services, M = the nominal stock of money, P = an index of prices of goods and services included in Y, and V = income velocity.

Transposing, we have:

$$P = \frac{M}{(Y/P)} V \tag{3}$$

where Y/P = real income or output.

In this context, it is important to distinguish between real and nominal cash balances, between alternative analytical assumptions about whether an economy is open or closed, and about whether there is central-bank intervention to maintain fixed exchange rates or a regime of nonintervention (otherwise known as floating rates). In a closed economy the stock of nominal money is determined by the central bank, but the real value of money balances is determined by the demands of the public. Indeed, change in the price level is the principal adjustment mechanism equating the demand for and supply of real money balances.

In an open economy with fixed exchange rates, received theory holds that international trade is essentially like interregional trade, so that there is no important autonomy for an individual country. Prices, at least those of internationally traded goods after adjustments for transportation costs and the like, are given by world, not domestic, markets. Indeed, because prices tend to uniformity through speculation and arbitrage, there are no important distinctions between world and domestic markets. An individual country, especially if small, is essentially a price taker.

With fixed rates and an open economy, received balance-of-payments theory concludes that balance-of-payments adjustments plus the required intervention by the central bank to maintain fixed rates yield the result that changes in the stock of money respond to changes in a country's demand for money. In other words, nominal money demand determines nominal money supply, and the stock of money (rather than prices) adjusts to changes in the public's demand for cash. The adjustment process, in response to an initial increase in the demand for money, envisages that if people wish to shift into money, they must shift out of goods or out of securities. Reduced demand for goods leads to reduced imports and expanded exports, while reduced demand for securities, by causing interest rates to rise, at least transitionally, leads to capital imports. Thus, starting from balance-of-payments equilibrium, either the current account or the capital account, or both, move into surplus.

The rules of the fixed-exchange regime require central-bank intervention to prevent appreciation. The central bank must buy foreign exchange, and it offers its own newly created base money to do so, which causes a multiple expansion of the money stock. The process of increasing the money stock continues until the public's demands are satisfied. On the other hand, an increase in foreign money and prices leads to domestic inflation, both because there is no essential difference between domestic and foreign prices and because the initial balance-of-payments surplus will cause the central bank to increase domestic money.

The same processes hold for deflation.

To pursue a price path different from the world's, a country must alter its exchange rate from time to time. Similarly, a country must alter exchange rates in order to achieve control over its money. Indeed, exchange appreciation or depreciation may be interpreted as a necessary element in achieving a desired money stock. (Controls are a form of disguised variation in exchange rates.)

Turning now to an open economy with no central-bank intervention in foreign-exchange markets, a single country is essentially back in the closed economy case because it can pursue an autonomous monetary policy. Exchange rates vary to clear foreign-exchange markets, and with no intervention there are neither surpluses nor deficits. As in the quantity equation described above, the price level will tend to depend on (1) real output, (2) the stock of nominal money (determined by the central bank), and (3) the public's demand for real balances. Exchange rates will tend to be related in part to relative price levels.

Stability of velocity implies corresponding stability in the relationship between nominal money and nominal income as in equation (1) and in the relationship between nominal money per unit of output and prices as in equation (3). It does not necessarily imply stability in the relationship between money and prices because, especially in the short run, real income may also respond to monetary change. If money and output are independent and output is given, the stability of velocity implies stability of the relationship between money and prices. Some analyses make these assumptions, especially in considering long-run questions. Although there is some evidence that in the long run output depends on such real variables as productivity and stocks of resources and that output is essentially independent of money, there is no such dependable empirical case in the short run. Indeed, although there are numerous studies showing the numerical or functional stability of velocity in the short period covered by business cycles, there is no apparent stability or predictability regarding how changes in income are broken down into changes in prices on the one hand and changes in output on the other. In addition, more complex models of short-run price-level determination, which include additional variables, have yet to yield satisfactory results. This is why the focus of this study is on longer-period relations.

Money and Inflation in the United States and
Other Major OECD Countries, 1960–73

If V is a constant, changes in the price level depend only on changes in $M/(Y/P)$, the quantity of money per unit of output. As Table 3.3 shows, income velocity has been close to a constant in the United States since at least 1960, when M_2 (currency plus all commercial-bank deposits less large certificates of deposit) is used as the measure of money. Velocity differed little from its mean value of 2.36, despite the variability of interest rates, fiscal and monetary policies, inflation, growth, and other economic, social, and political

circumstances that could reasonably be expected to alter velocity and
the demand for money. The standard deviation was only 0.03, or 1.34
percent of the mean. The same constancy of velocity is also reflected
in the high correlations of M_2 on GNP and in the close relationship of
prices to M_2 per unit of output. The essential constancy of M_2 velocity
is the most striking and puzzling datum in this research and perhaps
in recent monetary history.

Figure 1 shows the close association between the U.S. CPI and
the ratio of nominal M_2 to deflated GNP. Nominal GNP was deflated
by the CPI, which makes up most of the GNP deflator. The regression
equation is

$$P = \underset{(.30)}{.88} + \underset{(37.62)}{.99} \; \frac{M_2}{\left(\dfrac{Y}{P}\right)} \tag{4}$$

with $r^2 = .99$ (t values are in parentheses). The constant term is
virtually zero, and the regression coefficient essentially unity. This
means that prices have varied proportionately with nominal money per
unit of output. The high correlation means that the relationship is
dependable, which is evident from Figure 3.1.

FIGURE 3.1

United States: Index Numbers of Prices and Money (M_2) per Unit of
Real Output, 1960–73
(1965 = 100)

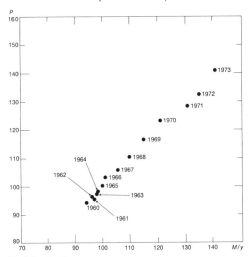

Source: Table 3.3.

FIGURE 3.2

"Rest of the World": Index Numbers of Prices and Money per Unit of
Real Output, 1960–73
(1965 = 100)

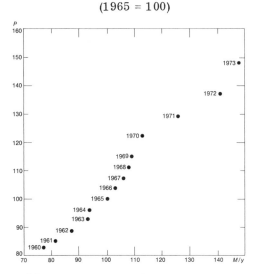

Source: Table 3.2.

Velocity has also tended to be relatively constant since 1960
for the nine OECD countries in our survey, for which M_1 (currency
plus demand deposits) is used as the measure of money. Figure 3.2
shows the same close association between the weighted averages of
prices and the nominal stocks of money per unit of output for these
countries as in the United States.*
The regression equation is

$$P = 6.87 + .96 \frac{M_1}{\left(\frac{Y}{P}\right)}$$
$$\quad (1.50) \quad (22.66)$$

(5)

with $r^2 = .98$. The regression equation is very close to equation (4)
for the United States and may be interpreted in the same way. The
constant term is positive but small and close to zero, and the regression coefficient is close to unity but slightly lower than the .99 estimate for the United States.

---

*See pp. 62–65 for a more detailed description of data sources.

Constancy of income velocity also implies a similarly close association between the nominal stock of money and nominal GNP. Figure 3.3 shows the scatter for index numbers of U.S. nominal money (M_2) and nominal GNP. The regression equation is

$$Y = 2.03 + .98 M_2 \qquad (6)$$
$$(1.28) \quad (76.42)$$

with an r^2 of .99. As in equation (4), the constant term is essentially zero and the regression coefficient is very close to one, both of which are implied by constant velocity.

For the nine major OECD countries the regression of nominal money (M_1) on nominal GNP is

$$Y = 6.87 + .96 M_1 \qquad (7)$$
$$(2.08) \quad (44.12)$$

and the coefficient of determination (r^2) is .99. The results are similar to equation (5). Figure 3.4 shows the scatter diagram of the weighted index numbers of nominal money and nominal GNP for these countries.

FIGURE 3.3

United States: Index Numbers of Money (M_2) and GNP, 1960-73
(1965 = 100)

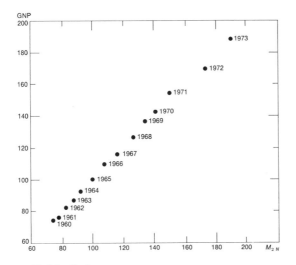

Source: Table 3.3.

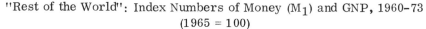

FIGURE 3.4

"Rest of the World": Index Numbers of Money (M_1) and GNP, 1960-73
(1965 = 100)

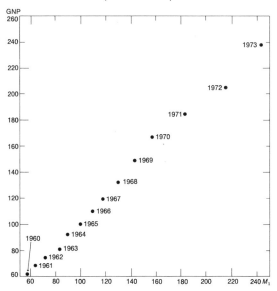

Source: Table 3.2.

Although income velocity has tended to be constant in the United States when M_2 is used as the measure of money, it turns out that there has been an upward secular drift of velocity when M_1 is used. * Nevertheless, as Figure 3.5 shows, there has been a close association between M_1 and GNP since 1960.

In the 1960s M_1 velocity tended to increase an average of 2.7 percent per year. The same long-period drift continued in the 1970s. The sense in which velocity is used here conforms to equation (1), which suppresses the constant term, making average velocity equal to marginal velocity.[4] Regression equations (4) and (6) tested whether average and marginal velocities were equal for M_2. The evidence shows that the constant term is essentially zero.

For M_1, average velocity is rising, but marginal velocity is relatively stable. This follows from the regression of M_1 on GNP,

*For the data and a more detailed analysis, see Table 3.3 and accompanying text.

FIGURE 3.5

United States: Index Numbers of Money (M_1) and GNP, 1960–73
(1965 = 100)

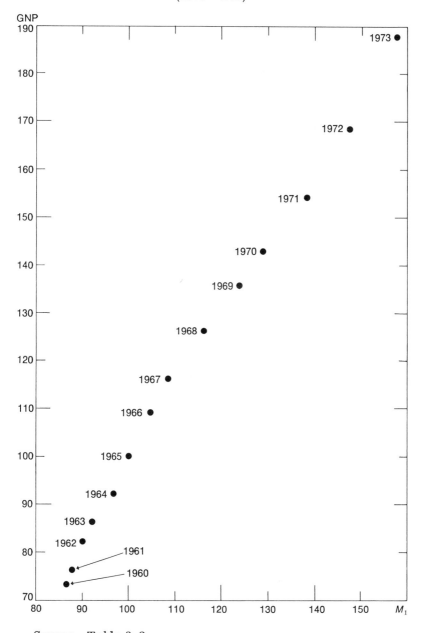

$$Y = -55.30 + 1.54 \, M_1 \qquad (8)$$
$$ (-14.85) \quad (47.42)$$

$(r^2 = .99)$, because marginal velocity is positive and the constant term is negative.

To test the relationship between prices and money per unit of output for M_1 as in equation (3), which depends on constancy of average velocity, obviously requires an adjustment of the data to take into account the secular drift of M_1 average income velocity. If this were done, it would approximate the close relationship when the M_2 measure is used.

Money and Inflation in Latin America, 1950-69

As equation (3) indicates, stability of income velocity implies that inflation will be related positively to a country's money-supply growth and inversely to its growth of real income. To illustrate and test the proposition further, consider the inflation experience of 16 Latin American countries over the 1950-69 period summarized by Robert C. Vogel.[5] Vogel calculated the means and standard deviations of the inflation rates of the 16 countries as measured by consumer prices as well as the means and standard deviations for money-supply growth and real-income growth, where money was defined as currency and demand deposits (M_1), and real income was estimated as nominal GNP deflated by the country's CPI. The average annual rates of inflation for the period ranged from 43.0 percent for Uruguay to a mere 0.3 percent for El Salvador and 1.1 percent for Venezuela (see Table 3.1).

Using ordinary least squares I estimated the regression equation across 16 countries:

$$P' = a + bM' + c \left(\frac{Y}{P}\right)' \qquad (9)$$

where P is the mean annual rate of inflation, M is the mean annual money-supply growth and (Y/P) the mean annual real-income growth, all measured as percent per year. The regression results were:

$$P' = 1.35 + 1.05 \, M' - 1.38 \left(\frac{Y}{P}\right)' \qquad (10)$$
$$ (0.57) \quad (22.31) \qquad (3.55)$$

with an R^2 of 0.98 (t values are in parentheses).

The results strongly confirm that secular inflation is associated with an increase in money per unit of output. The regression co-

TABLE 3.1

Inflation and Related Statistics for 16 Latin American Countries, 1950–69

	Rate of Inflation*		Money Supply Growth*		Real Income Growth*		Velocity	
	Mean	S.D.	Mean	S.D.	Mean	S.D.	Mean	S.D.
Uruguay	43.0	34.9	40.1	33.3	0.7	6.3	5.96	0.82
Bolivia	41.3	55.9	41.6	58.1	3.0	22.8	11.77	5.58
Brazil	35.1	21.5	38.2	22.1	3.9	4.3	4.17	0.39
Chile	28.2	14.6	35.2	12.8	4.6	6.4	11.35	1.74
Argentina	26.4	23.4	24.6	11.8	2.4	7.3	4.14	1.01
Paraguay	12.5	17.5	15.4	14.2	5.5	4.1	11.27	1.21
Colombia	9.2	8.2	16.5	5.5	5.4	3.9	6.56	0.50
Peru	8.5	5.8	13.4	6.0	5.7	7.4	8.38	0.64
Mexico	5.3	5.3	11.3	4.3	6.9	4.6	8.22	0.52
Nicaragua	3.4	6.1	8.6	11.1	3.7	7.5	8.85	0.94
Ecuador	3.0	3.3	8.8	8.2	4.7	3.7	8.00	0.62
Honduras	2.1	3.4	8.0	8.7	4.0	3.9	10.21	1.11
Costa Rica	1.9	2.2	9.0	7.9	5.7	3.4	6.16	0.41
Guatemala	1.1	2.8	5.9	7.4	3.9	3.1	9.47	0.78
Venezuela	1.1	2.8	7.9	8.8	6.8	4.8	6.70	0.50
El Salvador	0.3	1.5	3.5	6.9	4.6	3.5	7.58	0.62

*Percent per year.

Note: S.D. is the standard deviation. Inflation is measured by the consumer price index; money supply is currency plus demand deposits; and real income is nominal GNP deflated by the consumer price index.

Source: Robert C. Vogel, "The Dynamics of Inflation in Latin America, 1950–1969," American Economic Review, March 1974, p. 103.

efficients are elasticity estimates. The elasticity of the inflation rate with respect to the money-supply growth is essentially 1.0, which indicates that the differences in the 20-year inflation experience among the 16 countries are directly proportional to differences in their respective rates of monetary growth, holding real income constant. The elasticity of the inflation rate with respect to real income is -1.38. The standard error of the regression coefficient is 0.39, so that it, too, does not differ significantly from -1.00, which means that inflation differences among the 16 countries are inversely proportional to differences in their respective changes in output.

I separated the 20-year period into two decades, 1950-59 and 1960-69, and ran the same regressions. The results were essentially identical for both decades as well as for the period as a whole. Results for five-year periods were also identical.

Another implication of the stability of velocity is that variability in the growth rate of money leads to variability in either the rate of inflation or changes in output, or both. Using Vogel's figures for the standard deviations of the same variables as measures of their variability in the regression of the form of equation (9), I found:

$$P'' = -1.19 + 1.0\, M'' + .09 \left(\frac{Y}{P}\right)'' \qquad (11)$$
$$\quad\;\; (.80) \quad (5.53) \quad\;\; (.09)$$

with an R^2 of 0.88.* These results indicate that Latin American countries with more variable year-to-year changes in their rates of monetary growth experienced correspondingly more variable year-to-year changes in their inflation rates and that the variability of inflation is directly proportional to the variability in the rate of monetary change. There is no apparent association between the standard deviation of real income and the standard deviation of inflation, because of the high simple correlation between the independent variables (the standard deviations of money and output), but a still higher simple correlation between money and prices that, taken together, masks the separate influence of the variability of real income on the variability of prices.

These statistical results are consistent with Vogel's findings based on different statistical tests and using more complex models to test several alternative hypotheses using annual data for pooled regressions.[6]

---

*The double prime (") notation refers to standard deviations of the rates of change of the variables.

INFLATION IN THE 1960s

I turn now to the worldwide inflation of recent years, with special emphasis on 10 major industrial OECD countries. These are
the United States, Canada, Japan, France, Germany, the United Kingdom, Italy, Belgium, the Netherlands, and Switzerland. For convenience, I shall refer to the 10 as the "world."

The First National City Bank of New York has estimated a
weighted average of percentage rates of change in money (M_1), GNP,
and the CPI for the 10 countries, using 1970-71 exchange rates to
convert all figures to dollar equivalents before weighting each country
by its relative GNP in the base period.* The United States is approximately half the total for the "world." For some purposes I have separated the U.S. figures from the aggregate and also have added data
and calculations based on the M_2 measure of money.

Tables 3.2, 3.3, and 3.4 contain these data for the "world"
less the United States, for the United States, and for the "world."
They also contain the implied percentage changes in real GNP (with
the CPI used as the deflator) and in income velocity. In addition to
these data (with 1965 equaling 100), index numbers have been con-
structed for the levels of money, nominal GNP, prices, real GNP,
and income velocity, and these figures are also shown in Tables 3.2,
3.3, and 3.4. Later, I will discuss the relationship between U.S.
monetary policy and that of the "rest of the world," as well as the
special importance of the "dirty" floats of 1971 and 1972 and of the
movement toward floating rates in 1973 in shaping the path of monetary change and, thereby, of world inflation. (See Table 3.5 for the
total and average annual percentage changes in these variables for the
1960-73 period and selected subperiods.)

The decade of the 1960s tended to be a period of worldwide inflation, as measured by official price indexes. During the first half
of the decade, inflation outside the United States both exceeded and
had greater variability than U.S. inflation. As Table 3.3 shows, the
CPI in the U.S. increased every year between 1960 and 1965, and
the rate of increase ranged from 1 percent to 1.7 percent. However,
given many of the biases in the construction of the index, many economists have believed that these changes in the official index were consistent with stable or even slightly declining prices. For the "rest
of the world," as Table 3.2 shows, the rise in the index of consumer

---

*The weights were as follows: United States, .5042; Belgium,
.0144; Canada, .0440; France, .0793; Germany, .1033; Italy, .0493;
Japan, .1111; the Netherlands, .0175; Switzerland, .0115; and the
United Kingdom, .0658.

TABLE 3.2

"World" Less United States: Changes in Money Supply, Nominal GNP,
Consumer Prices, Deflated GNP, and Income Velocity,
Annual Data, 1960-73

Year	Money (1)	GNP (2)	Consumer Prices (3)	GNP Deflated (4)	Income Velocity (5)
Percentage changes					
1960	9.94	13.28	2.30	10.97	3.33
1961	13.54	11.75	2.94	8.81	-1.68
1962	12.02	9.37	4.31	5.09	-2.55
1963	13.73	10.44	4.62	5.81	-3.19
1964	9.43	11.90	3.48	8.42	2.58
1965	11.26	8.96	4.32	4.64	-2.09
1966	8.83	9.60	3.85	5.75	0.77
1967	8.77	8.61	3.03	5.58	-0.16
1968	9.24	10.81	3.67	7.14	1.57
1969	9.94	12.55	3.51	9.04	2.60
1970	9.74	12.69	6.49	6.20	2.94
1971	17.47	10.61	5.87	4.73	-6.86
1972	17.31	11.07	5.75	5.33	-6.23
1973	13.05	16.20	8.43	7.76	3.15
Index numbers (1965 = 100)					
1960	56.78	60.76	82.46	72.85	107.34
1961	64.47	67.90	84.89	79.27	105.54
1962	72.22	74.26	88.54	83.30	102.85
1963	82.13	82.02	92.64	88.14	99.57
1964	89.88	91.78	95.86	95.57	102.13
1965	100.00	100.00	100.00	100.00	100.00
1966	108.83	109.60	103.85	105.75	100.77
1967	118.37	119.04	107.00	111.65	100.61
1968	129.31	131.90	110.92	119.62	102.19
1969	142.16	148.46	114.82	130.44	104.84
1970	156.01	167.30	122.27	138.52	107.93
1971	183.27	185.05	129.44	145.08	100.52
1972	214.99	205.53	136.89	152.81	94.26
1973	243.05	238.83	148.43	164.67	97.23

Note: Weighted averages of data from France, Germany, Japan, the United Kingdom, Italy, Belgium, the Netherlands, Switzerland, and Canada. 1973 figures are preliminary estimates.

Sources: Unpublished data made available by private communication with First National City Bank of New York; Federal Reserve Bank of St. Louis, Rates of Change in Economic Data from 10 Industrial Countries (March 14, 1974).

TABLE 3.3

United States: Changes in Money Supply, Nominal GNP, Consumer Prices, Deflated GNP, and Income Velocity, Annual Data, 1960-73

Year	Money M$_1$ (1)	Money M$_2$ (1)	GNP (2)	Con- sumer Prices (3)	GNP De- flated (4)	In- come M$_1$ (5)	Ve- loc- ity M$_2$ (5)
Percentage changes							
1960	-0.10	1.00	4.10	1.60	2.50	4.20	3.10
1961	2.10	5.20	3.30	1.00	2.30	1.10	-1.90
1962	2.20	5.80	7.70	1.10	6.60	5.40	1.90
1963	2.90	6.50	5.40	1.20	4.20	2.40	-1.10
1964	4.00	6.30	7.10	1.30	5.80	3.00	0.80
1965	4.20	8.00	8.30	1.70	6.60	3.90	0.30
1966	4.50	7.80	9.50	2.90	6.60	5.00	1.70
1967	3.90	7.60	5.90	2.90	3.00	2.00	-1.70
1968	7.00	8.90	8.90	4.20	4.70	1.90	0.00
1969	6.30	6.70	7.60	5.40	2.20	1.30	0.90
1970	4.50	4.40	5.00	5.90	0.90	0.50	0.60
1971	7.10	11.80	8.00	4.30	3.70	0.90	-3.80
1972	6.50	10.20	9.40	3.30	6.10	2.90	-0.80
1973	7.40	9.60	11.60	6.20	5.40	4.20	2.00
Index numbers (1965 = 100)							
1960	85.94	73.51	73.52	93.93	78.03	85.64	100.05
1961	87.75	77.35	75.95	94.87	79.82	86.58	98.14
1962	89.68	81.85	81.80	95.92	85.09	91.25	100.01
1963	92.28	87.14	86.21	97.07	88.67	93.44	98.91
1964	95.97	92.60	92.34	98.33	93.81	96.25	99.70
1965	100.00	100.00	100.00	100.00	100.00	100.00	100.00
1966	104.50	107.78	109.50	102.90	106.60	105.00	101.70
1967	108.58	116.01	115.96	105.88	109.80	107.10	99.97
1968	116.18	126.38	126.28	110.33	114.96	109.13	99.97
1969	123.49	134.82	135.88	116.29	117.49	110.55	100.87
1970	129.05	140.73	142.67	123.15	116.43	111.11	101.47
1971	138.21	157.30	154.09	128.44	120.74	112.11	97.62
1972	147.20	173.37	168.57	132.68	128.10	115.36	96.84
1973	158.09	190.01	188.12	140.91	135.02	120.20	98.77

Source: Federal Reserve Bank of St. Louis, Rates of Change in Economic Data for 10 Industrial Countries (March 14, 1974).

TABLE 3.4

"World": Changes in Money Supply, Nominal GNP, Consumer
Prices, Deflated GNP, and Income Velocity, Annual Data, 1960-73

Year	Money (1)	GNP (2)	Consumer Prices (3)	GNP Deflated (4)	Income Velocity (5)
Percentage changes					
1960	4.88	8.65	1.95	6.70	3.77
1961	7.77	7.49	1.96	5.53	-0.28
1962	7.07	8.53	2.69	5.85	1.46
1963	8.27	7.90	2.90	5.00	-0.37
1964	6.69	9.48	2.38	7.10	2.79
1965	7.70	8.63	3.00	5.63	0.93
1966	6.65	9.55	3.37	6.18	2.90
1967	6.32	7.24	2.96	4.28	0.92
1968	8.11	9.85	3.94	5.91	1.74
1969	8.11	10.05	4.46	5.59	1.94
1970	7.10	8.81	6.19	2.62	1.71
1971	12.24	9.29	5.08	4.21	-2.95
1972	11.86	10.23	4.51	5.72	-1.63
1973	10.20	13.88	7.31	6.57	3.68
Index numbers (1965 = 100)					
1960	69.66	66.80	88.02	75.36	92.14
1961	75.07	71.08	89.74	79.53	95.35
1962	80.38	77.93	92.16	84.18	96.74
1963	87.03	84.08	94.83	88.39	96.39
1964	92.85	92.06	97.09	94.67	99.08
1965	100.00	100.00	100.00	100.00	100.00
1966	106.65	109.55	103.37	106.18	102.90
1967	113.39	117.48	106.43	110.72	103.85
1968	122.59	129.05	110.62	117.27	105.65
1969	132.53	142.02	115.56	123.82	107.70
1970	141.94	154.54	122.71	127.07	109.54
1971	159.31	168.89	128.94	132.42	106.31
1972	178.20	186.17	134.76	139.99	104.58
1973	196.38	212.01	144.61	149.19	108.43

*M_1 data used for the United States.

Source: Unpublished data made available by private communication with First National City Bank of New York.

prices ranged from 2.3 percent to 4.62 percent during the same period.

In the latter half of the decade the inflation rate was relatively stable outside the United States and varied between approximately 3 to 3.85 percent per year. For the United States the inflation rate continued to rise from 2.9 percent per year in 1966 to 5.4 percent per year in 1969, before peaking at 5.9 percent per year in 1970.

In the 1970s, the U.S. inflation slowed to 4.3 percent in 1971 and 3.3 percent in 1972, before rising abruptly to 6.2 percent in 1973. Inflation tended to accelerate through 1973, and on a January 1973 to January 1974 basis the increase in the CPI was 9.3 percent. For the "rest of the world," starting in 1970, the inflation rate exceeded the U.S. rate and, as in the United States, there was a slight tendency for the inflation to moderate in 1971 and 1972 before the sharp rise in 1973. In 1973 most of the other nine countries experienced inflation at rates close to or exceeding the U.S. rate. From January 1973 to January 1974 consumer prices increased 7.4 percent in Germany, 7.9 percent in the Netherlands, 10.3 percent in France and 23.1 percent in Japan. Over the 14-year span between 1960 and 1973 the inflation rate in the "rest of the world" exceeded that of the United States in every year but 1969 and 1970.

For the United States over the 1960-70 period as a whole, as Table 3.5 shows, inflation averaged 2.5 percent per year, or a total of 31.1 percent for the 10-year period. For the "rest of the world," inflation averaged 4.0 percent per year, or a total of 48.3 percent.

Regarding money and GNP outside the United States, money increased by 174.8 percent in the decade, or 10.6 percent per year on average. The rise in nominal GNP of 175.4 percent was virtually the same as the increase in money. Although there was some variability in "rest-of-the-world" velocity on a year-to-year basis, income velocity in 1970 was almost the same as it had been in 1960. "Rest-of-the-world" output increased a total of 90.1 percent, or an average of 6.6 percent per year.

For the United States during the 1960-70 decade M_1 increased a total of 50.2 percent, or at the average rate of 4.2 percent per year. Nominal GNP increased 94.1 percent, 6.9 percent per year, and M_2 increased 91.4 percent, or at the average annual rate of 6.7 percent. U.S. deflated GNP rose a total of 49.2 percent, an average of 4.1 percent per year. Unlike the "rest of the world," U.S. M_1 velocity continued its rising secular trend at the average rate of 2.7 percent per year. It turns out that for the later 1970-73 period, this secular trend of velocity increased at the identical mean rate of 2.7 percent per year. M_2 velocity was essentially constant in the 1960s and in the 1970s as well.

TABLE 3.5

"World" Less United States, the United States, and the "World"; Intraperiod Changes in Money, Nominal GNP, Consumer Prices, Deflated GNP, and Velocity, 1960–73 and Selected Subperiods

| | "World" Less United States | | United States | | | | "World" | |
	Percent Change over Period	Average Annual Rate of Change	Percent Change over Period M₁	M₂	Average Annual Rate of Change M₁	M₂	Percent Change over Period	Average Annual Rate of Change
1960–73								
Money	328.1	11.8	84.0	158.5	4.8	7.6	181.9	8.3
GNP	293.1	11.1	155.9		7.5		217.4	9.3
Prices	80.0	4.6	50.0		3.2		64.3	3.9
GNP deflated	126.0	6.5	73.0		4.3		98.0	5.4
Velocity	-9.4	-.8	40.0	-1.3	2.7	-.1	17.7	1.3
1960–70								
Money	174.8	10.6	50.2	91.4	4.2	6.7	103.8	7.4
GNP	175.4	10.7	94.1		6.9		131.3	8.7
Prices	48.3	4.0	31.1		2.5		39.4	3.4
GNP deflated	90.1	6.6	49.2		4.1		68.6	5.4
Velocity	.6	.05	29.7	1.4	2.7	.1	18.9	1.7
1970–73								
Money	55.8	15.9	22.5	35.0	7.0	10.5	38.4	11.4
GNP	42.8	12.6	31.9		9.7		37.2	11.1
Prices	21.4	6.7	14.4		4.6		17.8	5.6
GNP deflated	18.9	5.9	16.0		5.1		17.4	5.5
Velocity	-9.9	-3.4	8.2	-2.7	2.7	-.9	-1.0	-.3
1960–65								
Money	76.1	12.0	16.4	36.0	3.1	6.3	43.6	7.5
GNP	64.6	10.5	36.0		6.3		49.7	8.4
Prices	21.3	3.9	6.5		1.3		13.6	2.6
GNP deflated	37.3	6.5	28.2		5.1		32.7	5.8
Velocity	-6.8	-1.4	16.8	-.05	3.2	-.01	8.5	1.6
1965–70								
Money	56.0	9.3	29.0	40.7	5.2	7.1	41.9	7.2
GNP	67.3	10.8	42.7		7.4		54.5	9.1
Prices	22.3	4.1	23.2		4.3		22.7	4.2
GNP deflated	38.5	6.7	16.4		3.1		27.1	4.9
Velocity	7.9	1.5	11.1	1.5	2.1	.3	9.5	1.8

Sources: Tables 3.2, 3.3, and 3.4.

42

First Half of the 1960s

As Tables 3.2 and 3.5 show, in the first half of the 1960s the stock of money outside the United States increased at relatively high rates, as did nominal GNP.* From 1960 to 1965 "rest-of-the-world" money increased slightly faster than nominal GNP, as income velocity tended to decline. Although there was less stability on a year-to-year basis than for the 1960-65 period as a whole, over the period money increased at a mean annual rate of 11.65 percent (with a standard deviation of 1.79), nominal GNP increased at a mean annual rate of 10.95 percent (with a standard deviation of 1.65), and velocity declined at an average of 0.60 percent per year.

For the United States over the same period these relationships were less stable for M_1, but were highly stable for M_2 relations. The mean annual increase in M_1 was 2.55 percent (with a standard deviation of 1.57), and the mean annual increase in nominal GNP was 5.98 percent (with a standard deviation of 2.03). M_1 income velocity continued its secular upward drift and increased at the rate of 3.3 percent per year. M_2 increased an average of 5.0 percent per year, with essentially no change in velocity.

During the first half of the decade of the 1960s, balance-of-payments considerations in the United States and concern for the loss of gold were important constraints on U.S. monetary expansion and were crucial in countering widespread pressures to inflate by monetary or other means.[7] The U.S. price stability relative to world inflation cited above was responsible for progressively larger current account surpluses (see Table 3.6), but U.S. government and U.S. private capital movements to abroad were large enough to result in official-settlements deficits in each year in the 1960-65 period. There was some tendency for a reduction in the U.S. deficit over the period, and by 1966 there was a small surplus on an official-settlements basis. From 1960 through 1965 the total U.S. deficit on an official-settlements basis was $12.1 billion, and the U.S. gold stock declined $5.43 billion, from $19.50 billion to $14.07 billion. The gold drain was a most serious concern for U.S. authorities who, at the time,

---

*These figures are biased upward by the rough estimating procedure we have used that depends on 1970-71 exchange rates. Given that foreign currencies in the early 1960s tended to be worth less relative to the dollar than they were in 1970-71, our procedure has resulted in overstating both nominal money and nominal GNP by the same degree. The estimates of prices and income velocity are independent of this bias. Thus, changes in the deflated GNP are also biased upward.

TABLE 3.6

U.S. Balance-of-Payments Measures, Annual Data, 1960–73
(billions of U.S. dollars)

Year	Current Account (1)	Basic Balance (2)	Nonliquid Short-Term Private Capital and SDR (3)	Errors and Omissions (4)	Net Liquidity[a] (5)	Liquid Private Capital Flows (6)	Official Settlements (7)
1960	1.8	-1.2	-1.4	-1.1	-3.7	0.3	-3.4
1961	3.1	0.0	1.2	-1.0	-2.2	0.9	-1.3
1962	2.5	-1.0	-0.6	-1.2	-2.9	0.2	-2.6
1963	3.2	-1.3	-1.0	-0.4	-2.7	0.8	-1.9
1964	5.8	0.0	-1.6	-1.0	-2.7	1.2	-1.5
1965	4.3	-1.8	-0.2	-0.5	-2.5	1.2	-1.3
1966	2.3	-1.7	-1.1	-0.3	-2.2	2.4	0.2
1967	2.0	-3.3	-0.5	-0.9	-4.7	1.3	-3.4
1968	-0.5	-1.4	0.2	-0.4	-1.6	3.2	1.6
1969	-1.0	-3.0	-0.6	-2.5	-6.1	8.8	2.7
1970	0.4	-3.0	0.4	-1.2	-3.8	-6.0	-9.8
1971	-2.3	-9.3	-1.7	-11.0	-22.0	-7.8	-29.8
1972	-8.4	-9.8	-0.9	-3.1	-13.9	3.5	-10.3
1973[b]	3.0	1.2	-4.2	-4.8	-7.8	2.5	-5.3

[a] Coverage of liquid banking claims for 1960–63 and of nonliquid nonbanking claims for 1960–62 is limited to foreign currency deposits only; other liquid items are not available separately and are included with nonliquid claims.

[b] Preliminary figures.

Column 1 = goods and services + private and government transfer payments.
Column 2 = current account + private and government long-term capital.
Column 3 = nonliquid short-term private capital + SDR.
Column 4 = errors and omissions.
Column 5 = basic balance + column 3 + column 4.
Column 6 = liquid private capital flows.
Column 7 = column 5 + column 6.

Source: U.S. Department of Commerce, Survey of Current Business, various issues.

were deeply committed to the fixed exchange-rate system and the gold
convertibility of the dollar. In addition, the gold drain was itself a
direct but partial constraint on monetary expansion.

Taking the 1960-65 period as a whole, "rest-of-the-world"
money increased $66.6 billion, or 93.6 percent. Total international
reserves increased $18.7 billion, or 51.0 percent, which was close
to 25 percent of the rise in international money. (This figure applies
to all countries, not merely the nine OECD countries in our "world.")
Of this increase, gold accounted for $9.4 billion. (The U.S. gold
stock declined $5.34 billion and essentially added this sum to the
"rest-of-the-world" international reserves.) Foreign-exchange holdings rose $6.2 billion, virtually all of which consisted of U.S. liabili-
ties. U.K. liabilities hardly changed over the period, so that they
were a progressively smaller proportion of world foreign-exchange
reserves. Holdings of other foreign-exchange assets were low and
changed little. The Eurodollar market was still in its infancy, and
apparently there were few foreign-exchange reserves held in non-
U.S. and non-U.K. currencies. Thus, it would seem that U.S. deficits contributed in an important way to the world monetary expansion,
to constraints on U.S. monetary expansion, and to the correspondingly
higher rate of inflation in the "rest of the world" than in the United
States. In addition, some elements of a modified specie-flow adjustment mechanism appeared to have been at work during this period.
Note that because money increased so much faster than reserves, it
suggests that foreign central banks need not have permitted the rise
in their reserve positions to have a multiplied effect on money, which
they apparently did. Indeed, the additional domestic credit creation,
and with it more money and more inflation, may have been desired for
other purposes, including the use of inflation as a means of attaining
long-run balance-of-payments equilibrium.

During the same period, the IMF also contributed to world expansion of money and thereby of prices because international reserves
in the form of reserve positions in the IMF by non-U.S. countries increased by $4.5 billion—from $1,250 billion at year-end 1959 to
$4,770 billion at the end of 1965.

Second Half of the 1960s

From 1966 to 1970 there was a period of accelerating inflation
in the United States, which for the first time exceeded the inflation
rate of the "rest of the world." Outside the United States inflation
was stable and in the 3.0 to 4.0 percent range.

The period was characterized by fixed exchange rates and a
rising tide of difficulties in maintaining the Bretton Woods system.

Major currencies were forced to revalue and their links to gold were further attenuated by the adoption of the two-tier system in 1968, which effectively eliminated gold convertibility of the dollar and thereby essentially placed the world on a dollar-exchange standard. The long-run impact of this fundamental change was masked by the fact that in 1968 and 1969 the U.S. balance of payments was in surplus on an official-settlements basis, mainly because of private short-term capital flows to the United States in response to high U.S. interest rates. Still another factor in these capital flows may have been the political disturbances in Europe, notably in Czechoslovakia and France. * (See Table 3.6 for U.S. balance-of-payments measures on an annual basis for 1960-73 and Table 3.7 for quarterly data, 1968-73.) In 1968 and 1969 world international reserves increased only moderately and actually fell for the total of European industrial countries. It was not until 1970 and 1971 that the system began to crumble and then to disintegrate.

As Tables 3.2 and 3.5 show, for the "rest of the world" over the 1965-70 period, money increased at relatively stable annual rates of between 8.8 percent to 9.7 percent per year. Reflecting a mild upward drift of velocity, nominal GNP tended to increase at more rapid rates. The five-year rise in velocity is virtually identical with the five-year mild fall in velocity during the first half of the decade. By 1970 income velocity had essentially returned to its 1960 value.

For the United States, rates of monetary change were highly variable, especially relative to the experience of the first half of the decade, and tended to be associated with later business-cycle changes in GNP. M_1 velocity continued its upward secular drift, but at a somewhat slower rate than in earlier years, reflecting at least in part the

---

*Walter Salant made the following interesting comment on these capital flows in a letter to the author in which he stated: "You attribute the U.S. surplus in 1968 and 1969 mainly to high U.S. interest rates. I think the political disturbances in Europe (Czechoslovakia, France) and the inability of European capital to go into gold at a price to which people had been accustomed was also a factor. I discussed this point in an article in the Quarterly Review of the Banca Nazionale del Lavoro in September 1969 . . . (see pages 298-300). I agree that the rise of interest rates in the U.S. was a factor but . . . I do not—nor did not then—think that was enough to account for the reversal. Without the termination of the gold pool's operations, I think the rise of interest rates in the United States would simply have raised interest rates elsewhere, and would probably even have done so without attracting much capital."

recession of 1969–70 and the usual cyclical decline in velocity during
recession periods. As Table 3.5 shows, for the 1965–70 period velocity increased an average of 2.1 percent per year, and in the first
half of the decade it increased an average of 3.2 percent per year.
For the decade as a whole, the mean increase is 2.7 percent per year,
which is precisely the value for the 1970–73 subperiod. M_2 increased
at an average annual rate of 7.8 percent, and M_2 velocity increased a
total of 1.0 percent, or about 0.2 percent per year.

Between 1965 and 1970 an expansion of international reserves
was part of the mechanism that resulted in continued monetary expansion. For the United States, of course, international reserves played
a minor direct role in its money–supply process, except that the $3.0
billion decline in the U.S. gold stock was a small moderating factor
in U.S. monetary growth. For the "rest of the world," international
reserves increased $22.5 billion in five years, or approximately 40
percent. The bulk of the increase, approximately 90 percent, was
accounted for by the rise in foreign–exchange reserves. Of the $21.0
billion increase in foreign–exchange reserves, $7.9 billion was in ad-
ditional dollar liabilities. The larger amount, $13.3 billion, is ac-
counted for by what the IMF data blandly label "other." Some of the
"other" foreign–exchange reserves may be in currencies other than
those of the United States or the United Kingdom, such as the Deutschemark or franc, but the collective wisdom of international financial experts appears to be that these reserves are mainly composed of Eurodollars.

In 1965 the total for the "other" category was $0.9 billion. By
1970 it had reached $14.2 billion. Thus, the development was both
new and major and contributed an important source of the rise in international reserves. Not only are the details of these connections obscure, but it is not at all clear how the development of the Eurodollar
market in its operation as a source of international reserves affects
received balance–of–payments analysis.

Between 1965 and 1970 IMF operations continued to increase international reserves and thereby to augment world monetary expansion.
First, there was an increase of $1.0 billion in non–U.S. reserve posi-
tions in the IMF. Second, the SDR was initiated in 1970 and approximately $3.1 billion of SDRs were created in 1970, $0.9 billion held by
the United States and $2.2 billion for the "rest of the world."

As Figure 3.6 shows, over the 1965–70 period as well as over
the entire decade of the 1960s, first differences in the U.S. money
stock (M_1) on an annual basis were inversely related to the U.S. official–settlements deficit, and have no apparent relationship to changes
either in international reserves or in foreign money. The inverse relationship between changes in U.S. money and the U.S. deficit would
also appear to be troublesome for received balance–of–payments doc-

FIGURE 3.6

First Differences of U.S. and "Rest-of-World" Money, First
Differences in Total International Reserves, U.S. Balance of
Payments, Official-Settlements Deficit, and First Differences in U.S.
Liabilities to Foreigners

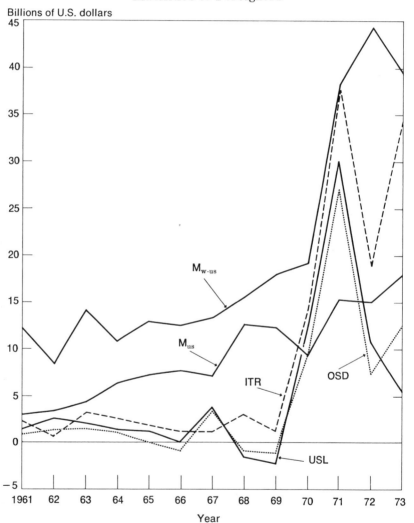

Note: $M_{w\text{-}us}$: first differences of money stock in rest of world;
M_{us}: first differences in U.S. money stock (M_1); ITR: first differences
in international total reserves; OSD: U.S. balance-of-payments official
settlements deficit; and USL: first differences in U.S. liabilities.

Source: Table 3.8.

48

FIGURE 3.7

U.S. and "Rest-of-the-World" Percentage Change in Money,
Quarterly Figures at Annual Rates, 1966–73

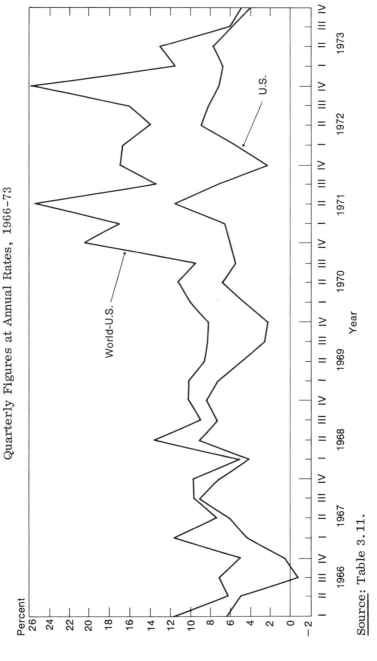

Source: Table 3.11.

49

trine. These annual data for U.S. and foreign money have a common
secular rise, but there is no close year-to-year synchronization of
the two. This, too, is troublesome in view of the fact that, as Figure
3.7 shows, during the 1966-70 period there was an almost perfect
synchronization of quarterly rates of change of U.S. money and of
the money of the other nine countries in our "world." I have no hypothesis to explain this striking phenomenon, which continued until
the third quarter of 1971. I have checked the data and, at least thus
far, do not believe these regularities are the result of the methods used
for estimating the data. Later the positive synchronization becomes
an inverse one for the six quarters covering the second half of 1971
and most of 1972. During 1973, the positive synchronization was resumed.*

1970-73: THE BREAKUP OF THE BRETTON
WOODS SYSTEM

By 1970 the scene had been set for the final breakup of the
Bretton Woods fixed exchange-rate system and the large-scale expansion of world money in 1971 and 1972, as central banks outside the
United States struggled to prevent or retard depreciation of the U.S.
dollar, which led to the virtual worldwide price explosion of 1973 as
well as to the abandonment in early 1973 of fixed rates and heavy central-bank intervention.

The year 1970 was a recession year in the United States, which
followed the restrictive and antiinflationary policy that started soon
after the 1968 presidential election. Essentially freed from major
concern about gold by the 1968 two-tier gold agreement, the Nixon
administration was able to focus attention almost exclusively on domestic matters and to follow the policy of "benign neglect" with respect
to gold and the balance of payments.

From a surplus of $2.7 billion in 1969, the U.S. balance of
payments shifted in 1970 to an unprecedented deficit of $9.8 billion.
"Other" foreign exchange, perhaps mainly Eurodollars, also increased

---

*The U.S. money data were taken from Federal Reserve sources
(before the February 1974 revision), and the rest-of-the-world money
figures were derived by subtracting the U.S. series from the "world"
money series as estimated by the First National City Bank of New York.
First National City Bank weights were used in making the calculation.
In examining quarterly data on the U.S. official-settlements balance,
we found no apparent direct relationship between these quarterly data
and quarterly changes in foreign money.

by approximately $7.0 billion. In other words, the Eurodollar market was itself adding a large volume of reserves, which apparently served as the basis for creating more money.

However, it was not until 1971 that the fixed-rate system began to give way. As Table 3.7 shows, in the first quarter of 1971 the U.S. deficit was at an annual rate of $22.5 billion, essentially all of which resulted from capital movements out of the United States. In the second quarter of 1971 the official-settlements deficit rose further, to an annual rate of $25.4 billion. These movements accelerated still further in the third quarter of 1971 and were responsible for the August 15, 1971 major change in U.S. policy. Despite these huge deficits, the U.S. gold stock hardly changed as foreign central banks, perhaps on the basis of earlier agreements, did not acquire gold. Although the U.S. gold window was publicly closed on August 15, 1971, it would appear that, de facto, the dollar had been inconvertible for at least nine months. Withdrawal of gold convertibility at the fixed $35 price for gold and the virtual absence of major U.S. intervention in foreign-exchange markets effectively withdrew U.S. commitment and support for the fixed-rate system and effectively left it to foreign monetary authorities to determine their own policies with respect to intervention. It also served to reduce world demands for dollars as reserve assets, as liquid assets, and as a substitute for domestic money, thereby adding further downward pressure on the dollar. Given foreign central-bank intervention, it tended to increase world money and thereby prices.

The dollar was permitted to depreciate relative to major currencies, initially by 10 percent, but foreign central banks generally continued to intervene to retard still further depreciation. Massive intervention both before and after the August 15, 1971 change in U.S. policy resulted in a U.S. official-settlements deficit of $47.5 billion (at annual rates) in the third quarter of 1971. Because the data are available only on a quarterly basis, it cannot be determined how much of the deficit and the associated foreign central-bank intervention took place before August 15 and how much intervention took place after August 15. However, it is clear that in the fourth quarter of 1971 large-scale intervention by foreign central banks continued, because the U.S. official-settlements deficit was $23.6 billion at annual rates. Thus, as 1971 wore on foreign central banks persisted in increasing the monetary bases in their respective countries by monetizing the large capital flows from the United States in their desire to impede the devaluation of the dollar.

To summarize, during the third quarter of 1971 the fixed-rate system came unhinged. Because of continued and large-scale central-bank intervention, much of the world had entered a period of negotiated rates and of dirty floats largely maintained by the intervention of sur-

TABLE 3.7

U.S. Balance-of-Payments Measures, Quarterly Data Adjusted at Annual Rates, 1968(I)–74(IV)
(billions of U.S. dollars)

Year and Quarter	Current Account (1)	Basic Balance (2)	Nonliquid Short-Term Private Capital and SDR (3)	Errors and Omissions (4)	Net Liquidity (5)	Liquid Private Capital Flows (6)	Official Settlements (7)
1968							
I	-0.7	-1.4	-0.5	-1.3	-3.2	1.9	-1.3
II	0.6	0.5	1.5	2.2	-0.2	8.0	7.7
III	0.3	-1.9	-0.7	1.4	-1.2	2.7	1.5
IV	-2.0	-2.9	-.6	-.5	-1.7	0.4	-1.3
1969							
I	-1.4	-1.2	-0.4	-3.9	-5.5	10.8	5.4
II	-2.4	-8.2	-1.3	-2.8	-12.3	15.8	3.6
III	-0.1	-4.6	0.0	-3.7	-8.3	6.3	-2.0
IV	-0.2	1.7	-0.8	0.8	1.7	2.3	4.0
1970							
I	0.6	-4.8	-0.1	-0.2	-5.2	-6.0	-11.2
II	0.8	-2.4	0.7	-1.7	-3.4	-4.5	-8.0
III	0.9	-1.4	1.1	-2.8	-3.2	-4.3	-7.5
IV	-0.5	-3.5	0.0	-0.1	-3.6	-9.0	-12.7

	1	2	3	4	5	6	7
1971							
I	0.6	-5.5	-1.4	-3.8	-10.7	-11.8	-22.5
II	-2.9	-12.0	-1.3	-9.6	-22.8	-2.6	-25.4
III	-2.7	-13.2	-2.6	-22.0	-37.8	-9.7	-47.5
IV	-6.2	-7.5	-1.4	-7.7	-16.6	-7.0	-23.6
1972							
I	-9.4	-15.1	-1.4	3.8	-12.8	-1.2	-13.9
II	-9.5	-7.4	1.9	-3.8	-9.2	5.8	-3.4
III	-7.6	-10.6	-1.0	-6.5	-18.1	0.0	-18.1
IV	-7.0	-6.2	-3.2	-6.0	-15.4	9.5	-5.9
1973							
I	-2.2	-3.5	-7.1	-15.6	-26.2	-15.7	-41.9
II	-1.8	-2.7	-5.7	1.9	-6.5	7.9	1.4
III	5.0	10.2	0.2	-4.4	6.0	2.5	8.5
IV*	11.2	0.8	-4.3	-1.1	-4.5	15.3	10.8

*Preliminary figures.

Column 1 = goods and services + private and government transfer payments.
Column 2 = current account + private and government long-term capital.
Column 3 = nonliquid short-term private capital + SDR.
Column 4 = errors and omissions.
Column 5 = basic balance + column 3 + column 4.
Column 6 = liquid private capital flows.
Column 7 = column 5 + column 6.

Sources: Federal Reserve Bank of St. Louis, Rates of Change in Economic Data for 10 Industrial Coun‐tries (March 14, 1974); U.S. Department of Commerce, Survey of Current Business, various issues.

plus countries to prevent dollar devaluation. This intervention increased their domestic money stocks.

As a result of these actions the expansion of world money accelerated sharply starting in the fourth quarter of 1970. As Table 3.8 and Figure 3.7 show, during the fourth quarter of 1970 "rest-of-the-world" monetary expansion, which had been in the 9.0 to 10.0 percent range for several years, dramatically increased to an annual rate of 20.4 percent for the weighted average of the nine countries. By the second quarter of 1971 the rate reached 25.5 percent. As Table 3.9 shows, the sharp increase in monetary expansion from 1970 levels was general among all nine countries except Italy, which had attained monetary expansion that averaged 22.4 percent in 1971 as the basis for comparison with a 1971 average figure of 21.0 percent. For a sample of other countries in the second quarter of 1971, money increased at annual rates of 30.5 percent in Japan, 19.4 percent in the Netherlands, 27.5 percent in Canada, and a more moderate 18.1 percent in Germany. For the entire year of 1971 the average for the rest of the world increased 17.5 percent.

A consistent picture is seen in what happened to international reserves. In 1971 alone, total reserves of non-U.S. countries increased $39.3 billion, or 50 percent, $26.8 billion of which directly consisted of dollar foreign exchange.

The same general situation for rapid increase of money outside the United States continued in 1972. Foreign central banks continued to acquire dollars to forestall the appreciation of their currencies vis-à-vis the dollar, perhaps to avoid reducing the short-run stimulus that an undervalued currency afforded export-and-import-competing industries. The United States wanted the same thing, dollar devaluation to stimulate exports.* The U.S. balance of payments remained in deficit all through 1972, at lower rates than in the second half of 1971 but totaling $10.3 billion for the year. Total international reserves also continued to rise at a rapid pace, only moderately less so than in 1971 and mainly in the foreign-exchange component of international reserves. Here, the mysterious "other" component of foreign-exchange reserves, presumably composed mostly of Eurodollars, increased by $13.7 billion, which exceeded the growth of dollar foreign-exchange reserves.

For 1972 as a whole, money increased an average of 17.3 percent among the nine countries in our sample outside the United States. Again, virtually all of the nine participated in the same general mone-

---

*One way to interpret these events is that there was competitive devaluation with important monetary implications that just happened to have severe inflationary impacts.

TABLE 3.8

U.S. and "Rest-of-the-World" Percentage Changes in Money (M_1), Quarterly Figures at Annual Rates, 1966-67

Year and Quarter	"World"	United States	"World" Less United States
1966			
I	9.0	6.5	11.6
II	5.6	4.9	6.2
III	3.0	-0.7	6.9
IV	2.7	0.4	5.0
1967			
I	7.9	4.2	11.7
II	6.6	6.0	7.2
III	9.5	9.2	9.8
IV	8.5	7.2	9.8
1968			
I	4.6	4.1	5.0
II	11.2	9.0	13.4
III	8.2	7.5	9.0
IV	9.1	8.2	10.1
1969			
I	8.8	7.6	10.1
II	6.8	5.0	8.6
III	5.4	2.3	8.4
IV	5.2	2.1	8.2
1970			
I	7.3	4.5	10.1
II	9.0	6.8	11.3
III	7.5	5.5	9.5
IV	13.2	6.0	20.4
1971			
I	11.7	6.5	17.0
II	18.6	11.7	25.5
III	10.3	7.3	13.3
IV	9.6	2.2	17.1
1972			
I	11.0	5.4	16.8
II	11.4	8.8	14.0
III	12.1	8.1	16.2
IV	16.5	7.3	25.9
1973			
I	9.4	7.1	11.6
II	12.2	7.7	12.8
III	5.8	5.6	5.9
IV	4.5	4.0	5.0

Sources: Estimates for "world" money made available by private communication with First National City Bank of New York; Board of Governors of the Federal Reserve System, Federal Reserve Bulletin, various issues for U.S. money data.

TABLE 3.9

Percentage Changes in Money, GNP, and Consumer Prices for 10 OECD Countries, Quarterly Figures at Annual Rates, 1971-73

	1971				1972				1973			
	I	II	III	IV	I	II	III	IV	I	II	III	IV
Belgium												
M	13.1	7.9	15.4	10.5	11.2	15.4	12.7	13.2	16.3	13.8	7.3	6.8
Y	15.8	16.6	13.6	12.2	6.7	16.8	1.1	33.8	10.6	7.2	3.1	n.a.
P	5.7	5.6	5.1	5.0	5.4	4.1	7.6	7.4	8.4	5.7	5.6	8.0
Canada												
M	20.2	27.5	24.2	26.3	33.0	35.2	10.5	6.0	13.5	8.0	8.5	n.a.
Y	9.8	14.1	13.2	8.2	9.7	13.5	6.4	15.2	21.1	11.8	9.9	n.a.
P	2.4	5.7	6.0	2.7	4.7	3.8	8.1	4.1	7.5	9.6	11.7	7.3
France												
M	20.0	8.7	11.7	9.5	14.7	13.3	19.6	13.2	3.2	16.6	2.4	4.2
Y	n.a.	n.a.	n.a.	n.a.	n.a.	n.a.	n.a.	n.a.	n.a.	n.a.	n.a.	n.a.
P	5.6	6.4	5.5	5.8	5.3	5.6	7.8	8.8	3.5	8.2	10.2	11.4
Germany												
M	10.3	18.1	12.1	18.9	9.7	13.7	18.2	10.5	8.6	2.2	-14.4	8.0
Y	13.9	6.9	10.2	3.6	23.0	-2.5	8.7	14.0	28.1	1.1	4.6	n.a.
P	9.4	5.9	3.5	4.6	8.1	4.5	5.9	7.3	9.5	6.3	3.8	8.3

Italy												
M	25.4	11.8	19.5	16.2	16.4	22.3	23.6	28.0	12.9	31.8	27.2	n.a.
Y	n.a.	n.a.	n.a.	n.a.	n.a.	n.a.	n.a.	n.a.	n.a.	n.a.	n.a.	n.a.
P	4.8	4.3	3.9	5.8	5.0	5.7	7.1	11.2	11.3	14.7	9.5	11.0
Japan												
M	31.0	30.5	28.8	37.9	5.5	25.4	1.0	71.9	21.5	31.1	8.3	12.2
Y	14.9	10.9	14.3	6.1	12.6	19.3	20.3	22.9	26.1	26.2	17.6	37.6
P	5.2	7.5	3.8	5.3	1.1	8.8	3.3	5.5	11.4	22.7	12.7	14.7
Netherlands												
M	23.0	19.4	7.3	15.6	18.8	26.3	23.9	3.1	16.9	7.0	-19.9	n.a.
Y	n.a.	n.a.	n.a.	n.a.	n.a.	n.a.	n.a.	n.a.	n.a.	n.a.	n.a.	n.a.
P	9.7	10.8	4.6	8.0	8.6	10.3	2.8	10.7	6.9	12.4	3.2	9.5
Switzerland												
M	24.1	22.2	18.8	19.1	20.9	4.7	6.3	-6.2	-4.1	4.9	-2.1	n.a.
Y	n.a.	n.a.	n.a.	n.a.	n.a.	n.a.	n.a.	n.a.	n.a.	n.a.	n.a.	n.a.
P	7.2	5.9	4.6	8.5	7.5	5.1	5.4	9.8	10.7	6.8	5.7	20.5
United Kingdom												
M	19.1	4.6	13.6	25.1	18.5	16.9	5.6	17.1	0.3	28.4	-10.8	n.a.
Y	3.5	17.0	24.8	5.8	5.5	9.4	11.2	20.1	35.7	-0.9	17.9	n.a.
P	10.1	11.9	9.1	5.9	5.1	4.6	10.4	11.3	5.4	13.3	6.1	14.4
United States												
M_1	6.5	11.3	6.6	2.1	5.4	8.5	8.5	8.7	7.1	7.7	5.6	4.0
M_2	13.6	14.7	7.8	7.4	11.0	9.8	10.8	10.2	8.8	8.8	7.9	8.9
Y	15.1	7.9	6.5	8.0	10.9	11.2	8.7	11.7	15.2	9.8	10.6	10.5
P	3.1	4.4	4.0	2.3	3.3	3.3	3.6	3.5	5.8	9.0	9.1	9.9

Note: n.a. = not available.

Source: Federal Reserve Bank of St. Louis, Rates of Change in Economic Data for 10 Industrial Countries (March 14, 1974).

57

tary episode. For several countries the rate of monetary expansion
increased—for example, Canada's money grew at 25.7 percent in 1972,
compared with 20.8 percent in 1971. In several countries the rate of
monetary expansion slowed a bit—for example, in the United Kingdom
the 1972 rate of monetary expansion was 13.9 percent, compared with
15.3 percent for 1971.

As Table 3.8 and Figure 3.7 show, for the first three quarters
of 1972 the rate of monetary expansion for the nine countries ranged
from 14.0 to 16.8 percent. Then, in the fourth quarter of 1972 it
shot up to 25.9 percent averaged across the nine countries. The coun-
try-by-country increases were far from uniform. In Japan money increased at an annual rate of 71.9 percent, up from 1.0 percent in the
third quarter of 1972. In Germany, the increase was 10.5 percent,
down from 18.2 percent in the third quarter of 1972, and in Switzerland money actually fell at an annual rate of 6.2 percent. In Italy
monetary growth continued to accelerate and was at an annual rate of
28 percent during the fourth quarter of 1971.

In early 1973 the remains of the fixed-rate system disintegrated
further. Massive capital flows forced the central banks of major countries to abandon fixed or negotiated rates as they were driven to cease
large-scale intervention in foreign-exchange markets in order to regain control over their domestic money stocks. However, before
abandoning fixed rates, foreign central banks acquired a large volume
of additional dollars as the U.S. official-settlements deficit in the first
quarter of 1973 reached an annual rate of a staggering $41.9 billion,
virtually all of which was accounted for by short-term capital flows.

The adoption of floating rates was not uniform. With large-scale
capital flight out of Italy into Switzerland in January, first Italy and then
Switzerland permitted their currencies to float. In February Japan announced that the yen would be allowed to float upward as multilateral
readjustments, including a 10 percent devaluation of the dollar in February, were hastily made to stem massive capital flows, especially
out of dollars. In March five of the European Community countries—
Belgium, Denmark, France, Germany, and the Netherlands—allowed
their currencies to float jointly vis-à-vis the dollar and other currencies, thereby permitting the dollar to depreciate still further.

These moves led to the elimination of the U.S. balance-of-payments deficit in the second quarter of 1973, which recorded an official-
settlements surplus of $1.4 billion at annual rates. The surplus con-
tinued to grow through the year as devaluation improved the trade balance and capital flowed back into the United States. Correspondingly,
total international reserve assets and their foreign-exchange component ceased growing in the second half of 1973. The dollar appreciated throughout most of the second half of the year.

TABLE 3.10

U.S. Official-Settlements Balance, and Changes in U.S. Money, in International Reserves and the U.S. Liability Component, and in Foreign Money, Annual Data, 1961–73

(billions of U.S. dollars)

Year	Change in Money (M_1) for United States (1)	U.S. Balance of Payments: Official Settlements (2)	Change in International Reserves		Change in Money for "World" Less United States (5)
			U.S. Liabilities (3)	Total Reserves (4)	
1961	3.0	-1.3	0.7	2.1	12.0
1962	3.2	-2.6	1.2	0.5	8.9
1963	4.4	-1.9	1.6	3.5	14.4
1964	6.2	-1.5	1.2	2.5	10.5
1965	6.8	-1.3	0.0	1.9	13.4
1966	7.6	0.2	-0.9	1.7	12.4
1967	6.9	-3.4	3.3	1.6	13.4
1968	12.8	1.6	-0.9	3.1	15.3
1969	12.2	2.7	-1.3	0.9	18.0
1970	9.3	-9.8	7.8	14.3	19.4
1971	15.3	-29.8	26.9	38.0	38.3
1972	15.0	-10.3	6.8	19.0	44.6
1973	18.2	-5.3	12.1	33.6	39.5

Sources: Federal Reserve Bank of St. Louis, Rates of Change in Economic Data for 10 Industrial Countries (March 14, 1974); International Monetary Fund, International Financial Statistics, 1972 suppl. and various issues; unpublished data made available by private communication with First National City Bank of New York.

The move toward floating rates meant that the rest of the world was able to call a halt to the rapid rate of monetary expansion that had been taking place since 1971. By the third quarter of 1973, monetary growth was down to 5.9 percent. The expansion of the money stocks of all countries but Italy slowed significantly, and in four countries the money stock actually fell (see Table 3.9). In the United Kingdom money fell at an annual rate of 10.8 percent; in Germany, 14.4 percent; and in the Netherlands, 19.9 percent. Preliminary estimates for the fourth quarter indicate that monetary expansion was again slowed and at the rate of 5.1 percent, as compared with a 25.9 percent rate a year earlier during the fourth quarter of 1973.

It is, of course, too early to determine with any degree of assurance that the major currencies will continue to float and that thereby foreign central banks will be able to maintain control over money to achieve price stabilization or other objectives. Although the lessons of recent history have amply demonstrated the hazards of the Bretton Woods system and of fixed rates, and of the incompatibility of fixed rates and stable prices, I am not at all convinced that there is yet sufficient understanding of these phenomena or of free markets to preclude the return to yet another and perhaps new engine of inflation.

As Tables 3.2 and 3.5 show, for the rest of the world over the 1971-73 period the increase in nominal GNP of 42.8 percent was less than the 55.8 percent increase in money in the three years. During 1971 and 1972, "rest-of-the-world" velocity fell sharply, and there was no worldwide increase in inflation. Velocity increased in 1973 but was still below earlier levels in spite of the rapid inflation during the year. I have as yet no hypothesis convincing to me to explain the temporary decline in velocity or the equivalent lag in the effects of the surge of monetary growth in 1971 and 1972. Perhaps a more complex distributed lag analysis will turn out to explain the temporary decline in velocity. Note that M_2 velocity in the United States also declined temporarily in 1971 and 1972. The temporary decline in velocity remains another puzzle in this research.

I examined the data for the nine countries separately and found that income velocity fell in all of them (see Table 3.9). For example, in 1971 and 1972 money in Canada increased at 20.8 percent and 25.7 percent, respectively, while GNP increased 8.9 percent and 10.6 percent. In Japan money increased 25.5 percent in 1971 and 22.1 percent in 1972, while nominal GNP increased 11.3 percent in 1971 and 14.5 percent in 1972. In Germany, money increased 12.1 percent and then 14.1 percent, while nominal GNP increased 10.07 percent in 1971 and 9.20 percent in 1972. In fact, during the two-year period, it was only in the United States that income velocity for M_1 increased. Of course, one possibility is that many people may have interpreted the sharp increase in money as temporary and subject to

TABLE 3.11

U.S. Official-Settlements Balance, and Percentage Changes in U.S. Money, in International Reserves and the U.S. Liability Component, and in Foreign Money, Annual Data, 1961–73

Year	Percentage Change in Money (M_1) for United States (1)	U.S. Balance of Payments: Official Settlements* (2)	Percent Change in International Reserves		Percentage Change in Money for "World" Less United States (5)
			U.S. Liabilities (3)	Total Reserves (4)	
1961	2.1	-1.3	6.31	3.47	14.8
1962	2.2	-2.6	10.17	0.80	9.5
1963	2.9	-1.9	12.31	5.55	14.1
1964	4.0	-1.5	8.22	3.75	9.0
1965	4.2	-1.3	0.00	2.75	10.5
1966	4.5	0.2	-5.70	2.39	8.8
1967	3.9	-3.4	22.15	2.20	8.8
1968	7.0	1.6	-4.95	4.17	9.2
1969	6.3	2.7	-7.51	1.16	9.9
1970	4.5	-9.8	48.75	18.26	9.7
1971	7.1	-29.8	113.03	41.04	17.5
1972	6.5	-10.3	13.41	14.55	17.3
1973	7.4	-5.3	21.04	22.46	13.1

*In billions of U.S. dollars.

Sources: Federal Reserve Bank of St. Louis, Rates of Change in Economic Data for 10 Industrial Countries (March 14, 1974); International Monetary Fund, International Financial Statistics, 1972 suppl. and various issues; unpublished data made available by private communication with First National City Bank of New York.

TABLE 3.12

Quantity and Composition of International Reserve Assets, Quarterly, 1967(IV)–73(IV)
(end of period, in billions of U.S. dollars)

Year and Quarter	Total Reserve Assets	Gold Stock*	SDR	Reserve Position in IMF	Foreign Exchange	U.S. Liabilities	U.K. Liabilities	Other
1967								
IV	73.6	39.5	—	5.7	28.4	18.3	8.2	1.8
1968								
I	72.7	37.8	—	5.7	29.1	17.3	9.6	2.2
II	73.2	38.6	—	6.6	28.0	15.9	8.8	3.3
III	73.4	38.7	—	6.6	28.2	16.4	8.8	3.0
IV	77.0	38.9	—	6.5	31.6	17.5	9.7	4.4
1969								
I	75.0	39.0	—	6.1	28.9	15.8	9.8	4.2
II	76.9	38.9	—	6.3	31.7	14.9	9.4	7.3
III	80.1	38.9	—	6.7	34.5	16.7	9.7	8.1
IV	78.2	39.1	—	6.7	32.4	16.0	8.9	7.4
1970								
I	80.7	39.1	3.3	7.2	32.4	18.4	7.1	6.8
II	84.5	39.1	3.2	7.1	35.2	19.4	6.9	8.8

III	87.4	38.6	3.2	6.7	39.0	21.7	7.3	9.9
IV	92.5	37.2	3.1	7.7	44.5	23.8	6.6	14.2
1971								
I	99.4	36.9	5.8	7.3	49.4	28.4	6.2	14.8
II	105.0	36.5	5.9	6.9	55.7	34.0	6.9	14.8
III	117.6	36.2	5.9	6.3	69.2	45.3	7.1	16.7
IV	130.6	39.2	6.4	6.9	78.2	50.6	7.9	19.6
1972								
I	138.8	38.6	9.6	6.9	83.8	53.8	8.4	21.6
II	147.2	38.7	9.1	7.0	92.4	54.6	11.1	26.7
III	153.7	38.8	9.4	6.7	98.8	60.1	8.2	30.5
IV	158.7	38.8	9.4	6.9	103.6	61.5	8.8	33.3
1973								
I	179.2	43.2	10.5	7.5	118.0	71.3	8.8	37.8
II	183.2	43.2	10.6	7.5	121.9	70.7	9.4	41.8
III	187.4	43.2	10.7	7.5	126.1	69.8	—	—
IV	183.2	43.1	10.6	7.4	122.0	66.8	—	—

*Gold valued at $35 per ounce before December 1971, at $38 per ounce from that date until February 1973, and $42.22 thereafter.

Source: International Monetary Fund, International Financial Statistics, 1972 suppl. and various issues.

later reductions, but I have not yet had an opportunity to test this or
several other plausible explanations. In any event, the evidence is
clear that the large increases in nominal expenditures in the United
States and in the "rest of the world" were the result of large increases
in money rather than in velocity.

The low level of velocity—in 1973 it was 11 percent below its
level in 1970, even after the rise in 1973—suggests a short-run source
of further inflation, even if foreign central banks are able to maintain
monetary growth at the 5 percent level. Given the 6.5 percent average growth in real GNP that was achieved over the 1960-73 period,
a 5.0 percent growth of money, and a return to 1970 velocity, we
should find that average inflation outside the United States will be in
the 10 to 11 percent range in the near future. Of course, if there is
an economic slowdown and if real growth is below average, prices
would tend to be correspondingly higher. Widespread slowdowns are
likely because sharp reductions in the pace of monetary growth tend
to affect real output and employment before prices. In any event,
if "rest-of-the-world" money continues to grow only at 5 percent, I
find it difficult to envisage a continuation of the inflationary surge of
1973, even with continued restriction of petroleum output by the oil
cartel. In fact, given the limitations on the upward flexibility of velocity, I would anticipate a sharp reduction in "rest of the world" inflation, provided a tight rein is maintained on monetary growth. If it
turns out that "rest-of-the-world" inflation is less than that of the
United States, we may again see market pressures for dollar devaluation. If so, that would be the time to ascertain whether foreign central banks are able to resist this market phenomenon by repeating
old errors of intervention in foreign-exchange markets. In addition,
high rates of monetary expansion may be resumed if foreign central
banks, believing that high rates of monetary expansion are a cure for
economic slack and unemployment, panic in the face of economic recessions.

For the United States during the 1971-73 period, domestic considerations in the formulation of monetary, fiscal, and other stabilization policies, including wage and price controls, overshadowed balance-
of-payments considerations. Over the three years, annual growth
rates of M_1, measured on the basis of annual averages of daily figures,
were between 6.5 and 7.5 percent, and for M_2, 9.5 to 12.0 percent,
the highest in the post-World War II period. As Tables 3.3 and 3.5
show, M_1 income velocity increased an average of 2.7 percent per
year, which was identical with the trend in the 1960-70 period. Consistent with earlier norms, M_1 velocity increased throughout the business-cycle expansion. Differing with earlier norms, M_2 velocity remained virtually constant throughout the entire period.

In recent years an important element in U.S. policy has been the pursuit of autonomy in the conduct of domestic monetary policy. Even before the acceptance of floating rates in 1973, we had effectively achieved that autonomy once gold convertibility was abrogated. It would seem that the United States has only itself to blame, not the anchovies in Peru or foreign inflation, for the myopia of public policy and for such a shabby record.

I have not mentioned the prices of soybeans, gasoline, or shoes or the prices of other individual goods in my analysis of worldwide inflation. This is not an inadvertent oversight. To be sure, there was some reduction in the output of several products when the pace of worldwide inflation accelerated in 1973, which would explain why prices of chicken feed and petroleum increased relative to other prices. Because, as Tables 3.2 and 3.3 show, aggregate output in the United States and in the "rest of the world" grew in 1973, the increase in the ratio of money to output, which was the proximate cause of the speedup of inflation, was the result of sharp increases in money, rather than decreases in output. In the United States, since 1971 both the M_1 and M_2 increases of money have been rising at the fastest rates since World War II. Prices have also been rising at the fastest pace since 1946. Since Federal Reserve actions determine the quantity of money, the Fed rather than the fish in Peru is primarily responsible for U.S. inflation woes.

I conclude with a few good words from Irving Fisher, written in 1912:

The whole civilized world is now eager to know whether in the future the high cost of living is to advance further, recede, or remain stationary. Opinions are plentiful but data supporting them are few. Even the best forecasts I have seen appear to be based on a very incomplete comprehension of the problem. Many conceive it as a problem of ordinary supply and demand and discuss the general price level as they would discuss the price of wheat or any other commodity, overlooking the fact that the causes affecting price levels are as distinct from those affecting an individual price as the causes affecting the tides are distinct from those affecting an individual wave. [8]

ACKNOWLEDGMENTS

This study benefited greatly from the criticism and suggestions of John Auten, Gottfried Haberler, Samuel Katz, Wilson Schmidt,

Anna Schwartz, and Harvey Segal. William Rule was especially helpful in sharpening the analysis and in the preparation of the empirical sections. The First National City Bank of New York kindly made available unpublished estimates of world money, prices, and income. Drafts of several sections of the paper were first presented at a course I conducted on the Economics of Inflation at Virginia Tech's Reston Economics Program in the winter quarter, 1974. Some of the research reported here was supported by a grant from the National Science Foundation.

NOTES

1. Anna J. Schwartz, "Secular Price Change in Historical Perspective," Universities-National Bureau Committee for Economic Research, Conference on Secular Inflation, suppl. to Journal of Money, Credit and Banking, February 1973, p. 264.

2. Ibid.

3. Ibid., p. 265.

4. See Milton Friedman and David I. Meiselman, "The Relative Stability of Monetary Velocity and the Investment Multiplier in the United States, 1897-1958," report to Commission on Money and Credit, in Stabilization Policies (Englewood Cliffs, N.J.: Prentice-Hall, Inc., 1963), pp. 165-268, for a discussion of the difference between average and marginal velocity. This study also contains velocity estimates for earlier periods. It turns out that there has been a closer relationship between money and income since 1960 than before.

5. Robert C. Vogel, "The Dynamics of Inflation in Latin America, 1950-1969," American Economic Review 64 (March 1974): 102-14.

6. Ibid., pp. 112-13.

7. See James Tobin, The New Economics: One Decade Older (Princeton, N.J.: Princeton University Press, 1974).

8. Irving Fisher, "Will the Present Upward Trend of World Prices Continue?" American Economic Review 2, no. 3 (September 1912): 531.

4

EXTERNAL SOURCES
OF U.S. INFLATION
Wilson E. Schmidt

There is a widespread view that the inflation we have recently
gone through is a special one, a commodity inflation caused particularly by international forces, including two devaluations of the dollar.
Both the Federal Reserve and the Council of Economic Advisors hold
this view. It is, of course, understandable that the Fed and the administration should want to blame foreign events for U.S. problems.
But that position will not wash. No matter what one's view of the
cause of inflation, the fact is that more of our inflation has been made
at home than abroad.

Broadly speaking, there are three different explanations for
changes in the price level. One is the monetarist view, which puts
the main emphasis on the stock of money. A second is the Keynesian
view, which focuses on injections through investment, government expenditures, and exports and on leakages in the form of savings, taxes,
and imports. A third is the cost-push argument, which contends that
as costs rise, prices will be increased by businessmen.

All these explanations are well-known in the domestic context,
for they have been roundly debated in the scientific journals, in the
pages of the financial press, in the Congress, and elsewhere. Their
application to an open economy is perhaps less familiar.

"COST PUSH" AND THE OPEN ECONOMY

When applied to an economy with trade relations with the rest
of the world, the cost push argument goes as follows: A devaluation
of the dollar raises the prices of goods we buy on world markets,
raising the cost of production of items that use those imports directly,
forcing businessmen to raise the prices of their products. Even though

imports are only 5 percent of the U.S. GNP, the rise in costs and in prices will be more extensive than that figure would suggest, because the prices of substitutes produced in the United States will also rise— for example, the price of Detroit autos no doubt rises when the prices of imported cars rises. Also, the rise in prices of imports may also affect wage demands, which will press up the cost of living, spreading throughout the economy to a degree far more important than suggested by the role of imports in consumer expenditures.

Much the same thing can happen on the export side. When the foreign demand for U.S. goods rises, either because of a devaluation, which makes U.S. goods more attractive to foreigners, or through a world boom, prices of U.S. exports in dollars will rise. This sets off a round of cost increases. For example, price increases for U.S. machinery will work their way up through the economy.

The evidence to support this view of the inflationary effect of external forces is indeed impressive. For example, we know that domestic production that competes with imports is roughly equal to those imports. Thus, even though imports have a weight of only 1.35 percent in the Wholesale Price Index (WPI), 3.1 percent in the Consumer Price Index (CPI), and 5 percent in the GNP deflator, the impact of a change in import prices on these indexes should be greater than indicated by their weight.

Take, as another example, estimates of the effect of recent increases in our export and import prices on the WPI and the CPI. I should explain that the U.S. government does not publish data on the prices of exports and imports that appear in these indexes. But with the help of friends in the government, I have selected the product categories in these indexes that are heavily impacted by international trade. My calculations show that these items, which account for about a quarter by weight in the WPI, and which, of course, include the imports and their domestically produced substitutes, explained about one-third of the rise in the WPI since the second quarter of 1972. The same is true of the role of import-impacted components (including their domestically produced supplies) of the CPI.

These are the highest estimates I have seen, except for one that concludes that almost all of the increase in the CPI can be attributed to the effect of import prices on wages and thus on costs. But since wages rose no faster than before, it is hard to accept this result.

It should be emphasized that even these high estimates based on the cost-push theory leave by far the majority (two-thirds) of the explanation for inflation to domestic causes.

Where does the Keynesian (or fiscalist, or, better in this context, mercantilist) come out? A rise in exports injects new income into the country, raising spending and thus prices. In contrast, a rise in imports takes income out of the country, reducing domestic spending and prices.*

How does the foreign sector stack up as a source of inflationary pressure in this view of the world? The answer is a bit complicated because one must make some assumptions about imports. For example, if both U.S. exports and imports each rose $1, and if these imports substituted for purchases of U.S. goods, then the two increases would offset one another and no change in income would ensue in the United States. But if the imports rose as a result of the rise in income caused by the increase in exports, the rise in imports merely slows the rise in income, and the consequent rise in spending on U.S. goods, because part of the increased income is diverted abroad.

Depending on which view of imports one takes, one can explain between 21 and 8 percent of the rise in the demand for U.S. goods and services (the rise in nominal GNP) between 1972 and 1973. Between 1971 and 1973 the percentages are 15 and 2 percent.

Again, the bulk of the increase in demand came from home and not from abroad. Of course, it is possible to raise these percentages substantially, if one compares only exports of goods and the total output of goods, leaving services aside, as the Fed recently has done. But this is too Marxist for my taste.

THE MONETARIST VIEW

Finally, there is the monetarist view. As indicated, the monetarist emphasizes the stock of money, which, he contends, is in turn, regulated by what is called the "monetary base" (roughly, the reserves of the commercial banking system plus currency in the hands of the public), which is, in turn, regulated by the Federal Reserve.

The important point for the monetarist is that since August 15, 1971 (the date the president ended the convertibility of the dollar into gold), international transactions have not been able to affect the stock of money or the monetary base. The dollars that Americans spend for foreign goods, services, securities, and aid cannot leave the country: They must be kept in the United States by foreigners, held or spent in the country. Gold does not move, so the monetary base cannot change. As international transactions affect neither the stock

---

*It is this view of the world, for example, that has been used by some economists, in the light of the huge rise in oil imports, to recommend a tax cut, overlooking the effect of higher petroleum prices on the foreign profits of the oil companies and thus on the U.S. national income.

of money directly nor the monetary base, which controls the stock of money indirectly, international transactions cannot affect the price level.

For the monetarist, a rise in exports is not inflationary, as it is for a mercantilist. The dollars foreigners use to buy U.S. goods have to come from some other use in the United States, so that demand for something else is reduced when U.S. exports rise, if, of course, the stock of money is constant.

For the monetarist, too, when prices of individual commodities —say, imports—rise, the prices of other products will fall, simply because the monetary stock is fixed. Hence, the international cost-push inflation makes little sense to the monetarist.

A monetarist might make an exception for the two devaluations since 1971 that, by raising the price of gold, permitted a rise in the monetary base of $2 billion, compared with a total growth in the monetary base of $18.4 billion. However, they account at most for 11 percent of the inflation. And this is a weak exception, since the Fed can sterilize the increment by selling securities, as it appears to have done in the case of the second but not the first devaluation.

A stronger exception is the substantial deterioration we have suffered in our terms of trade since 1971. We would all agree that a fall in productivity in the United States would raise the price level as fewer goods and services would be available. When the prices we have to pay for imports rise, that is the same as a fall in productivity, because a given volume of exports yields us a smaller amount of imports. Between 1971 and 1973, U.S. terms of trade worsened by about 6 percent. But, given the small weight of trade in the U.S. GNP, this would cause less than one-half of 1 percent of the inflation in 1971-73.

A final exception has to do with the willingness of foreigners to hold U.S. money. There are no official figures on the portion of the U.S. money stock that foreigners own, but, using some preliminary work done by the St. Louis Federal Reserve, I estimate that the ratio of foreign-owned to U.S.-owned stock of money has risen from about 2.5 to 3 percent between 1971 and the present. This is, of course, understandable, since the devaluations of the dollar have made foreigners—both private and official—more content with the dollars they have and thus more willing to hold them, relative to Americans, than before. This rise in the share of stock of money held by foreigners is deflationary, as foreigners sell the United States something to get a larger share of its money, or as foreigners reduce the velocity of their U.S. money relative to that of U.S. citizens to increase their cash balances. In short, foreigners have exerted a stabilizing influence relative to Americans.

Again, even without counting the deflationary influence of the higher holdings of dollars by foreigners, the monetarist model indicates that very little, if any, of the U.S. inflation can be explained, by foreign transactions.

Whether one is a monetarist, mercantilist, or pusher, most of the blame for inflation lies at home. It is childish to point the finger at foreigners and foreign events, and, worse, it is downright misleading for policy. Export controls or appreciation of the dollar, which would have to be accompanied by import restrictions in order to balance our international transactions if exchange rates were fixed again, would not provide much help and in fact would raise prices, because U.S. productivity would decline as resources shift into less productive uses.

CHAPTER

5

THE ECONOMICS
OF DEVALUATION:
THEORY AND REALITY
Randall Hinshaw

I will begin by addressing myself briefly to each of the following: the effect of devaluation on the domestic price level, the effect of devaluation on the balance of payments, and the recent experience with floating exchange rates. For present purposes, I will use the terms "devaluation" and "exchange depreciation" interchangeably.

First, we will consider the matter of devaluation and the price level. In the case of a large country like the United States, it has often been contended in the financial press and elsewhere that devaluation would have very little effect on the domestic price level. After the February 1973 devaluation of the dollar, for example, Herbert Stein, chairman of the president's Council of Economic Advisers, when asked what the price effect of the devaluation would be, was quoted as saying: "My guess is that we're talking in the neighborhood of a one-tenth or two-tenths cf a percentage point in the consumer price index, or not much more than that."[1] It is interesting to note that those who were reported to have disagreed with him at the time were not thinking in much bigger terms. For example, Senator William Proxmire, one of Stein's critics, thought that the impact on the price level would be a "full percentage point."[2]

In my opinion, both of these gentlemen greatly underestimated the effect of devaluation on the U.S. price level. While there were clearly other factors at work in 1973, the chief culprit accounting for the alarming increase in the price level—certainly in the first half of the year—was devaluation, by which we mean not only the February devaluation but also the subsequent depreciation of the dollar and, in some degree, the delayed effect of the December 1971 devaluation and accompanying depreciation.

There were other factors. In January 1973, for example, the administration abruptly terminated Phase 2, a rather tight period of

control on prices, and followed this with the much looser Phase 3.
This meant that a large number of prices went up almost immediately,
although it should be stressed that many of the prices that went up
would, in the absence of price control, have gone up earlier as a result of the December 1971 devaluation. The price-control program
never did apply to food prices, but here there was another factor operating—namely, the Soviet wheat deal, which undoubtedly had an appre-
ciable effect on the price of wheat. And then, of course, at the end of
the year there was the Middle Eastern oil embargo that sharply increased petroleum prices. These were factors in addition to devaluation, although I would argue that part of the rise in petroleum prices
earlier in the year was a direct result of dollar devaluation.

THE NARROW VIEW OF DEVALUATION'S EFFECTS

Why did Stein and members of the financial press think that devaluation would have little effect on the U.S. price level? They were
thinking of the impact on the price level as being derived exclusively
from a rise in import prices. They assumed that the impact would
therefore be small, since U.S. imports are small in relation to the
U.S. GNP (the figure was 4.8 percent in 1972).

Theirs was a far from adequate way of looking at the problem.
What dollar devaluation does is raise the dollar prices of internationally traded goods, exportables as well as importables, as a group:
immediately in the case of primary products, such as food and raw
materials, and more gradually in the case of so-called differentiated
products, such as automobiles. Here one must distinguish between
purely momentary and lasting price effects. In the case of dollar
devaluation, the price of U.S. beef, for example, for a very short
time fell, in foreign currency, below the prices prevailing elsewhere.
This meant that U.S. beef was selling at a terrific bargain. And of
course what happened was that meat brokers immediately came in and
bought all their beef from the United States until the price of U.S.
beef was in line with beef prices elsewhere. Thus, the dollar price
of beef rapidly rose. We could see that happening before our eyes
early in 1973, and the same thing happened in the case of soybeans
and other primary products. In the case of differentiated products,
the price effects were a little slower, but in 1974 General Motors
and other automobile producers raised car prices because, they said,
of big increases in the cost of raw materials.

In popular writing about devaluation, one frequently sees the
statement that devaluation lowers the price of exports and raises the
price of imports. People who talk this way are actually talking in
terms of different currencies. Devaluation of course does raise the

domestic-currency price of imports, and it may also lower somewhat the foreign-currency price of exports, but its main impact on export prices is in terms of domestic currency, and this effect is upward.

I say that the main impact is on the domestic-currency price of exports because most countries account for only a small fraction of world demand and world supply. In the case of a really small country, such as Iceland, the effect of a devaluation is immediately to raise the price of imports and of exports, in Icelandic currency, by about the same proportion as the increase in the price of foreign currency. If Iceland devalues, as it occasionally does, and if the price of foreign currency is raised, say, by 50 percent, this means that, in Icelandic currency, the import price level goes up by about 50 percent, the export price level goes up by about 50 percent, and the overall commodity price level goes up by almost that much. In terms of foreign currency the effect of an Icelandic devaluation on world prices is in general microscopic, because Iceland is such a tiny part of world demand and world supply.

Now in the case of a country as big as the United States the situation is different, but not thoroughly so. The United States is a big country, and it accounts for a substantial fraction of world demand and world supply, although in most cases that fraction is less than one-fourth. For example, if we compare U.S. production with world production for 1971, we find that the United States accounted for only 11 percent of world production of iron ore, 17 percent of world cattle production, 19 percent of world cotton production, and 22 percent of world production of copper ore. There are one or two cases where the fraction is much larger. For example, in 1971 the United States accounted for 46 percent of world production of corn and for 56 percent of world production of natural gas, but these figures are far from typical.

In the case of U.S. consumption in relation to world consumption, the story is much the same. In 1971 the United States accounted for 14 percent of world sugar consumption, 14 percent of world cotton consumption, 22 percent of world consumption of steel, 25 percent of world consumption of natural rubber, and 28 percent of world consumption of tin. Again, there were cases where U.S. consumption accounted for a greater fraction. For example, the United States in 1971 accounted for 44 percent of world consumption of synthetic rubber, but in most cases the fraction was between one-seventh and one-third.

Now since the United States, big as it is, accounts for only a rather modest fraction of world demand and world supply for most commodities, the principal impact of dollar devaluation on commodity prices is the upward effect on dollar prices, rather than the downward effect on prices expressed in foreign currency. In other words, the effect of dollar devaluation and depreciation is to raise the U.S. com-

modity price level by not much less than the rise in the weighted dollar price of foreign currencies. On a weighted basis, the price of
foreign currencies in terms of dollars is in the neighborhood of 20
percent higher than in 1969. We would guess that the U.S. commodity
price level was 15 to 17 percent higher than in 1969 simply because
of the approximately 20 percent rise in the dollar price of foreign
currencies. Of course, the U.S. commodity price level has risen by
more than 16 percent since 1969 but, as I have already admitted, factors other than devaluation have also been at work.

DEVALUATION AND THE BALANCE OF PAYMENTS

We now come to the second part of this inquiry: the effect of
devaluation on the balance of payments and, in particular, on the balance of trade. Here, my point of view differs sharply from that of a
number of other economists and from that prevailing in the financial
press. In 1973 there was an article in the Wall Street Journal that deplored the rise in U.S. prices following dollar devaluation, on the ground
that it was tending to wipe out the favorable effect of devaluation on
the trade balance.[3] Contrary to this view, I would regard the rise in
prices not only as an inevitable accompaniment of devaluation but as
an essential part of the adjustment process. The problem is that the
foreign buyer needs to be placed in a position where he can outbid the
U.S. buyer for a portion of the world output—U.S. and foreign—that
was formerly going to the U.S. buyer.
    That is exactly what happens when devaluation is successful.
The price level goes up, and those consumers whose incomes do not
rise that much—or do not rise at all—are likely to curtail their consumption in real terms. The result is an increase in exports and perhaps a reduction in imports—in technical language, a reduction in real
absorption, resulting, if all goes well, in a favorable effect on the balance of payments.
    Of course, there are many ways in which this process can be
thwarted, and we could easily spend a great deal of time discussing
that. But, in a very real sense devaluation, when successful, improves the balance of payments by means of a rise in the price level.
In the early months of 1973 one of the popular efforts to explain the
rapid rise in U.S. meat prices was the alleged sudden emergence of
a Japanese taste for beef. However, the sudden development was not
a dramatic change in Japanese tastes. It was the rapid decline of the
dollar in terms of the yen, a decline that increased U.S. beef exports
to Japan by placing the Japanese consumer in a position to outbid the
U.S. consumer for an increased portion of U.S. beef output.
    Now the incomes of some people automatically rise as a result
of devaluation. For example, devaluation raises the incomes of farm-

ers producing soybeans or other commodities that have gone up in
price, and such people may buy as much at the higher price level as
they were buying before at the lower price level. But the incomes of
many people (such as college professors) do not automatically go up
with devaluation. Thus, following devaluation, a cut in real absorption relative to real output is likely to occur, and, if it does occur,
there will be an improvement in the trade balance. This is the way,
in my opinion, that devaluation works, when it works.

Of course, there are many devaluations that are not successful,
and one of the main reasons for failure is that the higher price level
caused by devaluation may induce the government to resort to unwise
monetary and fiscal policies. The higher price level can be guaranteed to induce labor unions to press for higher wages. Thus, there
are likely to be new pressures to increase the price level of a kind
that will not help the balance of payments at all. In other words, there
will be pressures that will tend to increase the level of real absorption. If real absorption rises faster than real output, the trade balance will decline, and the devaluation may merely have served as a
shot in the arm.

In this connection, it is interesting to note that the administration's efforts at price control, far from improving the trade balance,
may have had exactly the opposite effect. Until the middle of 1971,
just before President Nixon introduced his price freeze, the U.S.
trade balance (including services) remained in surplus; the surplus
was somewhat smaller than in earlier years, but it was still a surplus.
Then, in August 1971, the president slapped on a three-month price
freeze. The freeze was followed by Phase 2, which, while somewhat
less rigid, was a program of rather strict price control. This holding down of prices, instead of improving the balance of trade, appears
to have had exactly the opposite effect. Beginning with the fourth
quarter of 1971, the trade balance went into substantial deficit. This
development was at least partly due to the fact that, at the artificially
depressed prices, a considerable amount of U.S. output that otherwise
would have gone to the foreign buyer was diverted to the U.S. buyer.
In other words, the holding down of prices, instead of increasing exports, had the opposite effect by stimulating domestic expenditure on
exportables. It should be noted that the trade balance remained in
heavy deficit until early 1973, when Phase 2 was replaced by the much
more lenient Phase 3.

FLOATING RATES

I will conclude with a few words about the experience with floating exchange rates. In March 1973 the Common Market countries,

with certain exceptions, agreed on a joint float in relation to the dollar; the exceptions were countries that wished to float independently. Earlier, a number of other countries, such as Canada and Switzerland, had floated their currencies. As a result, lately, all of the major currencies have been floating, either in cooperation or on a national basis.

Under this floating regime, the dollar declined rather sharply during the second quarter and early summer of 1973. I was unhappy about that decline, because I felt that it was having a very significant effect in boosting the U.S. price level. Accordingly, I was glad when the Federal Reserve decided in July to intervene in the foreign-exchange market. Earlier, I had advocated intervention, which was notably successful in reversing the downward trend in the dollar, because I was persuaded that the declining dollar, by raising the U.S. price level, was involved in a vicious circle. The dollar was not falling toward some lower equilibrium level, but was actually creating lower and lower equilibria by raising the price level and by encouraging inflationary fiscal and monetary policies. It was a situation that could go on indefinitely, with the dollar going down and down, and the price level going up and up. Luckily, the Federal Reserve intervened; the trend was immediately reversed, and the dollar gradually climbed during the remaining months of 1973. The rising dollar was not sufficient to arrest the rise in the U.S. price level, because there were other price-raising factors (notably, the oil crisis), but the price level during the latter half of 1973 rose less than it would have if the dollar had not been appreciating during this period.

Because I think the monetary authorities should intervene in the exchange market from time to time, I am not happy about the term "dirty floating." The only kind of floating that makes sense to me is managed floating, where the monetary authorities keep a very close eye on exchange rates and occasionally intervene not to maintain exchange rates at inappropriate levels but to discourage one-way hot-money movements, by making them a very risky undertaking. Of course, speculation is riskier under a floating-rate regime than under a fixed-rate regime, and in that respect the experience with floating has been encouraging, but this is partly because the monetary authorities were willing to intervene last July. The case for intervention is very much like the case for using stabilizing fins on a ship. During smooth weather, they are not needed and the ship can be "freely floating," but the moment the weather gets the least bit rough, the captain should not hesitate to intervene by ordering their use.

NOTES

1. Wall Street Journal, February 14, 1973.
2. Ibid.
3. Robert E. Winter, "The Dollar Devaluation Is Not Likely to Spur Exports of U.S. Goods," Wall Street Journal, March 8, 1973.

CHAPTER

6

THE ECONOMIC CONSEQUENCES
OF DEVALUATION OF A
RESERVE CURRENCY COUNTRY
Arthur B. Laffer

In May 1970, May 1971, August 1971, December 1971, February 1973, and after, the U.S. dollar was devalued by substantial
amounts. The initial series of devaluations was triggered to a large
extent, if not entirely, by the U.S. domestic employment situation.
The implicit economic model underlying the U.S. decision to devalue
was the so-called elasticities model of the trade balance.

The implications of the elasticities model in one of its simplified
forms provided policy makers with a virtual panacea. By devaluing,
one could raise domestic output and employment, and there would be
no tendency for the budget to go into deficit on a full employment balance basis. In fact, the actual deficit should shrink as a result of the
higher tax receipts due to higher income and employment. In addition,
the total cost in terms of higher inflation would be small indeed.

The increase in prices, as an initial effect of the devaluation,
would be the percent rise in import prices times their share in the
appropriate index. In the U.S. case, this means that a 10 percent devaluation would lead to a total increase in the consumer price index
(CPI) and wholesale price index (WPI) of at most one-half of 1 percent
and no increase whatsoever in the GNP deflator.

Though the subtleties of different versions of the elasticities
approach may vary between expositors, the structure of the relationship was as described. After both the Camp David devaluation of August 15, 1971 and the devaluation of the Smithsonian agreement in December 1971, the Council of Economic Advisers described these devaluations as leading to more U.S. jobs. Perhaps the most difficult
problem was political: (1) turning the concept of a currency devaluation into a politically acceptable option, and (2) convincing other governments to abstain from competitive devaluations or other forms of
"retaliation."

All told, the logic of the employment effects of devaluation was as follows. First, a devaluation worsens the terms of trade. Second, with the price of imports relatively higher, fewer would be imported. U.S. exports abroad would be relatively less expensive and foreigners would buy more. While the nominal trade balance may or may not improve, any constant price index of the trade balance would show improvement. Thus, the domestic economy would reduce net absorption from abroad and hopefully increase domestic output, as opposed to solely reducing domestic demand. In most of the versions of this elasticities scenario, the reduction in net absorption from abroad was analogous to an autonomous expenditure increase and thereby would have magnified effects. The effects of an improvement in the trade balance are precisely analogous to an increase in either government purchases or investment. That is, the total increase in output will be compounded by the multiplier.

ERRORS OF THE ELASTICITIES MODEL

While it is not the purpose of this chapter to recapitulate all the logical errors in the above approach, [1] it is worth noting that the elasticities view has several critical pitfalls. In the first place, it implies an explicit yet arbitrary principle of "allocation of frustrations." Basic to the outcome of the elasticities analysis is the assumption that the resulting increase in foreign demand for U.S. exports and the decrease in U.S. demand for imports will be followed by an improvement in the U.S. trade balance. However, if one concentrates on export-demand curves, the logic leads to a worsening of the constant-price trade balance. With exportables relatively less expensive, the devaluing country would increase domestic purchases of exportables while producing less, leaving fewer goods available for foreigners to buy. Likewise, foreigners would purchase less, while producing and exporting more of their now relatively higher-priced export goods. In all, if we concentrate on exportable excess-demand curves, we find that the trade balance, using a constant-price index, worsens. Obviously, the elasticities theory alone cannot be used to predict an unambiguous trade-balance effect.

On this point, empirical research into national propensities to import and export might carry the theory. However, the approach also suffers from the presumption that devaluations will affect relative price changes per se. In other words, the theory postulates that the rise in prices in the devaluing country (and the fall in prices elsewhere) will be less than the change in the exchange rate. If quantities of goods demanded depend upon relative prices and not upon absolute prices, it would be difficult to get such an anomalous result. With price differences arbitraged away, any change in an exchange rate must result in inflation rates in the devaluing country. If it were not offset, then at least one good would sell at two different prices at the same moment in time. This clearly should not happen in a competitive market.

Even though the theory relating exchange-rate changes to the trade balance is found wanting, it is possible that empirical work would show positive results. Unfortunately, there is little solace to be obtained here. In his recent study of wholesale prices, Moon Hoe Lee found himself unable to reject the view that inflation relatives fully offset exchange-rate changes.[2] Looking at nine of the major developed countries for the period 1900-72, exchange-rate changes were roughly associated with equivalent changes in relative price levels. I obtained similar results for more recent devaluation experiences on an anecdotal basis.[3]

The trade-balance results are equally unsupportive. Looking at some 15 postwar episodes, I was unable to find any systematic evidence of resulting improvement.[4] Three years after devaluation, 11 of the 15 countries had larger trade-balance deficits (measured in home currencies) than in the year of devaluation, and 10 of the 15 had larger deficits than in the year prior to devaluation. Even two years after devaluation, eight of the 15 countries had larger deficits in their trade balances than the year immediately preceding the devaluation.

Whatever its shortfalls, the elasticities mechanism was the modus operandi of the U.S. devaluation policy. It is surprising just how little the overall balance of payments on an official-settlements basis played a role. It was not until much later that concern was expressed on the level of reserves and the overall balance of payments. Thus, the U.S. proposal of reserve bands did not come until the level of unemployment had fallen quite sharply.

MONETARY POLICIES AND RESERVE CURRENCIES

Given the inadequacies of the elasticities perspective, a reexamination of the structure of international monetary flows is timely to the comprehension of the 1971-74 policy and its implications. In the traditional monetary approach to the balance of payments as currently espoused, any increase in a country's internally created money supply will lead the country to an overall balance-of-payments deficit. Likewise, the rest of the world will run a balance of payments surplus. Via the payments deficits and surpluses, the money supplies of the surplus countries will expand, and the money supply of the original country will tend to recede. In all, the effect of an increase in any country's internally created money supply will be an increase everywhere as the money is distributed.

In essence, the modern view of the monetary approach still treats money as if it were gold,[5] considering its distribution to be related to a country's income.[6] Therefore, surplus and deficits are little more than the difference between autonomous increases in the stock of money and equally autonomous increases in the demand for money.

While the analysis is correct as far as it goes, it does not describe the workings of the Bretton Woods agreement very accurately. With the introduction of the reserve-currency support system, the results of the monetary analysis are profoundly altered.* To see the force of this form of the intervention system, assume the following:

1. It is the responsibility of all nonreserve-currency countries to maintain the fixity of their rates to the reserve currency;

2. All nonreserve-currency countries hold minimal (assumed here to be zero) amounts of the reserve-currency country's money in its reserves;

3. All reserves are held in the form of interest-bearing securities obtained in the market of the reserve-currency country;

4. Supplies of the reserve-currency country's currency obtained by the central bank of the nonreserve-currency country and used to support the exchange rate are obtained by either borrowing in the reserve-currency country or by selling securities in the reserve-currency country;

5. Supplies of domestic currencies used to support the exchange rate by the nonreserve-currency country are net augmentations to the home country's money stock.

While these assumptions do not precisely fit the Bretton Woods era, they are very representative.

Using these assumptions, first imagine an increase in the domestic money supply via an open market operation of a nonreserve-currency country—say, country B. By increasing the money supply and reducing the total quantity of bonds, the private sector will have an incipient excess supply of money and an incipient excess demand for bonds. Via price arbitrage, the slightest tendency for interest rates to fall in country B will lead to attempts to purchase foreign

---

*The following discussion is based entirely upon Fischer Black.

securities—those of the reserve-currency country, country A. In order to acquire country A's securities, the citizens of country B must first convert their holdings of their own currency into country A's currency at their own central bank.

The central bank of country B, in order to satisfy the demand for country A's currency, must sell bonds in country A and acquire A's currency. The central bank then recovers its own currency while releasing its newly acquired balances of A's currency. The private sector then takes A's currency and uses it in A to buy an equivalent amount of bonds in country A. This process continues until all excess demands and supplies are brought back into balance.

Working it all out, the net effect of the open-market operation in the nonreserve-currency country is literally nothing. While, initially, the money supply increases and bonds decrease, the operation is quashed by the intervention system. The central bank, in order to support its exchange rate, is forced to reissue debt in the reserve-currency country and repurchase its own currency. The debt issued in the reserve-currency country is repurchased by the private sector of the nonreserve-currency country. The process continues until the original open-market operation is exactly offset. This result in no way depends upon the relative size of the country, only on its form of intervention. Thus, the nonreserve-currency country can have no effect whatsoever on its monetary policy.

Now imagine that the reserve-currency country, country A, expands its money supply via an open market purchase of bonds. As before, country A's private sector will have an excess supply of money and an excess demand for bonds. Again, interest rates will tend to fall and A's citizens will attempt to purchase securities in the nonreserve-currency country, country B. To do this, they must acquire B's currency at B's central bank. B's central bank will create new money to purchase A's currency, and A's citizens will buy up B's bonds with the new stock of B's currency.

However, B's central bank will not hold A's currency but instead will use it to acquire interest-bearing assets in A. This full process will continue until B's money supply has increased by the same proportion as the original increase in A's money supply. B's central bank will have been forced to acquire an equivalent amount of bonds. In all, A has complete control over its money supply, and because of its support mechanism, B must follow A's lead precisely.

The essence of these assumptions, which are basically the Bretton Woods agreements, is that the reserve-currency country strictly controls the world's monetary policy. All nonreserve-currency countries can have no effect while the reserve-currency country has 100 percent control. As opposed to the traditional monetary approach, no mention of size in any form need be made.

PARITY CHANGES AND RESERVE CURRENCIES

Working from the models developed in the previous sections, we can now derive the implications of parity changes in a reserve-currency framework. First, using a gold-exchange standard model, a devaluation per se is equivalent to a reduction in the devaluing country's money stock and an increase in the revaluing country's money stock. The reduction in the devaluing country's money stock occurs because prices rise due to the devaluation, thus causing a reduction in the real value of the nominal money stock. In the revaluing country, precisely the reverse occurs and the real-money supply rises.[7] As a result of the money-stock changes, there is a once-and-for-all deficit for the revaluing country and, obviously, a once-and-for-all surplus in the devaluing country. These deficits redistribute the money balances at the new exchange rates according to relative sizes.*

The essence of the gold-exchange standard-like analysis typified by the monetary approach is that adjustment takes place according to size. Thus, the effects of exchange-rate changes are strictly symmetrical across countries of equal size. In all cases, the originator of the exchange-rate change is immaterial.

Adding the same set of assumptions set out earlier that describe a reserve-currency country world, the implications become clear. If the nonreserve-currency country devalues, then its citizens will develop an excess demand for money and an excess supply of bonds. They will sell their bonds in the reserve-currency country and convert the proceeds at their own central bank. Thus, the nominal stock of money will rise in the nonreserve-currency country and the central bank will reacquire an equivalent amount of securities from the reserve-currency country with its proceeds of the reserve-currency country's currency. This process will continue until the money supply of the nonreserve-currency country has, in percentage terms, risen by the full amount of its devaluation. Prices in the nonreserve-currency country will also rise by the full percentage amount. As a result of all this, of course, the nonreserve-currency country will have an official-settlements surplus exactly equivalent to its purchase of the reserve-currency country's securities.

The reserve-currency country, on the other hand, is literally unaffected by the exchange-rate change. Its prices should not be materially altered, its money supply left fully intact, and its monetary policy should remain unchanged. The essence of this example is that, under this support system, a change in the exchange rate is the

---

*In general, the surpluses and deficits must occur through the capital accounts and not the trade balance.

only way a nonreserve-currency country can have any effect on its nominal quantity of money. As noted earlier, a normal open market operation in a nonreserve-currency country can have no effect. An exchange-rate change for a nonreserve-currency country is precisely identical to an open-market operation in a closed-economy context.

If the nonreserve-currency country revalues, an analogous set of reactions occur. The nonreserve-currency country's prices fall, it loses official holdings of reserves, and its nominal money supply falls. Again, the reserve-currency country is unaffected. This, however, is the only way a nonreserve-currency country can successfully affect an open-market sale of bonds.

The effects on the monetary policies of the two countries are identical whether the nonreserve-currency country devalues (revalues) or the reserve-currency country revalues (devalues). Only if the reserve-currency country is required to maintain some form of convertibility into, say, gold or SDRs, could the results vary. In such a case, a revaluation of the reserve-currency country imparts a deflationary bias to its economy, while a devaluation of the nonreserve-currency country has no effect. In essence, it was gold convertibility that imposed some semblance of discipline on the reserve-currency country.

To summarize, parity changes in a reserve-currency country model have effects exclusively upon the nonreserve-currency country. Its prices and money stock do all the changing. As opposed to the monetary-approach analysis of devaluation, relative size is not important. The form of exchange-rate intervention dominates everything. Thus, a devaluation of a reserve-currency country's currency should result in little noticeable effects in the reserve-currency country. While it may run a temporary surplus in its balance of payments, its money supply should be unchanged and its price patterns should similarly be unaltered.

THE RECENT U.S. EXPERIENCE

Although the devaluation policy of 1970-73 was encouraged by the prevailing theory, the trade-balance results appear to be less than substantial. In general, the evidence referred to earlier tends to dispute those who profess to find significant relationships between exchange-rate changes and improvements in trade balances. Furthermore, there is little evidence to suggest any significant response of the U.S. trade balance to the perpetual inundations of dollar devaluations. In May 1970, when the United States embarked on its course of continuous devaluations, the trade balance surplus was roughly at a $6 billion annual rate. In April 1974, after some 20 to 30 percent devaluation of the dollar (depending on the specific formula used), the trade balance shows a surplus of $4 billion at an annual rate. Even the most pessimistic of the elasticities models of the trade balance would have anticipated at least a $10 to $15 billion improvement.

It is ironic to note that Germany, the country whose currency has appreciated the most against the U.S. dollar, reported one of its largest monthly trade surpluses in February 1974. It is rather disturbing that the whole move toward devaluation of the dollar was rationalized as a strategy to improve the trade balance.

However, the trade-balance behavior for the United States has been far from mysterious. It has long been recognized that changes in the trade balance are closely, but inversely, associated with changes in the growth-rate differential between the United States and the "rest-of-the-world."[8] In Figure 6.1 changes in the U.S. trade balance as a share of GNP are plotted against the inverse of changes in the U.S./ "rest-of-the-world" growth differential from 1959 through 1971. The fit is close.

Thus, while little can be uncovered to display a relationship between exchange-rate changes and changes in the trade balance, there are stable relationships between other variables and changes in the trade balance. In fact, from the graphs one cannot discern the time periods of major exchange rate changes, even as a residual effect.

Although the policy of the last four years has shown little effect on the trade balance, it has altered the role played by the United States in the world's monetary system. During the 1950s and 1960s there was little doubt that the dollar was the world's reserve currency. During this time one of the major characteristics of the United States was demonstrated stability of monetary policy and inflation. While these rates may not have been sufficiently stable for some policy-related issues, they were far more stable than in other countries. They were also amazingly stable given the monetary impacts of the U.S. official settlements balances. A $30 billion deficit such as occurred in calendar year 1971, magnified through the money multiplier, could have resulted in a money-supply change of upward of $50 to $100 billion, using the traditional monetary approach to the balance of payments.

The consistency of the growth rates of monetary aggregates in years like 1971 complies closely with the concept of a reserve-currency country developed in this Chapter. Even in 1967, when much of the world devalued, U.S. prices and monetary growth rates show little out of the ordinary. The balance of payments, on the other hand, demonstrates a considerably greater amount of volatility. Basically, the United States had complete control over its own as well as other countries' monetary policies. To paraphrase Robert Mun-

FIGURE 6.1

"Rest-of-the-World" Bilateral Trade Balance with the United States,
1959-71

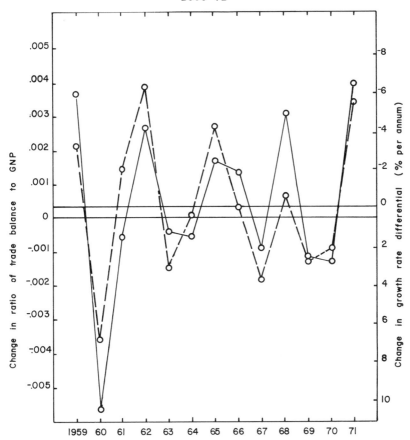

Legend:
Change in trade balance/GNP ratio ————————————————
Change in growth rate differential — — — — — — — — —

Note: The vertical scales have been so arranged that the dashed
line represents either the explanatory variable (right scale), or the
prediction of the dependent variable derived from the regression
(left scale).

Source: Arthur B. Laffer and R. David Ranson, "Canada,
United States. and the Rest of the Developed World: A Study in the
Integration of Markets," presented at Waterloo University Confer-
ence, 1972.

dell, the burden of adjustment fell disproportionately on the nonreserve-currency countries.[9]

From the end of 1971 to February 1973 the United States made rapid progress in acquiring some semblance of symmetry with the world monetary structure. In fact, by the actions of February 1973 the United States was able to sever successfully much of its reserve currency role. Irrespective of the wisdom of such a move, the overt behavior of major economic variables clearly changed. At that moment, U.S. prices started to resemble those of other countries. Double-digit inflation became a cliché, prime rates rose to more than 11 percent, and the WPI registered gains of more than 20 percent over 12-month intervals. Even monetary growth rates showed signs of increased instability, as well as inordinately high averages. In all, the U.S. experience since February 1973 underscores the movement of the United States away from the role of a reserve-currency country. The explicit U.S. intervention into the foreign-exchange market only lends credence to this view.

In all, U.S. experience for the postwar period is remarkably like that described by the model of a reserve-currency country. Exchange-rate changes were analytically analogous to those implied by the reserve-currency country model. The only major deviation from this approach appears to be the post-February 1973 period. Since February 1973 both policy actions and observed data have correlated more significantly with the implications of the traditional monetary approach. Which model will be more appropriate in the future remains to be seen.

NOTES

1. See Arthur B. Laffer, "Exchange Rates, the Terms of Trade, and the Trade Balance"; Arthur B. Laffer, "The Balance of Payments and Exchange Rate Systems"; Robert Mundell, "Devaluation," in Monetary Theory (Pacific Palisades, Calif.: Goodyear Publishing Co., 1971), pp. 86-97.

2. Moon Hoe Lee, "Excess Inflation and Currency Depreciation," Ph.D. dissertation proposal, Graduate School of Business, University of Chicago (Spring 1974).

3. Arthur B. Laffer, "The Bitter Fruits of Devaluation," Wall Street Journal, January 10, 1974, p. 10.

4. Laffer, "Exchange Rates, the Terms of Trade and the Trade Balance."

5. Arthur B. Laffer, "An Antitraditional Theory of the Balance of Payments Under Fixed Exchange Rates," mimeographed, University of Chicago, 1969.

6. For an interesting description of the doctrinal thread of this approach, see Jacob Frenkel, "Adjustment Mechanisms and the Monetary Approach to the Balance of Payments: A Doctrinal Perspective," mimeographed, University of Chicago, Department of Economics, March 1974.

7. Mundell, "Devaluation," in Monetary Theory, pp. 86-97.

8. Arthur B. Laffer, "Do Devaluations Really Help Trade?"

9. Mundell, op. cit.

CHAPTER

7

A EUROPEAN VIEW
OF THE FUTURE
OF GOLD
Alfred Matter

Defying all the efforts of the theorists, gold, which Keynes summarily dismissed as a barbarous relic, has today lost little of its age-old mystique. Particularly in environments like the present one, when political and economic uncertainties are rife, gold is widely acclaimed as being the one safe refuge when the chips are down. Nor does it seem at all likely that it has outlived its role in the international monetary system; its function has merely undergone some modification. The gold-specie or full-gold standard, under which the gold supply was to all intents and purposes synonymous with the money supply, was succeeded first by the gold-bullion standard and then, in the process of time, by the gold-exchange standard. Nowadays, gold is no longer in circulation, banknotes are no longer redeemable in gold, and gold itself has had to be supplemented by other forms of reserve asset.

THE MONETARY ROLE OF GOLD

I will begin by examining the monetary role of gold. It is, after all, the big imponderable at the present time and is likely to have a lasting influence on the price trend, the pattern of private demand for gold and, indeed, the quantity of the metal produced. Stored in central-bank vaults, there are well over 30,000 tons of gold, representing approximately half of the entire world output over the past 400 years; however, in Zurich, the biggest international gold market, a mere four to six tons are traded daily.

Under the Bretton Woods System, which was conceived in 1944 but lost two of its main pillars in 1971 when the convertibility of the dollar into gold was suspended and the regime of fixed exchange rates at least temporarily abandoned, gold no longer held the central role it had enjoyed under the gold standard, but it did retain a number of important functions. For instance, it continued to serve as a standard for currency par values and as a monetary reserve. In addition, the dollar was convertible into gold so that it, too, by implication, had basic reserve status. Gold plays an important role for the International Monetary Fund (IMF), which was also established under the Bretton Woods Agreements, and member countries are required to pay a portion of their IMF quotas—as a rule 25 percent—in gold. The IMF, moreover, adopted gold as a standard for its operations. Special Drawing Rights (SDRs), a new reserve asset allocated for the first time in 1970, although not in fact redeemable in gold, do carry an absolute gold-value guarantee. Their unit of value is defined as being equivalent to 0.888,617 gram of fine gold. In the event of a general increase in the price of gold, this would imply a corresponding increase in the value of SDRs in national currency.

THE GOLD POOL

During the 1950s the gold market was liberalized, and until 1960 it proved possible to keep the market price in line with the monetary gold price without a heavy cost in the way of intervention. At the end of 1960, however, large U.S. payments deficits, linked with rumors of a dollar devaluation after the presidential elections, triggered the first crisis of confidence in the dollar and resulted in a panic flight into gold. The price on the London gold market rapidly outstripped its monetary equivalent and by October 20, 1960, had climbed to $40 an ounce. After some initial hesitation, the U.S. Treasury intervened. A year later, in the autumn of 1961, the United States, the United Kingdom, Germany, France, Italy, Switzerland, the Netherlands and Belgium got together to form a gold pool with a view to jointly controlling the price of gold. The pool members undertook to sell gold for dollars and vice versa, whenever the Bank of England, as agent, deemed this to be desirable.

The share of each country in these syndicate operations was established according to a set scale. The members undertook to abstain from buying or selling gold on the market for their own account. Up to March 1968, the pool was largely successful in stabilizing the price on the London market in the region of the monetary price. In the years when the Soviet Union was selling large quantities of gold, the pool absorbed substantial quantities of the metal. When, however, the pound sterling, the second key international currency, came under pressure and had to be devalued in November 1967 at a time when the U.S. balance of payments was running a heavy deficit, there was a renewed run on gold which the pool was eventually unable to cope with. Any further plundering of official gold reserves for the benefit of private speculators would clearly have been pointless. France had already withdrawn from the pool prematurely in June 1967.

THE TWO-TIER GOLD MARKET

Thus, in the spring of 1968, the remaining seven members of the pool found themselves faced with the choice of either raising the official price of gold or, alternatively, creating a dual market. As it turned out, they opted to discontinue their interventions. From that moment on, the price trend was governed by the interplay of market forces; the price for monetary transactions was, of course, still maintained at $35 an ounce.

The splitting of the gold price revealed for the first time the extent to which American and European conceptions of the future of monetary gold diverged. At the time, the only point of unanimous agreement was that monetary gold stocks should in future not be used to supply the private gold markets. If the American view had prevailed, the central banks would have had to offer an additional assurance, namely to abstain at long term from buying gold, not only from the market but also from newly mined stocks held by the South African central bank. As several European central banks did not subscribe to this point of view and were only prepared to abstain from buying gold if the price on the free market exceeded the monetary price by a substantial margin, it was decided to adopt the following, less binding formula: "The Governors believe that henceforth officially held gold should be used only to effect transfers among monetary authorities, and, therefore, they decided no longer to supply gold to the London gold market or any other gold market. Moreover, as the existing stock of monetary gold is sufficient in view of the prospective establishment of the facility for Special Drawing Rights, they no longer feel it necessary to buy gold from the market. Finally, they agreed that henceforth they will not sell gold to monetary authorities to replace gold sold in private markets." As has since been apparent from the discussions surrounding the reform of the world monetary system, this makeshift solution in reality only served to gloss over the fundamental differences of opinion; in no sense were they settled.

At the end of 1969, when the free market price no longer exceeded the official one and, at times, actually lay below it, the United States announced its willingness to compromise with regard to South Africa. In an agreement initially concluded between the two main partners and subsequently also between the IMF and South Africa, it was decided that the latter should be allowed to sell gold to the IMF at the monetary price of $35 per fine ounce prevailing at the time, subject to certain conditions. From the creation of the two-tier market in March 1968 until the end of 1970, national monetary gold stocks, together with those of international organizations, rose by some $1.19 billion.

IMMOBILITY OF MONETARY GOLD

Until the beginning of 1971, the gold price on the free market diverged only minimally from the official price. As time went on, however, the repeated bouts of monetary unrest steadily widened the gap. After the first devaluation of the dollar in August 1971, and even more so after the second in February 1973, the gold price started to take off on the free market, thus providing clear proof of its close relationship with the dollar rate. Prior to the second dollar devaluation, the gold price had climbed to $65-$70, and eventually to over $125, prompted by the continuing weakness of the dollar. When the dollar rate started to firm between July and November 1973, the gold price also began to ease again.

The effect of the huge discrepancy between the artificially low level of the monetary price, which showed comparatively little upward reaction to the two dollar devaluations, and the dramatically increased market price was to totally immobilize gold as a means of settling balances between Western central banks. Understandably, no central bank was willing to sell its gold stocks at a fictitious official value that bore no relation to the market.

It has been obvious for some time now that the gulf between the two gold prices is a source of trouble in the international monetary structure, which should be removed as soon as possible. The rescinding of the 1968 agreement in November 1973 was a half-hearted step toward remobilizing gold stocks. Since then, central banks have been authorized to sell gold at the free market price. However, the question of whether or not they should also be allowed to buy gold at a price in excess of the official one is still very much a subject of controversy. The American view is that, since the agreement has now been rescinded, Article IV, paragraph 2 of the IMF Statutes is again applicable. This clause stipulates that no member shall buy gold at a price above par value plus a margin prescribed by the fund. The European view, on the other hand, with France as its leading proponent, is that this article is no longer relevant. The reason is that it was applicable to the gold parity system, which today is only of theoretical importance since the dollar/gold link has been severed and other leading currencies have made the transition to flexible rates.

The fact that the 1968 Gold Pool agreement has now been formally abandoned is of little material significance since, for the pur-

poses of inter-central bank settlements, gold is still traded at its
previous fixed price. Thus, the dual price system continues to operate. There is, however, little likelihood of monetary gold being sold
on the market, especially as long as central banks are prohibited from
buying it. The reasons for this are twofold: first, the market is thin
and consequently any large-scale selling would soon lead to a price
collapse; second, except in a dire emergency, a central bank would
be extremely reluctant to part with its safest reserves when it knows
there will be no possibility of replenishing them at a later date. Today no one, with the possible exception of the United States, is in favor
of this doubtful method of demonetizing gold. For this reason, none
of those central banks that were a party to the 1968 agreement has so
far been active in the market.

The agreement between the IMF and South Africa was likewise
invalidated in December 1973. In point of fact, it had already become
totally unrealistic back in 1971 when the gold price first started to
rise, as South Africa was able to find very profitable outlets for her
gold on the free market.

THE NEAR-TERM OUTLOOK FOR MONETARY
GOLD IN THE AFTERMATH OF THE
OIL CRISIS

Since the outbreak of the oil crisis, finding a solution to the gold
problem has become more topical and urgent than ever. There can
be no question of deterring the remobilization of gold reserves and
SDRs with their gold value guarantee any longer. The obvious course,
in view of the current state of emergency, would be to activate monetary gold stocks by raising the official price to a realistic level and
thus draw on the extensive reserves lying latent in the undervalued
monetary gold price. The effect of adjusting the official price to the
market price would be to virtually quadruple the value of world gold
reserves (not counting the Eastern bloc) from their present level of
approximately $45 billion to between $180 and $200 billion. Aggregate
monetary reserves would consequently be nearly doubled, reaching a
total of about $350 billion.

As far as the ways and means of adjusting the monetary gold
price to the reality of the free market are concerned, there is widespread agreement in Europe and the United States that simply refixing
the gold price at a correspondingly higher level is not a viable solution as, sooner or later, it would be bound to encourage renewed
speculation. On the other hand, the solution put forward at the beginning of 1972 by Professor Franz Aschinger, whereby the official price
would be merged with the market price, is finding more and more ad-

herents in both camps, i.e., among those advocating demonetization
and those in favor of consolidating the role of gold in the monetary
system. Under this system, the official gold price would be scrapped
altogether and monetary authorities, including the IMF, would be able
to deal in gold among themselves at a market-related price.

On April 22-23,1974 in Zeist, the Common Market countries decided to press ahead jointly in this direction. Even before the outbreak
of the energy crisis, the Nine were very keen to mobilize monetary
gold as, under the snake-in-the-tunnel system, central bank settlements that were intended to be adapted to the monetary reserve structure of the debtor country, have so far never functioned properly owing
to widespread reluctance to part with either gold or SDRs. Under the
scheme now agreed upon by the EEC, central banks would be free to
deal in gold among themselves at a market-related price as well as
to buy and sell the metal on the free market. According to the U.K.
view, however, gold buying on the free market should be made conditional on there being no significant quantitative increase in monetary
gold stocks.

In all probability, the Americans will feel able to agree to floating the central bank price of gold by constantly adjusting it to the free
market price since it represents a step toward their goal of demonetization. On the other hand, any scheme allowing central banks to buy
gold on the market is likely to be met with a doctrinaire veto in the
United States. Nevertheless the fact remains that, as long as gold
buying is not allowed there is no prospect of any selling on the market
either, for the reasons I have already outlined. An outright buying
ban is, therefore, unacceptable to Europeans, especially to France
and Italy. The U.K. solution already alluded to would represent a
reasonable compromise: central bank purchases would only be permitted to the extent that they did not result in any quantitative increase
in monetary gold stocks.

If the United States declines to participate in the Common Market
scheme, it is to be feared that the Nine—under mounting pressure from
countries like France, Italy, and Belgium, which have the highest proportion of gold in their monetary reserves and thus stand to benefit
most—will decide to go ahead on their own. The resulting formation
of two separate blocs would be a matter of great regret.

SOME TECHNICAL ISSUES

Implicit in the mechanics of merging the two gold prices are a
number of technical problems that have so far remained in the background but carry the seeds of future controversy. Once the official
fixed gold price has been scrapped, gold will no longer be able to func-

tion as a value standard for currency parities. Loss of this function, which would be welcomed by the United States as a step toward demonetization, would not involve any serious consequences as the most important currencies are at present in any case floating and the Committee of Twenty is already working on a project to define the value of SDRs in future in terms of a basket of leading currencies. The newly defined SDRs could also serve as a yardstick for establishing parities.

A further important issue is how to regulate central bank access to the free market. Inter-central bank transactions at a market-related price have the big advantage of mobilizing gold without at the same time causing price fluctuations on the free market. At the present time, however, with the exception of the Arabs, few industrial countries have such a favorable balance of payments situation that they can afford to sell foreign exchange for gold. The Arabs, for their part, will certainly not be prepared to take unlimited quantities of gold into their central bank reserves. As a rule, they prefer interest bearing investments; they may keep a certain proportion of their capital, say around 10 percent in gold, but then only for motives of risk diversification. If the only remaining outlet open to the central banks, which need their gold for balance-of-payments settlements, is the free market, this situation could easily provoke a price collapse there, particularly since at present, quite apart from the basic question of whether official gold buying on the free market should be permitted, few central banks would in any case be willing or able to buy quantities of the metal.

Three possible alternatives for limiting price fluctuations on the market resulting from central bank sales are currently up for discussion:

1. A "negative" commitment by the central banks not to sell gold when the price dips below a certain level, or conversely, not to buy gold, when the price exceeds a certain level.

2. A "positive" commitment by the central banks to act in concert to support the market and to designate an agent who would adhere to certain margins.

3. The central banks themselves would not deal directly on the market but create a "buffer stock," managed by an agent who would be charged by the monetary authorities to sell or buy gold in such a way as to ensure orderly conditions in the free market. Possible candidates for the function of agent would be the IMF, the Bank for International Settlements, or perhaps the European Monetary Fund.

Of these three possibilities, the second must be virtually discarded at the outset, as it would be tantamount to fixing a new official gold price.

A further problem, which has so far hardly been discussed, is the revaluation of gold stocks in central bank balance sheets after the two gold prices have been merged. This move would result in substantial book profits that could well arouse the cupidity of governments and politicians and generate a considerable wave of inflation. In general, the whole question of the inflationary potential inherent in revaluing monetary gold stocks will require very careful scrutiny, particularly in the context of the other interim measures planned for coping with the balance-of-payments disequilibrium caused by the massive increases in the price of oil. Total oil revenues accruing to the oil-producing countries in 1974 are estimated at between $80 and $105 billion, whereas the most they can import in the way of goods and services will not be more than $30 to $35 billion. They will thus be left with a surplus of between $50 and $70 billion. Some idea of the magnitude of this amount can be gauged from the fact that the growth in the monetary reserves of all those countries whose balance of payments was in surplus in 1972, was only of the order of $23 billion. The problem is aggravated by the fact that the Arab states are for all practical purposes outside the network of official monetary arrangements of the non-Communist world inasmuch as they have only miniscule IMF quotas, are not parties to inter-central bank swap facilities, and, in some cases, are not even nominal members of the SDR scheme.

Adjusting the monetary gold price only offers a limited and temporary way out of the dilemma. In the long run, it can be no substitute for domestic economic measures in respect of regulating balance-of-payments problems. Quite apart from this consideration, only a handful of countries stand to gain from it. Approximately half of aggregate monetary gold reserves are held in West European countries, a quarter by the United States and nearly 13 percent by the IMF; central banks in Japan and the developing countries, for instance, hardly hold any gold at all.

For the developing nations, which hold little or no gold, the so-called oil facilities—special credits designed to finance oil-induced payments deficits—which are at present administered by the IMF, will be of crucial importance. The fund has announced that a number of oil-producing states have signaled their willingness to channel part of their new-found wealth into the special fund. So far, the sum in question has grown to approximately $2.7 billion, which, set against the increase in gold reserves that would result from adjusting the price, is of decidedly modest proportions.

LONG-TERM DEMONETIZATION OF GOLD?

The imminent floating of the official gold price also represents a step toward demonetizing gold in a long-term perspective. There

is a consensus that SDRs are destined eventually to become the primary reserve asset, as gold production is not adequate enough to allow any sizable quantity to be diverted for monetary purposes, and
limits are also to be set to the accumulation of further reserve currency assets. On the other hand, the majority of European countries
do not subscribe to the official U.S. view that gold should be completely eliminated from the monetary system both as a standard of
value and as an international liquidity reserve. It would, after all,
be short-sighted to squeeze out the very reserve element that still
enjoys the most confidence.

Gold as a reserve has a number of merits that gain in attractiveness the more troubled the times are. Unlike foreign exchange assets
whose intrinsic worth is at the mercy of the situation or the whims of
the authorities in the reserve currency country, no such risks are attached to gold. It is the only reserve embodying a real value and is
therefore marketable and utilizable at any time. Moreover, insofar
as it is kept within the country, gold has further advantages over
other reserve assets in that it is on hand in times of war or emergency,
is exempt from transfer restrictions, and runs no risk of being
blocked. Gold is, in fact, the ideal last-ditch reserve.

THE ROLE OF SDRs

In view of gold's popularity as a monetary reserve, it is illusory
to expect that a ban on central bank gold buying will suffice to deprive
the metal of its functions as a monetary reserve. No country, not even
the United States, is going to sell a significant amount of its monetary
gold until another form of reserve asset achieves the same degree of
confidence. If this were to be the case, gold would probably phase itself out of monetary reserves, without any ban on buying being necessary. In the final analysis, then, everything will depend on the role
of SDRs in a future monetary system. Previous experiences with
this asset do not exactly inspire confidence, however. Indeed, their
very first allocation was in contravention of the stipulations laid down
in the applicable statutes, as they were issued at a time when monetary reserves were growing at an unprecedented rate in response to
enormous American payments deficits. If they are to fulfill their intended function in a reformed monetary system, SDRs must be basically
redefined.

Among demands being made at present are the dropping of the
SDRs credit function and the abandonment of limits to the obligation
to provide currency. Such pressure for changes gives cause for concern as there is a growing danger of SDRs being used not merely for
temporary payments settlements but also for financing unilateral pur-

chases of goods and services. This would only serve to accentuate their already inflationary bias. Furthermore, it does not look as though a link between SDRs and development aid can be avoided since the project has already received the backing of a large number of industrial member countries. A link of this sort would not only give SDRs further inflationary overtones but also political ones as well.

At the present time, it is hard to imagine that SDRs, whose proper functioning depends in the last analysis on the extent to which the spirit of the agreements as well as the written and unwritten rules of the game are observed, will ever enjoy the same degree of confidence as gold.

FORECASTING THE GOLD PRICE

We are finally left with the question of what the future trend of the gold price on the free market will be. When we stop to consider that, up to the two-tier division of the gold market in 1968, an ounce of fine gold cost $35 and as recently as the beginning of 1973 could be had for $65, the temporary peak of over $190 reached at the end of 1974 seems astronomical. However, it is important to bear in mind that, from 1934 to the spring of 1968, the gold price was stabilized by artificial means and was thus shielded from the inflationary increases to which other products were subjected during this period. Nevertheless, in the years immediately following the two-tier division, the pattern of gold price movements on the free market was relatively stable. It was not until the climate progressively deteriorated as a result of permanent monetary crises, the threat of world currency erosion, and finally the energy crisis, that gold began to make up its long overdue price lag at a headlong rate. If we compare the price trend of other important metals such as copper, silver, and lead from 1934 up to the beginning of 1974 to that of gold, compressed between 1968 and 1974, it is evident that the latter still has considerable ground to make up. The gold market has, however, a number of unique features that distinguish it from other markets, so that no hasty conclusion can be drawn to the effect that the gold price will continue to rise at a faster rate than prices for other commodities.

The factors determining supply on the gold market are primarily new production from South Africa and a handful of other countries, and sporadic selling by the Soviet Union. World gold production (not including the Eastern bloc), of which South Africa accounts for 78 percent, has progressively declined from 1,275 tons in 1970 to 1,094 tons in 1973. The drop in South African production was connected with the fact that the rising gold price enabled the mining industry to work deposits with a lower ore-content, thus conserving its high-grade reserves, and to some extent postponing the more rapid decrease in production that appears inevitable after 1980. Moreover, not all of South African gold output reaches the market. When the balance-of-payments situation allows it, part is channeled into the country's monetary reserves, circumstances permitting.

The Soviet Union, the second biggest gold producer in the world with an annual output currently estimated at between 220 and 240 tons, probably chastened by her previous experiences, has for some time been pursuing a very market-oriented policy, dosing her sales according to the absorptive capacity of the market in order to obtain the best possible price. In times of stagnating demand, Russian practice is to stay off the market for shorter or longer intervals and then, when demand grows stronger, to take advantage of rising prices to engage in large-scale selling. On the other hand, the USSR also has bought when prices were low, thus exerting a stabilizing influence.

On the demand side, the needs of industry and the jewelry trade predominate. Between 1935 and 1971, these components grew steadily since gold was cheap in comparison with other metals as a result of having been kept at an artificially low price up to 1968. Prompted by the recent steep price increases, however, the search for substitutes has begun. In 1972, industrial and commercial consumption fell from a record 1,412 tons in 1971 to 1,254 tons. The year 1973 saw further shrinkage.

Of total industrial gold consumption in 1972, 64 percent was for jewelry, 9 percent for coins and medallions, 8.5 percent for electrical engineering and electronics, and 6 percent for dentistry. The rest was used for various other, mainly decorative purposes. Embodied in jewelry is virtually the entire hoarding demand from the East, primarily from India, Pakistan, and Southeast Asia, where it is not customary to keep gold in bullion form. Since its peak in 1970, Eastern demand for hoarding purposes has declined steeply as a result of the upward price trend. The days when it constituted the major constant in demand for the metal are now probably over, for the simple reason that the purchasing power of the masses in India and Pakistan cannot hope to keep pace with the escalating price. Indeed, the present price trend could, on the contrary, lead to a temporary tendency to liquidate hoarded stocks. There is already some evidence that this is, in fact, taking place. In 1973, however, there were also signs that the gold consumption of European jewelers, which had hitherto been increasing at a rapid rate, was also starting to flag. In the electronics industry, on the other hand, demand is still very buoyant. Nor is the price uptrend likely to have an adverse impact on demand in the dentistry sector. At longer term, it seems a safe bet that once the hectic price movements have ceased, demand for jewelry purposes in Western industrial countries will pick up to some extent, even with prices at a high level, as this would tend to enhance the metal's prestige.

Juxtaposing newly mined gold plus those quantities resulting from Russian sales against industrial and commercial demand shows that supply had to be augmented in 1972 from speculative sales and the liquidation of hoarded stocks in order to meet industrial demand; in 1973, the converse was true. Thus, the unexpectedly steep increase in the gold price since the beginning of 1973 can no longer be explained in terms of an upsurge in traditional demand. A number of factors including the dollar devaluation, the resulting uncertainty on the foreign exchange markets, the panoply of capital controls erected in most of the hard-currency countries, particularly in Germany and Switzerland, mounting inflation and booming commodity prices, have considerably enhanced the attraction of gold as an investment or speculative medium. Just how strong an element the monetary influence was is illustrated by the fact that between January and November 1973 the gold price moved virtually in tandem with the dollar rate of the Deutschmark.

In spite of the somewhat disappointing results of the lifting of the U.S. ban on private ownership of gold at the end of 1974, the demand for gold may yet receive a substantial fillip from this source depending on the success, or lack of it, of American policy makers in coping with the triple threat of recession, inflation, and the energy crisis.

The outbreak of the oil crisis has not only made gold more attractive by reason of the dwindling confidence in the majority of national currencies, but it has also given the question of gold sales from central bank stocks new topicality, since most industrial countries are having to reckon with large payments deficits caused by higher oil imports. As already mentioned, the central banks hold something in excess of 30,000 tons of gold, which represent an enormous supply potential when one considers that the amount of gold traded annually on the free market is only in the region of 1,200 tons. So far, however, they have not made use of the option they were given in November last year to resume gold sales on the free market. The Zeist Agreement has unsettled the market climate; for the moment, investment buying on any scale has petered out. As long as an element of uncertainty continues to surround the future actions of the central banks, there are unlikely to be any substantial price increases in the short term.

Without wishing to commit myself to the price of $200 plus mentioned in dealers' and central bank circles, or for that matter to any specific price, I nevertheless subscribe to the view that gold will continue to rise in value at long term. Its complete or partial elimination from the monetary system is hardly likely to occur for many years, if not decades. In his address to the World Banking Conference in 1974

in London, M. Rene Larre, General Manager of the Bank for International Settlements, expressed the opinion that the United States, in
view of its improved payments position, might, indeed, sooner or
later, review the possibility of replenishing its gold reserves by buying.

Apart from the price reductions liable to be provoked by central
bank sales, virtually all the other factors affecting the market tend to
point to an increase in the price of gold. The instability in the foreign
exchange markets is likely to continue indefinitely, inflation is certain
to persist, Western gold production will tend to decline, even if higher
prices enable less profitable mines to be worked, and industrial demand
will probably pick up again slowly, once the current phase of restruc-
turing of the market has run its course.

All in all, experiences with gold in recent years have tended to
confirm that the gloomier the times, the more brightly gold glitters
as a monetary reserve or private investment. Until such a time as
the industrial countries manage to restore a measure of economic and
political stability, it will lose none of its luster. At the moment, the
prospect of a return to stability is regrettably remote.

CHAPTER

8

THE U.S. POSITION
ON GOLD TODAY
Miroslav A. Kriz

The conflict between national policies and international imperatives is nowhere more pronounced than in the world's gold matters.
The official U.S. position on gold is that the historic decline of gold
should continue and that the role of Special Drawing Rights (SDRs, or
"paper gold") should be enhanced in the not too distant future. The
European Common Market countries, on the other hand, while agreeing that SDRs should be the principal reserve asset in the future monetary system, seek arrangements for gold in the interim period that
would make gold in the monetary gold stocks of governments usable
at market-related prices for official balance-of-payments settlements.

It would take a brave person to predict the outcome of U.S.-
Common Market discussions about gold. Following a visit by the Dutch
finance minister, Willem Duisenberg, on behalf of the Common Market, to the secretary of the Treasury, William Simon, on May 13, 1974,
both sides declared their willingness to settle the future role of gold,
including interim steps, by agreement on the widest possible international basis. Treasury Secretary Simon made clear his view that, in
considering any proposals, a primary consideration should be the assurance that any changes affecting gold would provide for a continued
evolution toward a responsive international monetary order.

Against this background, I shall now review the diverging positions on gold on the two sides of the Atlantic and venture a few judgments about the outcome.

CONFLICTING VIEWS ON GOLD

The U.S. position on gold is well known: Nothing must be done
to enhance what remains of the role of gold in international monetary

relationships. Their position is rationalized by three considerations that have been incorporated in the U.S. negotiating position on monetary reforms. The first of these considerations is that the supply of gold is limited, and, since private demands compete for this limited supply, what is left for official reserves is wholly unrelated to the needs of the international monetary system. Second, provision of liquidity by means of a rise in the official price of gold would be "inherently destabilizing" and would provide disproportionate benefits to a few nations. And, third, because of recent price gyrations, gold cannot provide a satisfactory and stable basis for the monetary system.

The U.S. official position on gold is being challenged on grounds of monetary pragmatism. No government wants to return to the gold standard. However, several governments do not share the U.S. Treasury's enthusiasm for international monetary arrangements altogether divorced from gold. The governments of leading European countries do not believe that the complete abandonment of gold would fortify the international monetary system.

The first of the three arguments the Treasury has advanced to substantiate its position on gold is questioned on two grounds. For one thing, the adequacy of the supply of gold depends not simply upon the quantity but also upon the price. Any commodity will be in short supply if a government imposes and rigidly maintains a wholly unrealistic price, as has been the case for gold since the 1930s. For another thing, when the gold price is appropriate, new gold coming into the international monetary system directly finances balance-of-payments surpluses—or supports dollars that do so—and thereby makes it possible for there to be a net surplus for the system as a whole. As Milton Gilbert, an American who is the economic adviser to the Bank for International Settlements, has shown, this net surplus gives an essential element of play to the adjustment process—an element that cannot be supplied in any other way.

The Treasury's second argument is invalidated by the experience of recent years when the obsolete official price has been a major factor in the international currency crisis and in the decline of confidence in the dollar. A gold price readjustment, generally recognized as necessary and made to stick by proper monetary and fiscal policies, would be a stabilizing contribution to the achievement of such basic objectives as sustainable economic advance and reasonable freedom in trade and payments. The assertion that a rise in the price of gold would provide disproportionate benefits to a few nations (South Africa, the Soviet Union, and Western Europe) is political fancy that must not be allowed to disturb and disrupt vital monetary relationships among the key nations.

The Treasury's last argument is the easiest to counter. For it overlooks the fact that the gold price rise in recent years owes a very

great deal to inflation in the United States and in other key countries
and to the chaotic conditions in foreign-exchange markets and in international monetary relationships.

The continuing interest in gold by the governments of gold-hold-
ing countries outside the United States is motivated not by gold-standard doctrines, reminiscences, or mystique but by powerful considerations of an eminently down-to-earth nature. Gold has the advantage
of being money over which no government has a direct and decisive
control—an attribute that is all the more assured since the largest
holder, the United States, has less than one-fourth of the world's
total monetary stock, as against more than two-thirds a quarter century ago. Furthermore, there are times and circumstances in which
no other money will do, because gold alone is universally acceptable
without question as the means of payment of last resort. However
unreal it may appear, the possibility that dollars might be blocked
cannot be altogether excluded for all time. And, last but not least,
the value of gold is not immutable.

THE SEARCH FOR ACCOMMODATION

Against this background of conflicting views about world gold
matters, the international monetary conditions and policies are likely
to shape up along one of two courses: "go-it-alone" for Europe, or
renewed efforts by the governments of all key countries in the world
outside the Soviet Union and the PRC to make use of gold to help safeguard their political and economic cohesion, to say nothing of their
prosperity.

The "go-it-alone" approach for Europe arose last year from
the Common Market's joint float designed to keep the member countries' currencies locked together—commonly known as the "snake."
The Common Market countries are still committed to settling debts
with a mixture of assets mirroring the composition of their monetary
reserves, but they refuse to part with gold. Italy refused to do so in
the summer of 1973, and France averted the danger of a massive
hemorrhage of gold when it floated the franc "temporarily" in January
1974. To defend the franc, the French government would have had to
borrow heavily from Germany and would have also had to deplete Bank
of France gold stocks. After the French float, the snake lost much
of its blood and the matter of snake settlements has become rather
theoretical.

In the broader sense, however, the matter is very much alive.
The oil crisis and its consequences for the balances of payments of
the principal Western European countries have placed the mobiliza-
tion of monetary gold stocks into a new perspective. It is not that the

European governments would want to offer gold to Arab countries for investment of oil surpluses. Rather, it is that the European governments will be much less worried about using dollars, whether owned or borrowed, when they have gold reserves carrying a higher valuation behind them.

Thus, the real significance of the Common Market move is to make the most of an international asset—gold—of which its members are, jointly, by far the largest holders. Under the pressure of the balance-of-payments consequences of increased oil prices, but also under the impetus of their own efforts to establish an economic and monetary union, the Common Market countries want to use gold as an active instrument of monetary settlements at market-related prices. Sooner or later, they might also offer or accept gold, at market-related prices, in settlements with third countries, particularly the Soviet Union. If this happened, the Common Market value for gold actually used in international settlements would look much more like an official price than the U.S. Treasury's $42.22 price, at which no settlements are made. It would be a recognition that the true price of monetary gold is not the present U.S. official price.

If this happened, and if the U.S. Treasury persisted with the $42.22 price, the world would be split into currency blocs. In a world exposed to strains and stresses, and possibly to conflicts, in its monetary and commercial relationships, it can be confidently predicted that gold would be catapulted into a position of unchallenged primacy in international payments and reserves. But such a course of events would prove disastrous for the economic and monetary cohesion of the world outside the Soviet Union and the PRC and, ultimately, for the balance of political and military power in the world.

The Common Market countries have strongly emphasized their preference to act with U.S. support. The obvious hope is that the United States will accept what the Common Market regards as a pragmatic solution to free gold for practical use, and that economic logic and political realities will thus prevail.

For the administration to reverse the earlier U.S. position on gold, it will be, first of all, necessary to admit that gold can be helpful as a monetary instrument. Policy makers fear to be identified as reactionaries for keeping gold in the picture. There are academics and commentators who regard a renewed use of gold as unscientific economics and retrogressive politics—the undoing of progress made toward what they call a "rational" (i.e., goldless) international monetary system. As Lord Robbins argued in his Keynes Memorial Lecture at the British Academy in 1973, today it is as unpopular to say that gold can help monetary discipline as it was for Keynes to advocate monetary expansion in the circumstances of the 1930s. However, it stands to reason that, in a world that is not ready to dispense with gold, gold must be enabled to function once again, if not as the center of the monetary universe (for the governments will not admit it), then at least as an active instrument of monetary reserves at realistic prices.

Economic logic and political realities also command a reversal of the U.S. position on gold on the ground of foreseeable balance-of-payments developments. There is the possibility that, sooner or later, the U.S. balance of payments will be in surplus and the dollar will strengthen on the foreign-exchange markets. The question will then be concerned with the kind of claims that will be acceptable to the U.S. Treasury against foreign central banks and governments. Of course, for a while, dollars will be repaid. But, it may be questioned whether, in the long run, as dollar balances are run down, the American authorities will accept nongold settlements in ever increasing amounts. A more probable outcome is that the European countries will be expected to use their own gold reserves, reflecting the fact that these reserves were accumulated during the dollar crisis at American expense.

FLOATING RATES AND GOLD

Finally, the experience with floating exchange rates points toward elaboration of guidelines or, perhaps, even to rules for orderly floating and safeguards against competitive depreciation of currencies. Guidelines and rules, if they are sensible and respected, may well evolve into what we started from: "stable but adjustable" parities. In the process of restoring reasonable order to monetary and trade relationships among the key nations outside the Soviet and Chinese spheres of influence, the renewed use of gold can be of decisive importance. Reasonable order in monetary and commercial matters is, of course, a vital national interest of the United States.

At a time when the United States and other industrial nations, with the possible exception of Germany, are exposed to two-digit inflation, much will be heard about the inflationary repercussions of a gold price readjustment. Evidently, governments could not minimize the necessity to hold down inflation firmly in the aftermath of a gold upvaluation, but, quite clearly, annual SDR allocations or further large increases in dollar reserves would be equally if not more inflationary. More determined and more skillful efforts to hold inflation in check will be required in any event, but the technical difficulty of sterilizing the bookkeeping profits derived from an upvaluation of monetary reserves is, more often than not, exaggerated beyond reason.

Views such as these will, I trust, be understood in Washington. If, starting tomorrow, the United States changed its antigold posture and raised the monetary price with the stated objective of reestablishing a meaningful convertibility of the dollar into gold and SDRs, Americans as well as people outside the United States would come to realize that the economic and financial strength of the United States will enable it to carry such a program. With an administration in Washington able to conduct effective fiscal and economic policies, with expectation of reasonable monetary stability, and with realistic interest rates in U.S. markets (and, consequently, with restoration of confidence in the dollar), many of the allegedly intractable problems of international liquidity and balance-of-payments adjustments would, as if by miracle, disappear.

To conclude, a currency is not judged on the basis of its past history but on its intrinsic strength and by the current and prospective monetary and fiscal conditions and policies of the country that issues it. A gold price adjustment should be looked upon not as a sin, but as a contribution to the achievement of such basic objectives as sustainable economic advance and reasonable freedom in trade and payments. The increase in the dollar price of gold in 1934 did not prevent the dollar from later becoming the foremost international currency. In short, the dollar would certainly not die from a rise in the gold price —provided that the rise was generally recognized to be necessary, and made to stick.

A U.S. reversal on gold would be understood and well received in a time of recessionary tendencies throughout the entire industrial world. It would help safeguard the political and economic unity of the Atlantic world (including Japan). It is called for by the overwhelming national interest of the United States. To make good use of the element in the international monetary system that can prove most helpful in the stormy weather ahead is plain common sense.

CHAPTER

9

THE GOLD STANDARD
AND ECONOMIC GROWTH
Donald L. Kemmerer

Because experience is a stern taskmaster, we seek to learn from the experiences of others and to pass down from one generation to the next the "do's and the don'ts" we have inherited and have ourselves painfully learned. That is a good part of what education is all about. But the facts learned must be accurate and the conclusions drawn must be correct. If we draw false analogies, we shall adopt wrong policies and meet up with further painful experiences.

For more than a century thousands of doctors bled hundreds of thousands of trusting patients in order to cure them. Doctors bled Louis XIV of France 200 times during the last year of his life. George Washington's doctor bled him to cure him of pneumonia, thereby ensuring his death. Since respected doctors with good intentions often employed this remedy, few laymen, or even other doctors, dared question it.

Similarly, an overspeculation in stocks culminating in 1720 in the dramatic South Sea Bubble in London led Parliament to pass supposedly protective legislation. But it set back the development of the corporate device for businesses by a century and also put banks in a bad light. President Andrew Jackson, a century later, gave the Bubble incident as an important reason for disliking banks, especially big banks. In 1833 he vetoed renewal of the charter of the Second Bank of the United States, which was performing useful central banking functions at the time. That bank's loss of power helped bring on the Panic of 1837 and a six-year depression. The confused situation so prejudiced many Americans against central banks that it was three-quarters of a century (1913) before the United States finally founded another, the Federal Reserve System, and was the last major nation to establish one.

THE UNSCIENTIFIC BIAS AGAINST GOLD

In both the above cases, faulty analysis and inapplicable parallels did great damage and delayed progress for approximately a century. In today's more scientific age it is difficult to conceive that we would be guilty of such gross errors. Yet I believe the inclination in many quarters to dismiss the gold standard as an outmoded, undesirable monetary system falls in the same category as the prejudices in favor of bloodletting or against corporations and central banks. The decision to dismiss gold is hardly the consequence of an impartial examination of the facts. It is perhaps noteworthy that the same 40 years that have seen so many economists turn to the use of mathematics and achieve a more scientific image have also seen many of them take the attitude that they must be "committed" to a socially desirable viewpoint. Being "committed" is usually more emotional than scientific. The profession has perhaps rarely if ever been more affected by diverse ideologies.

Down to 1914—indeed down to the 1920s—the gold standard was widely looked upon as the best monetary system man had yet devised. In a gold standard the money unit, whether the dollar, pound, or something else, is a fixed weight of gold in terms of which prices, wages, and debts are all stated and into which bank notes and deposits are convertible on demand. As late as 1922, the late John Maynard Keynes expressed approval of it. But within a generation Keynes was calling gold a relic of barbarism, and some years later economist Paul Samuelson said that almost everyone favoring the gold standard was 70 years of age or older. The overwhelming majority of economists had come to oppose it.

One must conclude that either an entire generation of economists was wrong (either the pre-1914 one or the post-1934 one) or else their priorities had changed radically. Before we go so far as to call one group or the other "wrong," we will discuss the way priorities apparently did change. If it was a matter of changed priorities, the gold standard in the first instance may have been well calculated to promote the goals favored by the earlier generation of economists but have been found to block attainment of the goals preferred by the more recent generation of economists. I think this is the situation, at least in part, although I may conclude that the goals of this generation of economists have less desirable results in the long run than those of the older generation. Also, the methods of the current generation for achieving them are likely to cause great damage. If it is strictly a matter of goals, the current economists should say so and stop accusing the gold standard per se of consequences for which it is not to blame. But let us look first at the contrast in goals.

The pre-1914 generation considered the stability of the buying power of the dollar to be of great importance. They wrote with approval of how savings led to the formation of capital and of how capital was a chief cause of the steadily rising standard of living. Also, the leaders of developing nations were encouraged to set up a stable monetary system so as to persuade foreign capitalists to invest in the development of those countries. This was still going on in the 1920s, and it was an important reason for the reestablishment of a domestic gold standard in many nations in that decade.

THE GREAT DEPRESSION TRAUMA

In contrast, since the traumatic arrival of the Great Depression, whose wounds may take longer to heal than those of the South Sea Bubble, the chief concern of legislators, labor leaders, and economists has been to maintain a high rate of employment. The Great Depression was accompanied by a severe price deflation (almost 40 percent), high unemployment, and many business failures. The monetary system at the time, the gold standard, was retained in the United States until early 1933. These developments are often lumped together in people's minds as things henceforth to be avoided at all costs. Indeed the "new economics" of that era, whose mentor was Lord Keynes, put more emphasis on price deflation and on unemployment as conditions to be feared than it did on the evils of price inflation. The ensuing generation of economists who continued to be influenced by Keynes' views became more interested in mathematical economics than in economic history and more fascinated by government planning (in which they expected to play a major role) than in letting the free-market forces set prices, wages, and interest rates. Many of these economists are in top advisory positions today. They seem either not to have realized that price inflation has happened far more often in history than has price deflation and has victimized far more people or else to be indifferent to that fact. A new generation, many of whom had suffered from unemployment in the Great Depression, increasingly accepted this analysis. The Employment Act of 1946 (there was fear the depression would resume after the war) epitomized the major economic goal of the recent generation much as the Gold Standard Act of 1900 reflected the major economic goal of its time. The oft-used solution to an unemployment or recession problem has been to increase the money supply, which has often led, in time, to price inflation. The rationale has been that we must put more buying power in the hands of the people. This stands in contrast to the beliefs of the earlier generation. They thought that increased amounts of capital, encouraged by thrift, saving, and stable prices, resulting in higher productivity,

were the surest way of increasing employment and of raising wage
levels.

We are approaching a situation today where we must choose between these two philosophies, these two sets of priorities. The
combined stable-price-level gold-standard priority terminated abruptly
with the Great Depression. It was even contended that the gold standard aggravated that depression. The combination of aims, achieving
full employment and avoiding price deflation and depression even at
the expense of mounting price inflation, has led to the current crisis,
an accelerating rate of price inflation. U.S. consumer prices have
risen by more than 10 percent annually in recent years. The United
States' record of price inflation used to be one of the best, compared
to those of the Western European nations; now it is in the middle, and
the record of the whole group is deteriorating. As temperate an economist as Milton Friedman is recommending that we adopt the antiinflationary devices developed in Brazil, a nation notorious for tolerating
a high rate of price inflation. Some economists are saying that man-
kind today does not know how to control inflation. More and more
Americans, even labor-union members, are beginning to ask whether
the current rate of price inflation is not too high a price to pay to
eliminate the threat of unemployment, because wage increases do not
keep up with price increases.

In times past, when price inflations and their side effects became
unbearable, the solution was to return to a precious-metal standard:
gold, silver, or bimetallic. The French returned to bimetallism in
1803 after the assignats and mandats fiascos; the English after the
Napoleonic wars returned to the gold standard in 1821; the Americans
likewise returned to gold following the Civil War, in 1879; the Italians
after years of depreciating money problems went onto gold in 1883;
the Germans after their World War I monetary debacle returned to
gold in 1924; and the French, Italians, and others in the later 1920s
similarly sought again the security of a gold-bullion standard. The
list could be made much longer, but today the built-in antipathy of a
generation taught by the late Lord Keynes to blame some of the sever-
ity of the Great Depression on the gold standard makes it very difficult for Americans to reconsider that money standard as a way of getting out of our monetary difficulties. The Europeans are much more
willing than are Americans to think again in terms of a gold standard.
After all, twice in this century price inflation has hurt them badly.

One of the most frequently heard arguments against a return to
the gold standard is that such a return would precipitate a depression,
which no Washington administration could tolerate, and that in the long
run the gold standard would hamper economic growth.

The modern gold standard dates from 1717 in England and from
the 1870s in most Western nations, or else from not long before that.

True, gold was used as money at least as far back as the sixth century B.C. And in the early nineteenth century several nations operated on a silver standard or else on a bimetallic standard. Bimetallism, in practice, generally turned out to be either a gold standard or a silver standard. But any one of these three possibilities provided a more stable money system than inconvertible paper. The United States went on a bimetallic standard in 1792. By 1853, if not earlier, this nation was in reality on a gold standard. In 1873 there were nine nations on the gold standard and by 1912 there were 41 of them. In its pristine form it lasted until World War I broke out in 1914. And most often in a watered-down form (gold-bullion standard or gold-exchange standard, or a mixture of them) it existed in 47 nations between 1919 and 1936, for various periods of years.

THE ECONOMIC GROWTH RECORD

Except for occasional lapses, the industrial revolution produced fairly rapid economic growth. The industrial revolution dates in Britain from about 1733, and it really got under way in the United States in the 1840s, although some would trace it to 1812. France, Germany, and Belgium made great industrial strides starting in the 1840s.

In short, the periods of rapid economic growth in these nations coincided rather well with the periods they were on the gold standard, or at least on a precious-metal standard. Logically, one is faced with three possible explanations for this broad correlation between the gold standard and economic growth. The first is that the gold standard and economic progress had nothing to do with each other; their parallel appearance was just a coincidence. The second is that economic growth leads nations to adopt the gold standard, rather than that the gold standard causes economic growth. To that some hostile critics would add, "And if they had not adopted the gold standard, they might have made greater economic progress than they did." The third is that the gold standard itself stimulates economic growth. Let us look at each of these three possibilities, first logically, and then historically.

Is it likely that the gold standard and economic growth have nothing to do with each other? Increased capital (in the economic sense of tools, plant equipment) is virtually indispensable to economic growth. With little capital, the production of finished goods takes place extremely slowly. But saving is a prerequisite to the accumulation of capital, and of course a sensible investment of those savings must follow. People are most likely to save when they have confidence that they can enjoy the fruits of their savings. This implies confidence in the strength of the government to keep order, to enforce contracts, and to provide a stable money system.

By tradition, gold is the most reliable money; it has been known and respected for more than 2,000 years in many parts of the world. There are sayings in many languages extolling the value and the dependability of gold. Two especially deserve mention here, namely, "Man prates, but gold speaks," and "We have gold because we cannot trust governments." It seems scarcely logical that countries desiring to foster economic growth, and hence wanting to encourage saving, would overlook the money system with the highest reputation for dependability.

In the early 1950s Imade a study of 30 major nations that since 1873 had been on the gold standard for from zero to 53 years (1873-1950). I divided them into two groups of 15 each. The 15 nations that had been on gold the longest were on it for 44 years on the average. The per capita income of these 15 in 1950 ranged (or as close as possible thereto) from $311 to $1,635, and male life expectancy at birth (a good indication of economic progress) ranged from 54.6 to 69.4 years. The second group of 15 nations had been on the gold standard an average of 18 years. They had a per capita income ranging from $93 to $282 and male life expectancy at birth of from 37.4 to 63.8 years. The records of the two groups in terms of involvement in wars, and especially lost wars, were very similar.

In conclusion, it would appear that there is a relationship between economic growth and the gold standard.

The second option is that as a result of their economic growth nations adopted the gold standard even though it may not always have been to their advantage. Generally, economic growth increases the number of well-to-do citizens. Usually persons with greater wealth strive to preserve their wealth. Wealthy individuals, with some conspicuous exceptions, tend to be conservative. When they invest savings from their rising incomes, they try to ensure that the dollars returned to them will be as valuable as those they are investing. Precious-metal standards provide monies that are difficult to inflate, and hence these monies tend to keep their value. Also, it is easier to carry on trade if both buyer and seller can trust the monies that will be exchanged for the goods bought and sold. Stable money encourages trade. It is probably true that some economic growth precedes a nation's decision to adopt the gold standard.

In eighteenth-century colonial America the British government sought repeatedly to restrain the inclination of colonial legislatures to issue large amounts of paper money. This was not, as is often presumed, because those legislatures had any power to force British merchants to accept the local pounds at par value in payment of debts. They did not. Rather it was because price inflation in the colonies made it difficult for local citizens to pay local shopkeepers and hence for the local shopkeepers to accumulate enough purchasing power to

buy English pounds to pay the English exporters! The colonial adminis-
trators of industrializing and economically growing Britain strove
valiantly to promote a more reliable money system in the colonies,
which were so important to Britain's trade. Britain was already on
the gold standard.

The late historian Charles A. Beard showed that the men who
drafted the federal constitution in 1787, and through it sought to out-
law paper money, were for the most part well-to-do businessmen and
lawyers. The United States went on bimetallism in 1792.

THE GOLD STANDARD AND THE
INDUSTRIAL REVOLUTION

In the last third of the nineteenth century, as the industrial revolution spread south and east to Italy, Austria, Russia, and Japan,
these countries emulated Britain and shifted from a paper-money or
a silver standard (silver was considered somewhat less reliable than
gold) to the gold standard. Germany's leader, Count von Bismarck,
along with others in Germany, admired many British institutions and
seized the opportunity of Prussia's victory over France in 1870, from
which Germany received Fr 5 billion in reparations, to copy Britain's
gold standard. Both Prussia and the south German states had respecta-
ble silver-standard systems, but as Germany was becoming more industrialized and her trade was growing, she desired to be in financial
step with other nations that were leaning toward the gold standard.
Some 25 years later Japan, also industrializing and also on a silver
standard, used some of the reparations from her victory over China
in 1894 to go over to the gold standard.

Other colony-nations, such as India, the Straits Settlements, and
the Philippines, only went so far as to adopt the gold-exchange standard, a sort of economy-class gold standard.

It is noteworthy, too, that at the close of World War I (which
had forced the world off gold in 1914) delegates from a large group of
countries agreed at Brussels in 1920, and again at Genoa in 1922,
that it was highly desirable to return to gold as soon as practical—
i.e., as soon as the nations again felt financially strong enough to do
so.

What is clear is that in some cases nations felt they had to
achieve a certain economic level before they could afford a gold standard. The fact that economic growth may have sometimes preceded
adoption of it does not make that standard any less desirable, unless
it can be shown that it thereafter slowed down economic growth. But
if Germany and Japan could have done better than they did in the 1880s,
1890s, and after by avoiding the gold standard instead of by adopting

it, both would have had to do fabulously well. Their industrial output, especially Germany's, and their share of world trade grew very rapidly indeed soon after they went onto gold.

The third choice is that it is logical to suppose that operating on a gold standard stimulated economic growth. There are reasons to believe this. Businessmen seek to reduce risks so as to enhance their profits. A major risk is fluctuations in the monies they must pay or will receive. Gold standards with fixed pars of exchange reduce this kind of risk to a minimum. It is logical for gold-standard monies to become the favored currency in which to do business and to carry on foreign trade. Capitalists seek to convert their funds into such dependable currencies. Consequently, nations protecting and respecting their own monetary units have liquid capital consistently flowing to them. Liquid capital can purchase economic capital, and economic capital, if well managed, will lead to economic growth. Indeed, as economic historian Walter W. Rostow showed some years ago, it takes a sharp increase in economic capital to launch a nation into its economic "take-off" period.

For most of the 200 years between 1717 and 1914 the pound sterling, based on gold, was the most respected currency of the world, and the "City" in London was the place to which capital flowed from all over the world for investment in Britain as well as from there to other investment centers. Loans were nearly always repayable in pounds. Those 200 years were for the most part years of great economic growth for Great Britain. From 1914 to the 1950s it was the U.S. dollar and New York City's Wall Street that functioned in much the same way. Except for the depressed 1930s, that was a period of much economic growth for the United States. A particularly rapid rate of growth during the 1940s compensated for the slow growth in the 1930s.

As centuries go, the nineteenth was a fairly peaceful one, with great economic growth and more than usual reliance on precious-metal monetary standards. Perhaps all these conditions help to explain why it was also a century of extraordinary price-level stability in many nations.

Between 1873 and 1896 the number of nations on the gold standard increased from nine to 27. By 1912 there were 41 nations on gold. It was the most highly regarded monetary standard of that era. From 1865 to about 1896 in the United States there was price deflation, and there were three significant depressions, but there was also tremendous economic growth in railroads, steel mills, shipping, textiles, and many other industries. Between 1897 and 1914 there was a gentle increase in prices, and there were two significant depressions. The economic growth continued at a sharp pace. Between 1865 and 1896 a score of nations adopted the gold standard, prices fell, and economic growth spurted; between 1897 and 1914 another 14 nations adopted the gold standard, prices rose, and economic growth continued. Only in the United States in 1896 did the price decline cause serious debate over whether this nation should stay on gold. But the alternative offered was a bimetallic standard; it probably would have quickly become a silver standard in reality. The electorate, however, voted to continue the gold standard.

EXPERIMENTS IN RETURNING TO GOLD

We will now see what actually happened in a half-dozen instances in the past 100 years when nations previously on paper-money standards and experiencing price inflation decided to stabilize and return to the gold standard. I shall draw on both my own studies on this subject and on Wesley C. Mitchell and Willard Thorp's Business Annals, an early (1926) publication of the National Bureau of Economic Research.

1. The United States, on a paper money standard (greenbacks) from the last days of 1861, decided in early 1875 to return to the gold standard, setting January 1, 1879 as the goal. No serious preparations were made until the spring of 1877. Resumption occurred on schedule with no difficulties whatsoever. There was a depression from 1873 through 1878. Returning to gold did not revive these hard times; on the contrary, four years of prosperity ensued.
2. Austria-Hungary, economically less advanced than Germany, was in a mild depression from 1894 to 1898, then enjoyed prosperity in 1899, and went onto the gold standard in 1900. Three years of depression followed this transition before a longer era of prosperity developed.
3. Italy left the gold standard in 1893 after four years of depression. She suffered through three more years of bad times and then conditions gradually improved over a six-year period. Italy returned to gold in 1902, and five years of prosperity immediately followed.
4. Germany's disastrous inflation of 1914-23 is probably the best known in modern times. The worst years were not during the war but the five years following Germany's surrender. Eventually the mark, worth 24.2 cents in 1914, was stabilized at 1 trillion old marks to one new one (again worth 24.2 cents). The five postwar years were largely one long depression. After Germany returned to a gold-exchange standard in October 1924, there was at first a halting revival. That was succeeded by several years of prosperity, actually among Germany's best in the interwar era.
5. Sweden maintained neutrality in World War I, but like virtually all nations she had to leave the gold standard shortly after hos-

tilities began. Price inflation followed. The krona, which was worth
26.8 cents in 1914, depreciated sharply during the war. Based on a
1914 price index of 100, prices were at 370 in 1920. Prices in most
other lands, including the United States, also rose during this period
then fell sharply in 1921. But whether prices were rising or falling,
Sweden was in a depression from 1917 to 1923. By 1922 the krona
was again at its 26.8 cent par of 1914. On April 1, 1924, Sweden returned to a gold standard and a mild prosperity set in.

     6. France was badly mauled in World War I but emerged on the
victorious side. The franc fell from 19.3 cents in 1914 to 2 cents in
early 1926. A strong premier, Raymond Poincaré, then came to
power and inaugurated policies leading later that year to a de facto
stabilization at 4 cents. In 1928 France adopted a gold-bullion standard with a franc of 4 cents. Its value had doubled since January 1926,
yet many observers still regarded the franc as slightly undervalued.
Prosperity began with Poincaré's taking office and lasted somewhat
longer in France than in nearby nations. France held onto her painfully achieved gold standard but the struggle was a grim one from
1934 to 1936, when the Great Depression finally swept her off gold on
September 25.

     These six examples, two involving quite disastrous price infla-
tions (Germany and France), suggest that prosperity is more likely
than not to follow a return to the gold standard, and that being off gold
but on a price-inflation binge is more likely than not to produce depressed conditions. Further confirmation is provided in a staff article appearing in the August 1959 issue of the New York Federal Reserve Bank's Monthly Review. It contains charts of price inflation
and of economic growth in 16 developing nations (1951-57). The eight
with the greater degree of price inflation had the least economic growth
of the 16.[1] This suggests strongly that continued price inflation is
not the best way to achieve maximum economic growth.

     Nicholas Kaldor, a Cambridge University economist and no par-
ticular friend of the gold standard, which he believes hurt Britain in
the 1920s, has written that he has found no evidence that the period,
1881-1920 in Britain, largely a gold standard era, was characterized
by high unemployment.[2]

     The plain facts of the matter are that the criticisms of the gold
standard we hear today were not voiced before 1922, and only a few
of them were voiced before 1929. The chief worry in the 1890s, and
again in the 1920s, was whether the world production of gold was adequate to fill the growing monetary needs. Most of the criticisms
heard since then on university campuses, in the media, and in learned
journals were developed to justify the general departure from gold in
the early 1930s and to rationalize the continuation since then of incon-

vertible paper-money currencies and to excuse the price inflations
arising from inability to control such paper systems. Let me mention
just a few of these criticisms, in addition to the one that returning to
gold would cause a depression and slow down economic growth:

    1. It would be very difficult to arrange an international agree-
ment among most nations to return to gold. If most nations do not return together, it will not work.
    2. There is not enough gold in the world today to support a
gold standard.
    3. There is really no scientific way of determining what the
new price of gold should be.
    4. People and governments will no longer submit to the disci-
pline of the gold standard.

    There are many more. There are also good answers to all of
them. Let me give you two. First, all nations need not go back to
gold together. They did not originally come on together. Britain
was on gold virtually alone for a century; others then joined her one
by one, as they saw fit. Second, there is enough gold today to return
to gold standards. At $35 an ounce the supply of gold may have
seemed limited, but when gold is priced at $180 an ounce, that is the
same as having five times as much as before. And the likelihood is
strong that the higher price will stimulate still greater gold production.
    In conclusion, the gold standard is a monetary system to which
nations suffering from the evils of price inflation in times past have
often turned. Despite some defects, it has indeed been the most successful monetary system yet devised by man. Contemporary complaints that it would cause depressions and slow economic growth are
based on the questionable analogy of one recent experience and on full
employment goals, the cost of whose attainment in terms of price inflation is beginning to appear exorbitant. It is high time that we examined the alternatives, and in doing so that we penetrated the shal-
lowness and historical inaccuracies of the received criticisms of the
gold standard. The opponents of that standard have had 40 years to
show that their inconvertible system is better. The steadily worsening price inflation, with its many undesirable social consequences,
shows that they have failed.

NOTES

    1. New York Federal Reserve Bank, Monthly Review, August
1959, pp. 122 ff.

2. Nicholas Kaldor, "Economic Growth and the Problem of Inflation," Economica 26 (August 1959): 214.

CHAPTER

10

INTERNATIONAL BANKING
IN THE MIDST OF WORLD
MONETARY DISORDER
Jack Zwick

It is hazardous to generalize about the way in which commercial
banks have been affected and are responding to world monetary disorder, for there are marked differences among banks and among the individuals who work for them. As in other fields, international banking
has its share of optimists and prophets of gloom. What I have tried
to do is to sort out available facts and opinions and classify them. I
will first discuss briefly trends and prospects for different categories
of commercial banks. (For purposes of discussion here a distinction
is made among large multinational banks that, because of their size
and far-flung international operations, are quite dominant; the so-
called regional banks in the United States whose international activities
are less extensive; and, finally, foreign banks that during recent
years have displayed a healthy appetite for expansion in the U.S. market.) With this perspective, we then can examine environmental conditions with a better appreciation of problems and difficulties. Finally,
I have some specific suggestions regarding how these institutions
might improve their international performances in this period of monetary confusion and uncertainty.

I would be remiss were I not to note one overriding impression
at the outset: International commercial banking is thriving! Admittedly, prosperity is not evenly distributed among all institutions.
One need only read last week's newspapers to recognize that business
is spotty in certain areas, most notably foreign-exchange dealing and
branch operations in London, which have been disastrous for selected
institutions. Nevertheless, most institutions with an appetite for international business have grown more rapidly in this area than in other
branches of their business, both in terms of footings and profitability.
Most are planning to expand. The pervasive sentiment is one of optimism, albeit guarded in selected quarters. This prosperity and opti-

mism are quite remarkable in view of the fact that most of the conditions since World War II that have stimulated the expansion of international banking no longer exist. Reference here is to such factors as fixed exchange rates, stability of the dollar, political harmonization, U.S. exchange controls, freer trade, and so forth. Perhaps the following observations will serve to shed some light on this apparent anomaly.

THE MULTINATIONAL BANKS

It is commonly known that the largest U.S. commercial banks are dominant in the international fields, yet the extent to which they dominate may be surprising. In the 1973 survey of banks reporting to the Federal Reserve Board, 19 multinationals accounted for 80 percent of total foreign assets reported by U.S. banks. While there are major differences among the banks categorized as multinational, they share certain major characteristics.

All have branches in London and additionally, for tax reasons, shell branches in either the Bahamas or the Cayman Islands. A few have extensive branch networks throughout the world, and many have branches in the money centers that, besides London, include Frankfurt, Paris, Tokyo, Hong Kong, and Singapore. The majority have additional foreign-branch applications pending with the appropriate regulatory authorities. All the banks not based in New York operate Edge Act corporations in New York to participate in the foreign-exchange market and other international business that originates there.

Unencumbered overseas by the Glass-Steagall Act restrictions that apply at home, many of these institutions have become active in investment banking and brokerage functions. In addition to underwriting, syndication, and the like, they have added congeneric financial services to their arsenals, such as leasing, factoring, consulting, and data processing. These activities are conducted by overseas entities established de novo or by established foreign institutions in which U.S. banks have acquired ownership interests.

A few of the multinationals are aggressively pursuing local commercial and even retail business in the national markets in which they operate. Yet for most, the servicing of international customers and participating in interbank business are the activities of primary importance.

U.S.-based international companies remain the coveted customers. Most of the multinational banks entered the international field following these corporate customers. Today, the banks endeavor to serve these corporations in a number of new ways. Besides such functions as syndicated lending, leveraged leasing, and international tax counsel, several multinational banks offer assistance with international money management. Reference here is to the functions enabling companies to move monies as quickly as practicable among the parents and operating companies, with minimal transfer costs. This activity invariably spills over into the design or redesign of reporting systems as well as advice regarding money-market investments, which may make sense on a hedged or uncovered basis.

The multinational bankers are not sure these days what corporations plan to do, now that U.S. exchange controls are off and no accepted monetary reform is within sight. Many bankers had expected U.S. corporations to dismantle their offshore financing vehicles and to return home for the external funding of foreign subsidiaries. These bankers are surprised to discover that many companies are content, at least for the time being, with conditions in the Euro- and national currency markets, and bankers are deferring plans to scale down staffs in London until a clear pattern emerges.

It is axiomatic that international business may well lead to domestic business, and banks are continuously trying to increase their share of commercial business here at home. It is quite significant that many multinational banks have begun recently to open out-of-state Edge Act corporation offices in commercial centers throughout the United States—for example, in Houston, Miami, New Orleans, Dallas, Chicago, San Francisco, and Los Angeles. Initially, these offices were only needed by out-of-town banks to conduct international business in New York. One gets the distinct impression that these recently established Edge Act Corporations are closely allied to expanded loan production activities. Perhaps these new offices of the multinationals will someday serve as command posts for interstate banking. In the meantime, the multinational banks continue to expand international staffs and spheres of overseas influence.

THE REGIONAL BANKS

Before turning to the multinational banks' response to the current monetary turmoil, it is helpful to consider the posture of the so-called regional banks. Thirty-one of these institutions reported foreign asset holdings in 1973 of slightly more than $1 billion, or about 10 percent of the foreign assets of the multinational banks. The international experience and expertise of these institutions vary markedly.

During recent years, the regional banks have developed small departments, ranging in size from five to 100 persons to develop and process the growing volumes of international transactions. Frequently, the international departments are headed by outsiders recruited from the ranks of foreign banks or foreign departments of U.S. multi-

national banks. It has been their job to develop international plans
that managements would accept, to develop new business, and to or-
ganize and oversee systems for processing the various banks' international transactions. (There is evidence that previous experience in
handling international transactions for large multinational banks does
not necessarily equip some of these bankers for planning or marshal-
ing internal support for international activities in smaller institutions!)
The headquarters staffs are busily engaged in trade financing, solicita-
tion and processing of corporate customers' international business,
correspondent bank relations, credit evaluation, supervision of affili-
ate operations, and the like. In many of the regional banks these functions are growing rapidly.

Still another activity of these institutions involves the formation
of Edge Act corporations located in areas outside the city in which the
parent bank is headquartered. These domestically organized subsidiaries serve as vehicles for foreign banking and investment, and some
40 regional banks are represented by Edge Act corporations in New
York City. Regional banks account for approximately 10 percent of the
total international or foreign business held by commercial banks in
New York. The New York offices are used by the regional banks to
obtain and process business that otherwise would be referred to cor-
respondents, to participate in the foreign exchange market directly,
and to conduct a variety of other affairs for the parent institutions.

In the mid-1960s many of these banks opened branches in London.
Still more banks opened branches in Nassau and the Cayman Islands
in 1969 when the Federal Reserve Bank authorized the creation of
shell branches so that the smaller banks could access the U.S. dollar
market and service their foreign customers. As it developed, however,
most of the shell offices began to mobilize dollars abroad for use by
the parents during the period of domestic monetary restraint in 1969
and 1970. Cast in this role, the branches were actually contributing
to the financing of an internal commercial-banking system of which
they are a part.

Many of these foreign branches have been able to conduct a moderate volume of business with foreign governments and other international institutions. Initially, most of this business was probably the
result of contacts developed by the parent banks. However, within the
last year or so, a number of the branches have been venturing out on
their own to arrange Eurocurrency loans for foreign official bodies,
including an increasing parade of borrowers from developing countries.
Basically, the principal motivation behind the opening of foreign branches
by most of the U.S. banks that entered the field in recent years has been
to meet the financial needs of their foreign customers, particularly
U.S. firms restricted by Office of Foreign Direct Investment (OFDI)
in their ability to finance foreign investment with U.S. source funds.

Thus, many of the banks essentially followed customers overseas in an attempt to retain their business.

Yet the degree to which the recently established foreign branches have been able to play a meaningful role in servicing their natural customers has been limited. Consequently, the largest proportion of the foreign branches' efforts has been concentrated in the interbank market. This market consists of a network of foreign commercial banks with reciprocal arrangements for holding deposits and extending credits.

Once a number of banks entered the interbank market, they have been open to a sizable inflow of deposits, despite the sharp decline in the demand for such funds by their own internal banking systems since 1970. To employ such resources the branches have begun to participate progressively in what is basically a brokerage rather than a traditional banking business. Banks from other countries—particularly from Japan—have also entered the race, and the competition in international capital markets has become even more aggressive. This development has led to a marked narrowing of lending margins, which in turn has had a significantly adverse impact on the profitability of foreign branches of U.S. banks, particularly in London. The story has circulated in London these days that while no U.S. regional bank wants to be the first to close its London branch, several are queued up to be second!

THE PROBLEMS

In considering the problems posed for the multinational banks and for the regionals by the current crises, London is perhaps as good a point of departure as any. London is the heart of the interbank market, and, as noted earlier, a host of banks opened branches there in the mid- and late 1960s to assist corporate customers in complying with OFDI and parent banks to ease liquidity crises in the home market.

For many institutions, especially the newcomers, the bottom has been falling out almost since the moment they arrived in London. On the lending side, there has been a continuous withdrawal of prime names. European borrowers either were encouraged by their governments to use home markets or to avoid the Euromarkets beginning in 1970. At about the same time credit conditions eased in the United States, and parent banks no longer required advances from Eurobank branches. With the removal of the Interest Equalization Tax and restrictions on corporate borrowers (by OFDI) in 1974, still other borrowers replaced their Euroborrowings with domestic sources. To make matters worse, the Bank of England imposed severe restrictions

on sterling lending (ceilings and punitive reserve requirements) to
curb inflation, and this valued channel for deploying resources was
largely closed.

With more banks competing to service fewer international borrowers in London, it has become quite evident that borrowers of less
than prime standing have obtained accommodations at interest rates involving margins much narrower than could have been obtained during
earlier periods. Today, borrowers, many of them from developing
countries previously not accorded a prime rate, are able to obtain
funds on which the rate spread is set at as low as one-quarter of 1
percent. In addition, maturities of loans have lengthened considerably,
in a range of five years as recently as 1970 to as long as 15 years
offered during 1974.

Even without any bad debt experience, it is difficult for the newer
branches to operate profitably with these fine lending margins. Banks,
by mismatching the maturities of loans and bought deposits, could once
depend on a yield play to augment narrow spreads on lending. Now the
yield curve is almost flat, thus eliminating this possibility. Besides,
operating costs in London are rising dramatically from an already very
high base due to inflation, overcompetition among banks for professional personnel, and recent tax increases. As bad as these conditions sound for profitable commercial banking, circumstances are
even more difficult for those with the foresight to open merchant banks.

What can be said about prospects for banking in London under
these circumstances? Perhaps most important, there are credit evaluation and foreign-exchange trading problems that may bear heavily
on the outcome. Before I discuss these topics, I will consider prospects for the market in general terms.

Observers agree that a sizable part of both the medium-term
and long-term markets in dollars will remain in London due to the
relatively favorable terms on many of the loans and the desire to maintain foreign banking connections, especially in a world of floating exchange rates. This prediction holds not only for European borrowers
and lenders but also for a number of U.S. firms, for Japanese institutions, and for borrowers and depositors from the Middle East and
other developing areas. Borrowers, and especially depositors, will
proceed cautiously, however, until they are confident that the Bank of
England will not impose new controls on Eurocurrency operations.

The intensive competition for quality dollar business in London
will continue, and the better established, larger branches of the multinational banks have a decided edge. The multinational bank should
concentrate attention on staffing, improving control procedures, and
overall management in London to avoid the unexpected embarrass-
ment and to assure prosperity. The regional bank must face its dilemma squarely. Unless there is a reasonable prospect for adequate

natural business in London, the branch should be closed and Euromarkets accessed via less costly shell branches and, perhaps, a representative officer in London. For many, the full-service branch in London is a luxury that becomes more expensive with each passing day.

A second sensitive area, and one of prime import, concerns credit-evaluation procedures. While the intensity and depth of screening procedures vary dramatically among institutions, one suspects that many international departments are conducting the most cursory of analyses in their eagerness to build up footings in the interbank market.

Firsthand observations indicate that many lenders rely heavily on names and reputations rather than on credit analysis. Frequently, loan agreements are not structured in accordance with their purposes and cash-flow considerations. Loan organizers are presumed to have the requisite expertise and a number of lenders place their reliance on them rather than on their own credit analyses. Not much information is obtained regarding the borrowers and often the loan agreements contain inadequate documentation to provide adequate safeguards. Clearly, to the extent that such shoddy practices prevail we are living in the shadow of 1929.

Naturally, it is easier to discuss the problem than to effectuate remedies. Yet the hour is late for offending institutions to impose a rigid discipline on their international lending activities. Risks must be calculated in relation to capacity to sustain losses. Exposure limits for countries and regions must be established with care. Procedures must be set up and strictly implemented to ascertain country risk, foreign exchange risk, if any, and credit risk for each prospective international credit. If the implied risks are tolerable, and only if they are tolerable, designated officers must carefully weigh risks and costs in relation to available returns. This calculus takes into consideration not only explicit spreads but also overheads, allocated capital, and corresponding fees when obtainable. One suspects that the palliative for many institutions has three dimensions: systems design; recruitment of experienced international credit men; and management development to upgrade credit evaluation and control efforts. The multinational banks might also give thought to centralizing certain credit-evaluation functions as a control measure, now that U.S. capital controls are off.

Let us now turn to an equally vexing aspect of the international banking business, namely, foreign-exchange trading. Commercial banks that profess to be international believe they must be active participants in the foreign-exchange markets. During the floating-rate era, increased volume in foreign-exchange trading and wide fluctuations have created phenomenal opportunities both for profit and for loss, and well-known institutions have been on both sides of the ledger.

In preparing this chapter I spoke with a number of bankers regarding Franklin National Bank's widely publicized $25 million loss in foreign exchange. Commentators were almost evenly divided between those who believe the bank had adequate controls that the trader violated and those who question the adequacy of the controls themselves. At the risk of appearing supercilious, I side emphatically with the latter.

It has been my good fortune to work closely with a major bank noted for its expertise as a professional foreign-exchange trading institution. Always profitable in foreign exchange, this bank reported foreign-exchange earnings for 1973 equivalent to 35 percent of the bank's total earnings. It has devoted enormous energy and resources to perfecting and coordinating foreign-exchange trading operations in the United States and abroad to cope with floating-rate conditions, and it still is not completely satisfied. Intensive observation in this institution and discussions elsewhere leave me convinced that most foreign-exchange practices and controls in the industry are woefully inadequate.

Up-to-date information regarding the magnitude and composition of spot and forward positions on a worldwide basis are not always available, nor are advanced data systems to provide up-to-the-minute news items. Some institutions do not understand the determinants of foreign-exchange risk: Square positions are assumed to be riskless, overnight limits are presumed to limit exposure, and so on. The relationship (or nonrelationship) between daily trading and the longer-term prospects for currencies are not adequately appreciated. Sometimes senior managements take "a longer view" in a currency to assist the traders, and this can be disastrous. In some banks traders unwittingly compete for currencies with their counterparts in other branches. Many banks cannot quickly calculate profits or losses inherent in their positions, on which to base judgments. Most banks complain of a worldwide, chronic shortage of experienced and reliable traders. These are but a few of the deficiencies with which bank managements must contend to minimize chances of being added to the growing list of the unfortunate, which includes not only Franklin but such well-known names as Westdeutsche Landesbank and the Union Bank of Switzerland.

The last area of concern to many banks is the back-office problems that have accompanied expansion and a growing volume of international transactions. Increasingly, one hears complaints from the multinational banks' customers and the banks themselves, regarding inability to process payments and the like on a timely basis. This irritant is becoming more important to customers during the present era of high interest rates. The problems are not easily corrected by the giant institutions and, in my opinion, the weakness affords smaller institutions with a unique opportunity to compete with the majors for important and profitable international business.

PROSPECTS

The multinational banks hope that the British economy can survive and that London can remain open as a banking center. They are also hopeful that Italy's import restrictions will not tempt others and precipitate a trade war injurious to all. They would like to see restrictions relaxed in Japan so that Tokyo can become a major money center. And high on their "wish list" is the desire that U.S. regulations be flexible in order that a variety of financial services can be provided in the United States.

Yet these uncertainties are as much a stimulant as a deterrent. The multinationals have made substantial capital and manpower commitments to the international field since World War II. They now are planning to expand their businesses in traditional areas. Many are building new bridges to the Pacific basin, the Comecon countries and the Middle East. Indeed, they are anticipating a period of sustained growth despite the current disorders.

What about the regional banks? Notwithstanding their competitive disadvantages in certain facets of the international field, a vigorous international business is not only possible but essential for many of the regional banking institutions. Several of these banks have begun to discover that they have a competitive edge in trade financing; they can offer quicker service in this facet of the business, which is growing rapidly. They frequently can respond more rapidly to lending opportunities due to simpler loan-approval procedures. These banks are uniquely situated to participate in the financing of reverse investment—that is, investment by foreign companies in U.S. facilities. That these activities can be exceedingly profitable is attested to by those banks (recent entrants in the field) whose foreign departments contribute significantly to overall bank profitability. The international is one of the few areas in which growth is not closely circumscribed by the authorities. In the final analysis, an international component may even be necessary solely for defensive reasons: to hold corporate customers that may otherwise be picked off by the "full-service" institutions.

It is my firm conviction that many of these banks must begin now to design or revamp their international departments the better to serve corporations and traders in their respective market areas and to participate fully in the inflow of foreign direct investment. At the same time, and particularly in view of greater fluctuation and variability in the exchange markets, these institutions must develop up-to-date systems for planning and control of all facets of international activities and make provision for the recruitment and training of personnel to realize the full profit potential inherent in these activities.

FOREIGN BANK ACTIVITY IN THE
UNITED STATES

In conclusion, I would like to comment briefly on the activities
of foreign banks in the United States, a subject that has been discussed
widely in the general and financial press. Both economic and political
conditions during recent years have persuaded bankers throughout the
world that a presence in the U.S. market might be advantageous.
Numerous foreign offices have been opened here in the United States
(branches, agencies, and representative offices), especially in New
York and California. The foreign banks have engaged in a wide range
of commercial-banking, money-market, and securities activities.
With two or three exceptions, the foreign banks have not competed to
any significant extent with U.S. institutions for retail deposits.

As one of the early champions for the rights of foreign banks
operating here, I have always contended that these institutions play a
constructive role. Experienced in international financial matters,
they have stimulated U.S. banks to become involved in the international
field and extend their international services. These institutions help
keep U.S. financial centers from becoming parochial. Moreover, it
would be unjust to deprive foreign banks access to U.S. markets while
U.S. banks expand rapidly in foreign markets.

Foreign banks operating in the United States have been deprived
of some of the advantages enjoyed by U.S. institutions, most notably
Federal Deposit Insurance Corporation (FDIC) insurance for depositors. At the same time, it has been possible through separate entities to engage in business in more than one state and to conduct both
a commercial banking and securities business. These latter advantages enjoyed by foreign banks are the cause of the present controversy. Aggressive expansion, particularly by Barclays in New York and
by Lloyds in California, has provoked protest, especially from U.S.
banks, that they themselves are not extensively involved in the international field. By way of contrast, the major U.S. international banks
seek to avoid the imposition of any meaningful restrictions on foreign
banks operating in the United States, fearing reciprocal treatment
abroad that would inhibit U.S. banking activities in foreign markets.
The Federal Reserve Board has also become involved in the controversy, its concern stemming from questions relating to control over monetary policy.

Banking circles are rife with rumor regarding what will happen.
It is my belief that new legislation will place all foreign banks under
national control and that foreign banks will be permitted to continue
existing operations under a grandfather clause. Foreign banks will
be required to conform with existing prohibitions against interstate
banking and will also be prevented from engaging in both commercial

banking and securities activities. This suspicion has resulted in a
flurry of recent applications by foreign banks that seek to establish a
presence in various segments of the U.S. market prior to the imposition of any new restrictions.

CHAPTER

11

REMOVAL OF
U.S. CAPITAL CONTROLS
AND THE EUROMARKET
Y. S. Park

My subject is the future of the Euromarket, now that U.S. controls on capital movements are removed. On January 29, 1974, the U.S. government lifted three controls on international capital flows: first, the Interest Equalization Tax (IET), which had been in effect since 1963; second, the mandatory Foreign Direct Investment Program; and third, the Voluntary Foreign Credit Restraint guidelines (VFCR). Shortly after these controls were lifted, the London Economist ran a headline that read: "Two Revolutions Have Hit the Euromarkets at Once—the Bonanza of Arab Oil Money and New Competition from New York. Things Will Never Be the Same Again." It is questionable whether we should go so far as to call it a revolution to have U.S. capital controls removed, but such an expression is certainly an indication of the kind of excitement, or apprehension, that has been stirred up in international banking and financial circles by this new development.

THE EUROMARKET

What do I mean specifically by the term "Euromarket," in the context of my theme, "Removal of U.S. Capital Controls and the Euromarket"? I use the term to designate collectively those international financial markets developed in Europe and elsewhere, such as Eurodollar market, Eurobond market, Eurocredit market, Euroequity market, Asiadollar market, and so forth. Development of these markets has been influenced at one time or another by the three U.S. capital controls that I mentioned at the beginning. For example, growth of the Eurodollar market was greatly stimulated by the above three controls. When U.S. controls on capital movements were introduced

one after another (first, the IET in July 1963; next, the VFCR guidelines in February 1965; finally, the Foreign Direct Investment Program in January 1968), the Eurodollar market was able to grow very
rapidly, for these controls restricted access to the U.S. market on
the part of foreign borrowers for dollar funds, as well as on the part
of U.S. borrowers for funds for their foreign operations. So there
arose an increased demand for dollar loans abroad that in turn caused
an increased demand for dollar deposits abroad, which by definition
are Eurodollars. Eurodollars are dollar deposits at banks, either
non-U.S. banks or foreign branches of U.S. banks, that are located
outside the United States. Some say that U.S. controls increased the
money multiplier of the Eurodollar market. Others say that these controls increased the so-called primary deposits of the Eurodollar market—that is, there was an increased transfer of dollar deposits directly from the United States. Either through an increased Eurodollar
money multiplier or through increased Eurodollar primary deposits,
the market grew rapidly as a result of the U.S. capital controls.

In contrast to the Eurodollar market, which is a short-term
money market, the Eurobond market is a long-term bond market where
numerous international bonds are issued and traded. Eurobonds are
just one type of international bond, the other type being foreign bonds.
Foreign bonds are the same as domestic bonds, except that they are
issued by a nonresident foreign borrower. Yet, like domestic bonds,
foreign bonds are managed and underwritten by a national syndicate
of banks within the lending country; they are denominated in that country's currency and traded primarily by and among domestic investors
under that country's securities laws. In contrast, Eurobond issues
are managed and syndicated by an international group of underwriters
from many different countries, who sell these bonds to an international
clientele of investors. The bonds are denominated in any one of the
major national currencies, such as U.S. dollar or Deutschemark or
French franc, or they are denominated in one of the artificial units
of account, such as the Eurco, the European Unit of Account. These
units of account are not currencies; they are simply accounting concepts, a numeraire, a standard of value. Not far in the future, we
may even see a Eurobond issue denominated in SDRs.

These units of account are used in denominating certain Eurobonds, because investors in these bonds can be protected from the
exchange risk inherent in bonds denominated in a national currency.
Explanation of the differences and similarities among all these units
of account are too involved to be attempted here. Some Eurobonds
are denominated not just in one currency but in two or even three
currencies to give exchange protection to investors. In any case, the
distinguishing characteristic of Eurobonds, as compared to domestic
bonds or foreign bonds, is the fact that these bonds are issued and

marketed through an <u>international</u> syndicate of underwriters for a
Eurobond issue, in contrast to a national syndicate of underwriters
for domestic and foreign bonds.

THE EUROCREDIT MARKET

The Eurocredit market, which has sometimes been called the
medium-term Eurocurrency credit market, was originally thought of
as a bridge between the short-term Eurodollar market and the long-
term Eurobond market. It is true that the Eurocredit market started
out as a medium-term market, with the maturity of most loans falling
somewhere between five and seven years. However, the market is
not necessarily medium-term any more. Eurocredits of 10- or 12-
year maturities are quite common and you can even find 15- or 17-
year Eurocredits. Thus, the distinguishing characteristic of a Eurocredit is not the maturity of a Eurocurrency loan but the particular
mechanism of fixing its interest rate. For the interest rate of a Eurocredit is tied to the short-term Eurocurrency rate and the rate floats
every three or six months during the term of a loan. Thus, the Eurocredit market plays a bridge role connecting the short-term Eurodollar market with the long-term Eurobond market. The interest rate
of a dollar Eurocredit is fixed usually at the short-term, say three-
or six-month Eurodollar interest-deposit rate in London (called LIBO),
plus a spread or premium over the short-term Eurodollar rate. Depending upon the credit-worthiness of a borrower, the spread or premium may be anywhere from three-eighths of 1 percent for the very
best prime borrowers to 2.5 or even 3 percent for some of the least
creditworthy borrowers. The base-rate changes at the end of each
three- or six-month period, reflecting the new London interbank Eurodollar rate prevailing at that time.
    The Euroequity market is a market that is just developing. It
is a market where equity issues are being marketed on a Europe-wide
or international basis. For example, several years ago Ford Motor
Company placed a large secondary issue of its shares in tranches on
the various stock exchanges; those shares may be called Euroequities.
In late 1971 another U.S. company, Baxter Laboratories, Inc.,
floated a $12 million issue of convertible preferred stock in Europe
through an international syndicate. Also, there have been a fair number of convertible Eurobonds. However, if we classify convertible
Eurobonds as a Eurobond issue, the total volume of Euroequities
that have been placed so far is very limited, perhaps no more than
$100 million. Therefore, we can ignore the Euroequity market for
the purposes of this discussion. The Asiadollar market is an off-
shoot of the Eurodollar market, the only difference being that Asiadol-

lars are deposited in banks located in Asia, chiefly in Singapore. However, we can safely include this market as part of the Eurodollar market—except for the risk of hurting the pride of some Asian bankers. In any case, statistics on the Eurodollar market already include Asia-dollars as part of the Eurodollar market.

SIZE OF THE EUROMARKET

The description thus far of various Euromarkets leads us to conclude that we can consider only the three Euromarkets—that is, the Eurodollar market, the Eurobond market, and the Eurocredit market—in evaluating the impact of lifting U.S. capital controls on the Euromarket. What are the relative sizes of these three Euromarkets? As of the end of 1973, the size of the Eurocurrency market is estimated at more than $170 billion. The total volume of Eurobonds issued by the end of the first quarter of 1974 was about $26 billion. From 1971 through the end of the first quarter of 1974, the total volume of new Eurocredits was about $50 billion. This $50 billion figure for Euro-credits is only for those Eurocredits that the World Bank has been able to identify positively through tombstone watch or through other publications. Without doubt, a substantial volume of Eurocredits was extended before 1971 from the beginning of this market, which started around fiscal year 1965/66. Furthermore, a substantial volume of Eurocredits has never been publicly announced, so our $50 billion figure substantially underestimates the true volume, perhaps by as much as 25 percent. Therefore, it will not be surprising if the actual volume of Eurocredits that has been extended so far reaches the $70 billion mark from 1965/66 through the first quarter of this year. Clearly, when we talk about the future of the Euromarket, we talk about an enormous market that has absorbed almost $100 billion of medium- to long-term funds on an international scale and one that has more than $170 billion of Eurocurrency deposits from all over the world, ready to be tapped by borrowers and also ready to be transferred across national boundaries, when an occasion so demands.

As soon as the lifting of U.S. capital controls was announced, the Euromarket reacted swiftly. Eurodollar interest rates declined 50 basis points in one day. There was a brisk demand for Eurobonds that had been issued by U.S. companies, especially convertible Euro-bonds, because many dealers expected a great influx of U.S. invest-ors' money, after years of pent-up demand, eager to seek bargains in the Euromarket. Of course, that has not happened. When Euro-market traders finally found out that their expectation was not going to be met, rates went up and prices of Eurobonds declined rather substantially; this price decline was aggravated by rising short-term

rates in the U.S. money market, which made investors extremely reluctant to commit their funds to long-term securities. Many experts,
however, expected that U.S. investors, long prevented from purchasing Eurobonds because of the IET, would not come to the Eurobond
market and buy up Eurobonds, especially those that had been issued by
U.S. companies. Therefore, there would be a scarcity of Eurobonds
of U.S. companies, because these companies, which were forced in
the past to borrow in the Eurobond market to meet the requirements
of the Foreign Direct Investment Program, would now go back to the
U.S. market to raise long-term funds for their foreign operations. In
the U.S. market, the amounts raised could be larger than in the Eurobond market; the maturity could be longer; rates would be equivalent,
if not better; the underwriting fees would be lower; and the secondary
market support would be greater. Therefore, not only U.S. companies
but also foreign borrowers of long-term, fixed-rate funds would look
toward the U.S. market, now freed of restrictions.

As for the Eurocredit market, many expected to see increased
lending activity directly from the head offices of U.S. banks, which
were no longer restricted by the VFCR guidelines. Euromarket
branch offices of U.S. banks seemed likely to become less important
as a result, with some branches actually being closed to save money.
Increased direct-lending activity from head offices of U.S. banks would
reduce the demand for Eurodollar funds and thus reduce the demand
for Eurodollar deposits, which would mean a reduction in the size of
Eurodollar market. But there was also an opposite expectation that
the size of Eurodollar market would increase still further, because
Americans were free to invest dollars abroad. Some believed that
the outflow of dollars to the Eurodollar market would leave less money
in the United States, making it more difficult for U.S. borrowers to
obtain credit in the United States. I will consider this question more
closely later. For the moment, let us see what actually happened
(regardless of what was expected to happen) after the lifting of U.S.
controls.

As mentioned above, there was no exodus of U.S. investors in
search of Eurobonds, convertible or other. High short-term rates in
the United States tended to discourage U.S. investors from committing
their money to long-term, fixed-rate securities, be they U.S. domestic bonds or Eurobonds. There have been reports that several Eurobond issues planned by U.S. companies before the lifting of the controls were indefinitely postponed or canceled. In any case, the expected
flooding of the U.S. market by foreign issuers has not materialized
so far. In the Eurocredit market, there have been no discernible effects of the lifting of the controls. In fact, the market has been too
busy accommodating a flood of new business from oil-deficit countries
to think of anything else.

IMPACT OF THE LIFTING OF U.S. CONTROLS

If there has been any impact of the U.S. action, it has been primarily on the Eurodollar market, especially in the London dollar CD (certificate of deposit) market. According to informed sources in Eurobanking circles, during the first two months after control removal, $3-4 billion of new money flowed into the Eurodollar market from the U.S. market. A substantial part of this new money was invested in London dollar CDs, whose yield advantage over U.S. domestic dollar CDs was sometimes as high as 100 basis points or more. An institutional result of this development was the almost overnight establishment in New York of a trading market in London dollar CDs. While a number of dealers operate trading desks in both London and New York, a growing number of houses are trading from New York only, gaining access to secondary Eurodollar CDs through the large international money-brokerage community in New York. Due to increased arbitrage activity between U.S. domestic CDs and London dollar CDs, the yield advantage of Eurodollar CDs has narrowed substantially since the lifting of controls. For example, during the two months preceding the lifting of controls, the yield advantage for a six-month maturity was 137 basis points in favor of London on a weekly average basis, but it declined to 68 basis points during the following two months.

I have described so far what we may call "the immediate effect" of lifting U.S. controls on the Euromarket. However, this may not be indicative of what will happen to the market in years to come. To evaluate the long-term effects of lifting U.S. controls, we have to look more closely at the interrelationship between the Euromarket and the U.S. market. Consider, first, the relationship between the Eurobond market and the U.S. market.

Development of the Eurobond market has been more closely related to various U.S. control measures than development of other Euromarkets. In 1973 there was a conference in London on the Euromarket with many speakers emphasizing the significance of the year 1973 as the tenth anniversary of the Eurobond market. The year 1973 was also the tenth anniversary of the IET, and, indeed, there was a connection between the market and the tax. In July 1963 President Kennedy proposed the IET to restrict new purchases by Americans of foreign securities, issued both in the United States and abroad. Proposed primarily in response to the depletion of U.S. gold reserves by more than $7 billion during the period from 1958 through early 1963, the tax placed a charge, initially up to 15 percent, on all subsequent purchases by Americans of foreign-debt and equity securities of most developed countries. With their access to the U.S. market thus blocked, foreign borrowers turned to a novel concept—i.e., selling

bonds denominated in dollars through an international underwriting
syndicate to an international clientele of investors. The first such
issue was floated in July 1963, the same month in which the IET was
introduced. The issue was for an Italian company, Autostrade, which
operates and maintains Italy's national highway system. This $15
million Autostrade issue is considered the first Eurobond issue. Thus
there was a definite relationship between the origin of the Eurobond
market and introduction of the IET.

However, the Eurobond market was slow to grow, averaging
only several hundred million dollars each year, until 1965, when the
U.S. government introduced the so-called voluntary foreign direct investment program. The program required U.S. companies, on a voluntary basis, to restrict fund outflows from the United States. In
order to meet fund requirements for their foreign operations, U.S.
companies began to borrow in the Eurobond market. As a result, the
Eurobond market began to attract some attention in the United States.
When the 1965 voluntary program was replaced in 1968 by the mandatory Foreign Direct Investment Program, the volume of Eurobond issues by U.S. companies rose sharply. Compared to $562 million in
1967, U.S. companies borrowed $2.1 billion in 1968 in the Eurobond
market, almost four times as much. Since then, U.S. companies
have tapped, on the average, more than $1 billion each year in the
market. The question is, what will happen to borrowings by U.S.
companies in the Eurobond market, now that U.S. controls are lifted?
I expect a substantial transfer of issuing activity by U.S. companies
from the Eurobond market to the U.S. market, because of the advantages of the U.S. market over the Eurobond market mentioned above,
such as longer maturity, larger issue amount, lower underwriting
commissions, and better secondary market. However, some U.S.
companies will still continue to tap the Eurobond market. In late 1969
I made a survey of 112 U.S. companies that had borrowed in the Eurobond market and found that not all U.S. borrowings were done to meet
Foreign Direct Investment regulations. Some of their Eurobond proceeds were brought to the United States for domestic purposes. The
rationales for tapping the Eurobond market rather than the U.S. market were several. The absence of Securities and Exchange Commission (SEC) registration requirements would enable a U.S. company to
raise money quietly for various confidential purposes, such as for
not-yet-announced mergers or acquisitions. Eurobond issues also
helped to give visibility to the borrowing company in international financial circles. Also, some U.S. companies were desirous of pro-
curing nondollar currencies at a fixed rate, in order to hedge their
foreign-currency assets with foreign-currency liabilities. This was
conveniently accomplished by a Eurobond issue, denominated in that
foreign currency.

WILL FOREIGN BORROWING INCREASE
IN THE UNITED STATES?

Will foreign borrowers also abandon the Eurobond market in favor of the U.S. market, now that U.S. controls are ended? The answer is partially yes and partially no. There are several disadvantages of a U.S. bond issue by a foreign borrower, such as strict SEC registration requirements, the need to make more disclosures, different accounting rules, and the need to receive a credit rating by U.S. credit-rating agencies in order to be eligible for investment by many pension funds and savings banks. These factors will deter all but the most determined and most prestigious foreign borrowers from entering the U.S. market. And even those eligible foreign borrowers may prefer to borrow more through the private placement market, which does not require SEC registration, than in the public issue market. Interest rates may not be advantageous either, because U.S. investors are likely to demand a premium for foreign securities, which will wipe out any rate differential that may exist between the Eurobond and U.S. market.

The most obvious effect of lifting U.S. controls has been the narrowing of interest-rate differentials between the Eurodollar market and the U.S. money market. Before the lifting of U.S. capital controls, arbitrage operations between the two markets had been only one way, because while money could flow into the U.S. market without restriction, it could not flow out freely, due to U.S. controls. As a result, when overseas demand for dollars increased sharply due to an exchange crisis (people using dollars to buy, say, German marks to hedge against, or profit from, the potential revaluation of the Deutschemark), Eurodollar interest rates shot up dramatically, leaving a wide gap between Eurodollar rates and U.S. money market rates. For example, in 1971 the Eurodollar rate climbed to a dizzy 375 basis points above the U.S. commercial paper rate, as people rushed to borrow Eurodollars for conversion into German marks, Swiss francs, and the like. Such a wide yield differential will not occur again, because dollar deposits will flow out en masse to the Eurodollar market from the U.S. market as soon as Eurodollar rates rise marginally above U.S. money market rates. This prospect raises an interesting question: What will happen in consequence to U.S. money rates? The answer, that there will be no effect on U.S. rates, leads to the further question: Does the Eurodollar rate determine the U.S. rate, or vice versa? To put it another way, can the tail wag the dog? The answer is that the U.S. rate determines the Eurodollar rate, not vice versa. The explanation is simple. Assume that a depositor, American or not, transfers his deposit held at a bank in the United States to a Eurobank in, say, London. The depositor's original deposit in the U.S. banking system will decline, but the Eurobank's deposit in the U.S. banking system will increase. Thus, there is no net change in the total amount of deposits in the U.S. banking system. At the same time, the Eurodollar market gains an additional primary deposit, with a resulting increase in the size of the Eurodollar market. This means that the money supply—or, more precisely, that loanable funds in the Eurodollar market—can increase without affecting the amount of loanable funds in the U.S. market, hence without necessarily affecting the interest-rate level in the United States. However, when interest rates in the United States rise, Eurodollar rates also have to rise. Otherwise, Eurodollar depositors will transfer their deposits from the Eurodollar market to the U.S. market. This transfer affects the amount of loanable funds in the Eurodollar market, but, again, it does not affect the U.S. market.

I am not saying that creation of additional Eurodollars through transfer of dollar deposits from a U.S. bank to a Eurobank cannot affect the money supply in the United States. This transfer can affect the narrowly defined money supply, M_1, in certain circumstances. Suppose a depositor transfers his time deposit held at a U.S. bank to a Eurobank in London. If the Eurobank now keeps it as a demand deposit at its correspondent bank in the United States, then M_1 in the United States will increase, even though there will be no change in M_2, which is M_1 plus time and savings deposits at banks. On the other hand, suppose that the original depositor had only a demand deposit at a U.S. bank and that he subsequently transferred it to a Eurobank in London. If the Eurobank in London decides to keep it not as a demand deposit but as a time deposit at its correspondent bank in the United States, then M_1 will decrease, while there will still be no change in M_2. Because of this potential change in the proportion of demand versus time deposits in the transfer of a deposit to the Eurodollar market, there can also be a change in required reserves for the U.S. banking system as a whole. If the Federal Reserve does not counteract this, there will be a change in the reserve positions of U.S. banks and consequently in their ability to create credits. While this is theoretically possible, in practice the sums in question will not be substantial, or the Federal Reserve Board can easily neutralize them.

The narrowing of yield differentials between the U.S. and Eurodollar markets due to the removal of U.S. capital controls has a serious implication for the world monetary system. Whenever a change in the par value of a major currency appeared imminent in the past, the steep increase in Eurodollar interest rates, as well as scarcity of Eurodollar loans, restrained somewhat the ability of currency speculators to attack the currency involved, for these speculators had to weigh the potential gain from speculation against the high cost of speculative funds—i.e., the Eurodollar loans. Now, with the prospect of an almost unlimited supply of Eurodollars at a rate only slightly above the yield differential between the Eurodollar and U.S. markets, speculative attack on a currency must become too large to be controlled by central banks. This will pose a serious threat to any fixed exchange rate system, even one with a wider band. This leads in turn to a fundamental question: Would it be possible, or even desirable, to maintain a fixed exchange-rate system when there are no elaborate capital controls like the ones that the U.S. government finally lifted? I am afraid not.

EXPANSION OF EUROCREDITS

Finally, let us look at the effect of lifting controls on the Eurocredit market. I already observed that the lifting of U.S. controls has scarcely affected the growth of this market. The volume of Eurocredits expanded very rapidly in the spring of 1974, as several major oil-deficit countries, such as the United Kingdom, France, Italy, and Japan, came to this market for loans. According to the data collected at the World Bank, the total of Eurocredits extended during the first quarter of 1974 amounted to $14 billion, compared to $2.2 billion during the first quarter of 1973—an increase of more than 600 percent! Compared to 1973's total annual volume of $22 billion, a total volume of about $50 billion for 1974 will be no surprise. This tremendous increase in Eurocredit volume is mainly due to the oil price hikes. Because of the price hike, there is an increased demand for reserves by oil-deficit countries; there is also, of course, an increased supply of funds from oil-producing countries. However, removal of U.S. controls has also played, and is expected to play, a constructive part in growth of the Eurocredit market. One of the most disturbing factors in this market has been the potential for extreme fluctuations in Eurodollar interest rates, or even the outright unavailability of Eurodollars during an exchange crisis. Since the lifting of U.S. controls has removed this possibility or substantially reduced its significance, a main worry in the Eurocredit market has disappeared: for lending banks, the worry that no Eurodollar funds will be available for rollover of Eurocredits; for borrowers, the worry that they may have to accept a prohibitively high base rate (i.e., the London Eurodollar interbank rate).

As a result of the lifting of U.S. controls, there will also be some institutional as well as operational effects on U.S. banks. Some overseas lending activity by foreign branches of U.S. banks will be brought back to head offices in the United States. Some unprofitable Eurobanking branch offices will be closed, reduced in size, or combined with other branches. Many shell branch offices in Nassau and the Cayman Islands will be closed, though not necessarily all of them. These shell branches have been set up simply as bookkeeping facilities for Eurodollar business by medium to small U.S. banks, which could not afford a full Eurobanking branch office, while their head offices in the United States were prevented from engaging directly in Eurobanking business.

However, this retraction and consolidation by U.S. banks of their overseas Eurobanking branches will not be immediate or even substantial. There are definite advantages for Eurobanking branch offices that, free from Regulation Q, can accept time deposits of less than 30 days and also without interest ceilings. They are also free from Regulation D, and so they do not have to keep reserve requirements as do domestic banks. Also, the absence of formal restrictions on the capital/deposit ratio and the wholesale nature of Eurobanking will allow Eurobanks to gain a competitive edge over United States-based banks. Since Regulation M requires an 8 percent reserve require ment on U.S. bank liabilities to their foreign branches as well as on foreign branch loans to U.S. residents, this unduly favors non-U.S. banks operating in the Eurodollar market. The highly developed syndication power of Eurobanks in arranging a Eurocredit not only makes it easier merely to borrow but also to borrow a substantially larger amount—up to $2 billion or more in a single deal—than in the U.S. market. Longer maturity, more flexible amortization and prepayment schedules, multicurrency options, and the ability to take a lower margin due to the wholesale nature of Eurocredit business—all these factors make the Eurocredit market a powerful competitor of the U.S. credit market. Hence, we can expect a continued strong growth of this market in the future.

If my analysis is valid, it leads to optimism concerning the future of the Euromarket. Undoubtedly, there will be consolidation and readjustment here and there, due to the removal of U.S. capital controls. However, the overall development of the Euromarket will be toward more efficiency and more flexibility. And that is exactly what we are hoping for.

CHAPTER

12

THE GLOBAL
IMPACT OF THE
OIL PRICE RISE

Richard N. Cooper

The fourfold increase in petroleum prices that took place at the beginning of 1974 is probably the most severe single economic shock that the world economy has had to absorb since World War II. The impact of this increase on the world economy is a vast, complex subject, with many ramifications going well beyond economics. I will discuss several of the economic implications briefly, under five different headings, and then conclude with some remarks on the implications of these developments for the reform of the international monetary system on which governments have been working intensely for the past several years.

It is useful first to recall the magnitudes involved: Persian Gulf crude oil prices (f.o.b.) rose from about $2.12 a barrel in January 1973 to $3.68 a barrel in November 1973 to $7.61 a barrel in January 1974. Crude oil from other foreign sources experienced similar price increases. At 1973's volume, the price increases since October 1973 will raise payments for imported oil by nearly $70 billion, to $120 billion c.i.f. at ports of importation. With total world trade running around $500 billion, this represents a tremendous jolt to the world system of international payments and to living standards in all oil-consuming economies.

ECONOMIC EFFECTS OF THE PRICE INCREASE

It is useful to divide the economic analysis problem into five separate but obviously related components: short-term economic stabilization, terms-of-trade effects on real income, long-term substitution away from oil, short-term balance-of-payments financing, and long-term investments by the oil producers. I will dwell most exten-

143

sively on the problem of short-term financing, since that is the most
immediate problem for the world economy and also where the issue
of petroleum prices bears most directly on the international monetary
system. But it is useful first to touch briefly on the other economic
effects.

Economic Stabilization

The first problem created by the sharp increase in oil prices
concerns economic stabilization. In its economic effect, the large increase in oil prices acts like an excise tax imposed on all consumers
of oil, with the proceeds of the tax returned to the money market. In
the context of the United States alone, where the incremental bill for
imported oil will be an estimated $15 billion on the assumptions stated
above, this excise tax would be equivalent in its effects to a 10 percent
increase in personal income taxes (or, equivalently, a 1.5 percent income tax surcharge on all personal income), with the proceeds returned to the financial markets—for example, to reduce the short-
term public debt. Such a tax/investment combination would have a
substantial deflationary impact on the U.S. economy and would require
expansionist monetary and fiscal actions to offset it.
Reality is more complicated, not least because the increase in
oil prices is global, yet some of the "tax" proceeds from other countries will undoubtedly be invested in the United States, reducing the
net deflationary impact there but increasing it elsewhere (where, because of the higher dependence on imported oil, the deflationary impact will be proportionately stronger in the first place). Opening the
U.S. short-term money market to unrestricted foreign borrowing will
tend to cut the other way, reducing the deflationary impact abroad
and increasing it here. But the general point is that the increase in
oil prices, resulting in revenues that will be placed in liquid assets
rather than spent, will exert a short-run deflationary pressure on the
world economy. Some deflation from the exuberant 1973 was desirable in any case. But forecasters in the fall of 1973 already foresaw a
slowdown in 1974, and the oil price rise may result in overshooting
the mark. Here is an area for close coordination of national economic
policies, most logically at the OECD, to assure that the national actions are consistent and mutually supporting.

Price-Wage Inflation

In addition to requiring actions for stabilization, the increase
in oil prices will also require action, or at least exhortation, to pre-

vent a fruitless, inflationary attempt by many groups in society to preserve their real incomes. A sharp shift in the terms of trade, with the price of imports rising relative to the price of exports, is a new experience for Americans. It leads to a real loss of income, and there is nothing Americans can do internally to recoup it. They are faced with having to pay out roughly $15 billion more in exports than they had counted on to buy the imports they want. (They can, of course, and most likely will borrow the $15 billion and make the real payments later.) This lowers per capita real income in the United States by about 1.5 percent. The corresponding figure for other industrial countries is closer to 4 percent. Even the larger magnitude should be manageable in view of the rapid growth that all industrial economies have enjoyed in recent years—it is not much more than one to two years' growth in real income per capita. But the "man in the street" simply experiences a rise in the prices he must pay for gasoline, fuel oil, electricity, and so on, and he is going to want higher wages to compensate for that. Because the "tax" comes from outside the country, however, there is no way that collectively Americans can compensate for it; it requires a reduction in real income relative to what they would otherwise enjoy.

For this reason, I regret very much the virtual abandonment of the government guidelines on wage settlements after April 1, 1974. In these of all circumstances we need guidelines on wages, combined with a forceful explanation of the fact that in this case the increase in price is external to the country and thus cannot be recouped through higher money wages there (on the assumption that the OPEC countries will continue to raise oil prices in line with any inflation in the prices that they have to pay for imported goods). It is of course unfortunate that the increase in oil prices followed so rapidly on the heels of a sharp increase in food prices. (That conjunction may be more than a coincidence, since several Middle Eastern countries complained bitterly of the higher import prices they were having to pay, and they import food.) That was primarily an internal transfer, with U.S. farmers benefiting at the expense of urban wage earners, although in that instance the United States also charged more to foreigners. But when such a large price increase comes from outside the country, average living standards must fall, relative to what they would otherwise be, except insofar as the public is willing to borrow (ultimately, from the oil-exporting countries) in order to maintain them. This is an important point that has received too little attention, for if it is not widely understood, it will set off a further wage-price spiral that can be quelled only by generating substantial unemployment.

Substitution Away from Middle-East Oil

Over the longer term the higher oil prices will discourage consumption and will stimulate the search for substitutes. Our modern
industrial economies are remarkably resilient, and while they cannot
survive without energy, they can survive without Middle Eastern oil,
given enough time to adjust to the new situation. We cannot escape
the cost entirely, however, for the substitutes will be more expensive
than foreign oil was in the summer of 1973, at least in the absence of
technological breakthroughs that are now difficult to foresee. In the
longer run we can limit the monopoly profits of the owners of oil by
encouraging the entry of substitutes. But even after reducing our dependence on one source of supply, we still will be left with higher
energy costs than we have been accustomed to until this year.

Short-Term Balance-of-Payments Financing

The balance-of-payments financing problem arises because for
the next several years virtually all net oil-importing nations will be
in balance-of-payments deficit on conventional definitions. Indeed,
in future years the cumulative deficit (with its corresponding surplus
in the oil-exporting nations) will be staggering: It will worsen by the
$70 billion mentioned above, less an allowance for reductions in con-
sumption of oil and an allowance for increased purchases of goods,
services, and long-term investment (including repayment of debt) by
the oil-producing nations. At best, these two factors together are not
likely to amount to more than $30 billion, so unless oil prices fall
(as they may) there will be a deficit-financing problem of something
over $40 billion. *

----

*The arithmetic of oil payments is somewhat confusing, even af-
ter allowing for uncertainties in the amount by which consumption will
decline in response to such large price increases. Because of the cost
of production, costs of transport, and profits of the international oil
companies, there is a substantial discrepancy between the growth
payments for oil by importing nations and the net receipts for oil by
exporting nations. The staff of the Council on International Economic
Policy, for instance, reckons the cost per barrel of Persian Gulf
crude c.i.f. U.S. gulf ports at $9.09, of which an estimated $7.01 ac-
crues as revenues to the exporting country. The remainder goes to
shippers and the oil firms. But the increase in prices, $5.49 since
January 1973, goes wholly as revenues to the exporting countries.
It is this increased revenue, amounting to around $70 Billion on last

The first point to note is that in the aggregate these large purchases of oil will be self-financing: If the oil countries sell the oil at
all, they will automatically use the proceeds for something, if only to
build up interest-bearing deposits in the Eurocurrency market, which
is where much of the money is likely to go. The question is not, therefore, whether the oil-exporting nations will invest their surplus funds,
but rather where and in what form they will do so. My guess is that
most of the investment will be in highly liquid dollar assets, mainly in
the New York and Eurodollar money markets. These two markets are
the only places large enough to absorb on short notice the volume of
funds involved, without acute disruption. In the absence of offsetting
central-bank action, these two markets should be flush with funds.

What about the nations that need the funds to pay for the enlarged
import bill? They cannot hope collectively to pay in 1975 with goods
and services, so they must either borrow or draw on their accumulated
reserves. It is worth recalling that not too long ago many countries
deplored the surfeit of reserves, and indeed the managing director of
the International Monetary Fund (IMF) was unable to get approval for
an additional issue of the Special Drawing Rights (SDRs)—the last issue
was in January 1972. World reserves stood at $187 billion at the end
of September 1973, having risen by exactly $100 billion (measured in
dollars) from three years earlier. Some countries can comfortably
finance their oil payments out of reserves during 1975-76 and by the
standards of just a few years ago still have ample reserves. This is
precisely the kind of occasion that reserves are meant to be used for:
to smooth the transition to a markedly different condition.

But most countries do not have such a large cushion; the ability
to draw down reserves is substantial, but they will dwindle quickly
against the equally substantial additional payments for oil. These countries will have to borrow. As noted above, the funds will be globally
available, from the oil countries themselves. But they will not be
equally available to all countries that need them. Many countries will
have no difficulty raising the necessary funds through short- and me-

---

year's volume, that poses the financing problem. Some of the price
increase will of course affect payments in late 1973, so the increase
from calendar year 1973 to 1974 will not be this large, even if volume
does not drop.

A 50 percent increase in imports by the oil-exporting countries
would amount to about $10 billion. A 15 percent drop in world con-
sumption of oil, implying a short-run price elasticity of demand for
imports of .075, would cut the revenues of oil-exporting countries by
around $15 billion. A drop in oil prices would of course reduce the
revenues further.

dium-term borrowing from the banks that are the depositaries of the funds; the Eurocurrency market has grown apace in recent years, and a rapidly growing list of countries has had access to it. Thus, in the short run the financial markets will channel funds to where they are needed, provided countries are willing to borrow, and provided the large commercial banks are willing to lend.

The last qualification is an important one. While the availability of adequate funding at the global level is clear enough, each commercial bank must concern itself with the security of its own deposits. Arab money can be withdrawn from a single bank at any moment (since the funds are held in highly liquid form), and the sum can be sufficiently large, relative to the capital of the banks, such that the failure of a major debtor could damage the bank irreparably. It will therefore be necessary for central banks to provide some form of backstopping to the commercial banks, if the latter are to perform the necessary function of financial intermediation on the scale required in the present circumstances. The most expeditious way to accomplish this would be for the leading central banks to commit themselves, if necessary, to rediscount the medium-term bank loans to governments up to some maximum for each country stipulated in relation to its incremental oil payments. The very public announcement of such a backstopping commitment would have a salutory effort in calming financial markets and in encouraging commercial banks to make loans to countries that, one way or another, will have to be made anyway, if economic collapse is to be avoided.

Some countries have neither adequate reserves nor adequate credit worthiness to borrow extensively through commercial channels. Most of these are developing countries, and some may be able to borrow directly from the Arabs on commercial terms. The sums required for these countries—India, Bangladesh, and Uruguay are examples— are not large in comparison with the total problem, probably under $2 billion in 1974.

Two lines of approach are possible, and both may be necessary. The first is to lower the price of oil to these countries, either directly through discriminatory pricing by the oil-producing countries, under the rubric of solidarity within the Third World, or indirectly through loans on concessional terms by the Arab countries. The second is by financial intermediation on behalf of those countries, most expeditiously handled by the World Bank. The bank can borrow readily in financial markets on its own high credit standing, backed as it is by all member countries, and then it can re-lend in the form of program loans to the needy countries. The bank could not give concessional interest rates on such loans (some outside source of funding would be necessary for

that*) and it would not run any exchange risk, since the borrower
would borrow dollars to pay its oil bill in dollars. But obviously the
bank could not avoid the intrinsic credit risk involved in such lending,
and ultimately it might be called upon to reschedule the loans and in
other ways to convert nonconcessional loans to concessional ones.
The problem here is to provide financing to get through 1974 and 1975
without inviting utter collapse of some economies through inability to
pay for oil and oil-based products, such as fertilizers.

Long-Term Financing of the Oil Flows

The long-run substitution away from Middle East oil, along with
steady increases in consumption in the Middle East, will assure that
Arab oil producers will not go on adding without limit to their financial claims on the rest of the world. But in the rather long meantime,
they will be increasing those claims, and they will seek modes of investment other than short-term deposits and other liquid claims. In
effect, the oil producers are exchanging one kind of asset—oil in the
ground—for another: the more conventional financial assets. The possible problems associated with extensive Arab investment vary with
the form of investment, but this is not the occasion to provide a lengthy
analysis. Let it suffice to say that, broadly speaking, the Arabs can
put their assets into (1) deposits and other liquid claims, (2) long-
term bonds, (3) equity shares without controlling interest, (4) direct
investment in productive assets or real estate abroad, (5) real investment in productive assets at home (some of which would be imported),
and (6) commodity stockpiles, such as gold. All these alternatives,

---

*One possible source of such funding, advocated in a more gen-
eral context in Towards a Renovated World Monetary System (New
York: Trilateral Commission, 1973), would be the capital gains on
sales into the private market of official monetary gold, since the gold
is carried in reserves at $42.22 an ounce and has sold in private mar-
kets for more than three times that amount. Official sales would de-
press the price but not so much as to wipe out the gain, which could
then be appropriated to the World Bank, without any book losses to
the central banks or treasuries involved. Indeed, the IMF alone holds
more than $6 billion in gold, valued at the official price. Sales of as
little as $200 million of this a year would generate gains sufficient to
cover the full interest costs on loans to the most disadvantaged countries.

with the magnitudes under consideration (for example, initially $45 billion a year, declining steadily to zero after, say, six years, plus accrued interest, amounting to around $200 billion in 1980, all concentrated in relatively few hands), could have noticeable effects on the world economy, but none of them would be really alarming, if properly handled. Liquid assets can be shifted from one claim to another, possibly disrupting money and currency markets. But it is precisely this kind of disturbance that an international lender-of-last-resort, such as I proposed to the Joint Economic Committee last year, would be designed for: It could promptly and smoothly "recycle" any untoward movement of funds of this sort. The present central-bank swap arrangements represent a primitive form of such a facility, but they are now too small for the potential disturbances. A multilateral facility should be established in the IMF.

Bond and equity markets can always be manipulated for gain by any transactor large enough to influence the expectations and actions of others through price manipulation. But if such manipulation were discovered, it could readily lead to punitive response by the regulating authorities of the exchanges, and that would inhibit further manipulation. Direct investment abroad has certain problems associated with it, aired extensively in recent years in discussion of the multinational corporation. Some of those problems would be aggravated when the investor is a foreign government. But direct investments abroad by the Arabs will be slow in coming. And as has been said in connection with all multinational corporations, they represent hostages to the host government—a fact that augurs in favor of conventional business behavior. So we should be thoroughly relaxed about this prospect until events prove the contrary.

Finally, purchases of gold seem the least troublesome of all. Beyond relatively small amounts, purchases seem bound to drive the price up to a point at which future selling of any magnitude would impose capital losses on the seller. Hence unless they can play successfully on the psychology of other gold hoarders, oil-exporting nations should be wary of putting too much of their wealth into this form.

IMPLICATIONS FOR REFORM OF THE INTERNATIONAL MONETARY SYSTEM

The world has been engaged during the past two years, through the Committee of Twenty of the IMF, in trying to improve the functioning of the international monetary system, the rules of which gradually broke down in the late 1960s and early 1970s. This is not the occasion to review the many important details and disputes concerning such a major reform, but the sharp increase in oil prices does

have some implications for the reform effort as it has been conceived
so far, and they can be discussed briefly under three headings: the
balance-of-payments adjustment mechanism, the alleged "overhang"
of U.S. dollars in the international system, and restoration of convertibility of the U.S. dollar into some kind of reserve asset.

Balance-of-Payments Adjustment

The majority of governments apparently desired a return to a
system of relatively fixed exchange rates, despite the strong evidence
that without substantial flexibility in exchange rates of one form or
another the international monetary system is likely to break down periodically. The increase in oil prices convinced many governments
that exchange-rate flexibility is likely to be a feature of the international monetary system for some time to come, and hence they might
profitably turn their attention to making a system of managed flexibility work well. There is a special irony in this desirable turn of opinion, for the big increase in oil prices is one disturbance that adjustments in exchange rates cannot handle well. This major disturbance
involves relative commodity prices and is not monetary in origin;
monetary adjustments alone, such as changes in exchange rates, cannot solve the problem, since real consumption by the oil-exporting nations is not likely to rise much faster than otherwise, even with huge
appreciations of their own currencies, relative to all the leading currencies.

Where exchange-rate flexibility can be very helpful during the
next several years is in achieving the numerous secondary adjustments
that must take place between leading economies. The sharp increase
in oil prices will alter patterns of comparative advantage and of competitiveness among industrial countries, and the flows of long-term investment from the oil-exporting countries to other countries cannot
be known in advance and in any case are not likely to follow the same
pattern as that of the increased oil payments. Thus, after a transitional adjustment period there will have to be adjustments in trade
competitiveness between, say, France, Germany, Japan, and the
United States, and alterations in exchange rates can be very helpful
in bringing these necessary adjustments about. Since we do not now
know even the direction of necessary adjustment in some cases, a
period of exchange-rate flexibility managed to prevent highly erratic
movements in rates can be very helpful.

In the meantime, we should not hesitate to rely heavily on financing the oil deficits, as discussed above, until the new long-run
patterns become clearer to businessmen and governments alike.

The "Overhang" of Dollars

Until the fall of 1973 much concern was expressed about the excessive supply of dollars on the world scene, with international reserves having grown by $100 billion in the preceding three years. In the face of large oil deficits, these holdings of reserves now look very welcome, and indeed short-run financing of the oil deficits will involve transferring substantial amounts of these dollars to the oil-exporting countries. It is too early to tell whether they will be more or less willing holders of the dollars than their predecessors. It is conceivable that they will be restless about holding so much of a single currency and will try both to diversify their holdings into other currencies (thereby passing the dollars back to other countries) and to fund some of them into claims on the IMF denominated in SDRs, along the lines of the "conversion account" discussed by the Committee of Twenty. The latter course, however, is quite unlikely, at least for any magnitude. The Arab oil exporters are among the few who elected not to participate in the SDR scheme at all, and they are not likely to begin now that they are the great balance-of-payments surplus countries of the world. They will undoubtedly diversify their currency holdings somewhat, but under the present circumstances other countries are likely to look on the resulting increases in their dollar holdings with a less jaundiced eye than would have been true a year ago. Thus the "overhang" is likely to be much less of a problem than some observers have perceived it to be.

Convertibility of the Dollar

The United States suspended gold convertibility of the dollar for foreign official holders in August 1971. European countries made it clear in the Committee of Twenty discussions that restoration of convertibility, at least into SDRs, was a sine qua non of their participation in any overall reform of the monetary system. Under the present circumstances, the prospects for early restoration of convertibility have receded considerably (the Arab oil-exporting countries are not likely to be especially interested in convertibility into SDRs, and gold convertibility could be restored only at a very much higher official price of gold, a move that the U.S. government, for excellent reasons, has persistently opposed). Instead, we will see a prolonged period of exchange-rate flexibility, so that countries need not accumulate unwanted dollars, along with an increased willingness to hold dollars.

CHAPTER
13
EXCHANGE-RATE FLEXIBILITY, OBJECTIVE INDICATORS, AND INTERNATIONAL MONETARY REFORM

Thomas D. Willett
Nicholas P. Sargen

One of the major issues that has been debated in the discussions on international monetary reform is the type of adjustment mechanism that is appropriate, given the high degree of interdependence and capital mobility today in the international economy. This chapter examines a number of considerations bearing on this issue, including a discussion of the weaknesses of the "adjustable-peg" system and an examination of alternative forms of increased exchange-rate flexibility; a discussion of the system of reserve indicators proposed by the United States; and an analysis of the attitudes of the developing countries toward greater exchange-rate flexibility. In the concluding section, it is argued that for reform of the international monetary system to be successful a balance must be achieved between the need for international policy coordination and desires for independent policy. This balance can be attained by permitting a greater degree of exchange-. rate flexibility than under the adjustable-peg system, and by using a reserve-indicator scheme to apportion adjustment responsibilities (under a system based on par values or gliding parities) or to provide safeguards against competitive depreciations in floating situations.

THE NEED FOR GREATER
EXCHANGE-RATE FLEXIBILITY

There is fairly widespread recognition today that the Bretton Woods system, which had worked so well in the 1940s and 1950s, was not well equipped to cope with economic developments during the 1960s. One major source of difficulty with the system that had been noted by the early 1960s had to do with the provisions for increases in international liquidity. By the late 1960s, however, it had become apparent

that a significant and perhaps even greater source of difficulty with
the system concerned general questions of balance-of-payments adjustment, especially as to authority for adjusting mutual payments imbalances and the role which exchange-rate changes should play in the
adjustment process. In these matters, several of the crucial empirical assumptions made by the designers of the Bretton Woods system
turned out over time to become increasingly less appropriate.

One of the principal concerns of the designers of the Bretton
Woods system was to avoid a repeat of the competitive depreciations
of the 1930s. Viewed from this standpoint, the system was extremely
successful. Yet, as so often happens, the improvement was made at
the cost of moving too far in the opposite direction, as the major international monetary problems that emerged in the postwar period resulted from exchange-rate changes being too infrequent, rather than
too frequent.

The "adjustable peg," adopted as part of the Bretton Woods system, contained a strong bias against parity changes, and at the same
time permitted only a narrow range of fluctuations of market rates
about parity (1 percent on either side). While such a bias may have
been justified in a world in which "beggar-my-neighbor" exchange-rate
adjustments were anticipated, the international economic climate of
the postwar period had changed dramatically from that of the 1930s.
Perhaps the most important factor was a better understanding of
proper use of macroeconomic policy management, which considerably
reduced the economic incentives for competitive depreciation as a
means of exporting unemployment.

While the bias in the system against exchange-rate changes reduced the problem of mercantilist exchange-rate depreciations by
deficit countries, it at the same time exacerbated the corresponding
problem of the failure of surplus countries to appreciate their currencies when appropriate.* Yet maintenance of undervalued exchange
rates (and balance-of-payments surplus objectives) can be just as
disruptive to international exchange as attempts to maintain an overvalued rate.

———————————

*The term "devaluation bias" has come to be used to describe
the situation under the adjustable-peg system in which the number of
devaluations has exceeded the number of revaluations. Roper [Kyklos],
however, has pointed out that it is difficult to distinguish the "devaluation bias" from the effect of a shortage of international liquidity,
since if there is an inadequacy of international reserves and part of
this demand is satisfied by dollars, then the noncenter countries will,
on average, retain undervalued currencies to satisfy that demand.

The adverse effects of excessive exchange-rate fixity were further compounded by increased international economic activity in the postwar period, and in particular by the increase in capital mobility. Under the articles of Bretton Woods, it was not envisioned that this would present much of a problem, because the mobility of international liquid funds was at that time quite low and was further constrained in most countries by comprehensive systems of exchange controls. However, by the 1960s the picture had changed dramatically, and in the face of huge increases in the quantities of internationally mobile funds, the "one-way bet" presented by sticky exchange parities generated ever-increasing speculative or precautionary capital flows. Frequently, initial government reactions were to try to supersede or suspend market forces, with deficit countries attempting to finance the deficits and surplus countries to sterilize the inflows, rather than attempting to correct the fundamental disequilibrium. Delay in undertaking exchange-rate changes, however, ultimately increased the cost of adjustment once the changes did occur.

By biasing incentives against the use of exchange-rate adjustments, the adjustable-peg system also unnecessarily increased the degree to which policy coordination was needed for efficient operation of the system. At a time when the national degree of economic interdependence was increasing, and in the absence of effective mechanisms for bringing about international policy coordination, this proved to be a fatal deficiency.

During the 1960s there was a continuing debate over whether it was solely up to deficit countries to correct their payments imbalances, or whether surplus countries, too, had a responsibility. Given the cost of correcting large payments imbalances, substantial international tension was created. While there are several mechanisms in the Bretton Woods system whereby the international community can place formal pressure on deficit countries to adjust, the situation is not as satisfactory with respect to placing adjustment pressure on surplus countries. This question was not ignored at the Bretton Woods meetings, but Keynes' proposal for taxing excess reserve accumulations by surplus countries was not adopted. The only sanction that was formally implemented—the application of discriminating taxes against offending surplus countries under the provisions of the scarce currency clause—was so severe that it has never been used.

In the negotiations on international monetary reform, attention has been directed at the need to mitigate problems arising between deficit and surplus countries over balance-of-payments adjustment responsibilities, as well as over more general problems caused by excessive exchange-rate fixity. As part of an overall reform package, the United States has sought to create an effective mechanism for adjustment of payments imbalances that would place surplus and deficit

countries alike under agreed and broadly symmetrical rules and responsibilities for taking action to restore equilibrium. (The U.S. proposal for a system of reserve indicators is discussed in more detail
below, pp. 158-59.)

ALTERNATIVE FORMS OF
EXCHANGE-RATE FLEXIBILITY

As the shortcomings of the Bretton Woods adjustment mechanism
became more apparent in the late 1960s, considerable interest was
generated in the academic community about limited forms of exchange-
rate flexibility. These included suggestions to modify the adjustable
peg, either to permit more frequent and prompt parity changes or to
provide for wider exchange margins. A third type of arrangement
that was discussed was the "crawling-peg" or "gliding-parity" scheme,
which would permit small, continuous changes in parities. Each of
the above types of arrangement would fit into the basic framework of
the Bretton Woods system, but would require some modification of
the rules pertaining to parity change or to margins.

Proponents of the above schemes included economists who
favored some form of limited flexibility as a first best solution, as
well as economists who preferred flexible rates (with no intervention).
In the latter case, support for some form of limited exchange-rate
flexibility reflected the general feeling in the 1960s that floating rates
had little chance of being implemented, given the biases of central
bankers and members of the financial community against flexible rates.

The situation today has changed dramatically as a result of the
large, volatile capital flows of recent years, and the oil situation.
Floating rates subject to some official intervention are being experi-
mented with at least for the "interim" period, while interest in implementing a "crawling-peg" type of scheme as an international arrangement has waned considerably.*

The acceptance of flexible exchange rates is not necessarily in-
consistent with the views of proponents of a gliding parity system,
but it reflects recognition of the changed circumstances. McKinnon,
for instance, has noted that a gliding parity scheme was not intended
to insulate national economies from international commodity and financial markets, but rather that international markets had been relatively strong and stable in the postwar period, and could provide an

---

*This does not imply, however, that the "crawling peg" is no
longer relevant for individual countries, as a number of the developing
countries have implemented schemes of this type.

element of short-run stability to domestic economies. He acknowledged
that freely floating rates might be more consistent with highly unstable
commodity markets such as those prevailing in the 1930s, and that the
situation in the international commodity markets today undoubtedly has
influenced preferences for floating roles in the "interim."[1]

The adoption of floating rates was also influenced by the inability
of countries to harmonize their policies or agree on a consistent set of
objectives, which they must do if a fixed-rate system is to work
smoothly. Under fixed rates, the higher the level of capital mobility
between national economies, the more difficult it is for a country to
follow macroeconomic policies that are sharply different from those
of its trading partners. For a given difference in inflation rates, for
instance, the size of the resulting balance-of-payments disequilibrium
between two countries will increase as the level of interdependence between them increases.

Use of exchange-rate adjustments to offset the effects of differing sets of underlying economic or policy influences offered a means
of reducing the tradeoff between independence and efficient policy implementation. Differing policy objectives between countries can be
rendered consistent by adjusting exchange rates in line with the resulting differences in balance-of-payments trends. Appropriate use of
exchange-rate changes effectively increases the scope for following
independent policies, although there is also a price associated with
achieving monetary independence—namely, the costs that are incurred
as a result of increased uncertainty in the foreign-exchange market.

While the experiment with managed floating has not been long
enough to allow any definite conclusions, we at least have been able to
observe a system of more flexible rates in action. At a recent conference held at Williamsburg, Virginia, representatives from the business, banking, and academic communities assembled (as a sequel to
the Burgenstock conference) to consider what lessons have been
learned from a year of greater flexibility in exchange rates. The general feeling expressed at the conference by a number of participants
was that, while the system of managed floating had not worked perfectly, it had on the whole worked quite well and was probably the
only workable system at the present time.[2]

The main problems that had been encountered by representatives
of the business community stemmed from the relatively high volatility
of exchange rates in the spot market, combined with a thin volume of
trading in most of the forward markets. In this respect, the situation
of more generalized floating does not appear to have paralleled the
Canadian experience, where exchange rates remained relatively stable.
The volatility of exchange rates in this first year, in part may represent a transitory phenomenon: the business community and governments
can be expected to learn by doing.

It is a more difficult task to sort out the effects exchange-rate
fluctuations have had on other economic variables. Trade and investment flows, for example, have not been curtailed as many had feared,
although it is difficult to know what these flows would have been under
fixed rates. It appears that transactions costs, as measured by the
spread between buy and sell rates, have increased somewhat, but it
is not clear to what extent this is due to floating per se or to uncertainty created by events and in any event transaction costs remain only
a small fraction of 1 percent of the value of a transaction.

Managed floating appears generally to have been successful in
enabling countries to pursue more independent policies, and thus from
a political standpoint it has accomplished one of its basic objectives.
While there may be disagreements about the desirability of continuing
a floating system over the long run, it seems clear that acceptance of
the system in the interim has helped to reduce international tensions
fostered by disputes over responsibilities between surplus and deficit
countries. A good bit of the political trauma associated with exchange-
rate changes has been eliminated, as depreciations and appreciations
can be seen to be more the result of market forces than of overt government action. This in itself should reduce some of the barriers
that have stood in the way of acceptance of greater exchange-rate flexibility as an aspect of a reformed international monetary system.

THE U.S. PROPOSAL FOR A SYSTEM OF
RESERVE INDICATORS

An important issue that was addressed in the negotiations on international monetary reform had to do with establishing acceptable
criteria for deciding when some form of adjustment response was
needed, and for apportioning adjustment responsibilities between surplus and deficit countries. As part of an overall reform package, the
United States proposed that fluctuation in countries' reserve positions
be used as the main indicator for signaling the need for adjustment.

The proposal for a system of reserve indicators was motivated
by a number of considerations, but its main purpose was to avoid
much of the conflict that arose under the Bretton Woods system, pertaining to the apportionment of adjustment responsibilities. Under the
U.S. proposal, surplus countries as well as deficit countries could be
called on to undertake some form of adjustment response to correct
a balance-of-payments disequilibrium. While a number of criteria
had been suggested for use as presumptive rules or guidelines, the
single most valid indicator of an actual or emerging disequilibrium
was taken to be a persistent movement of a country's reserves in one
direction or another from some "normal" level. Once a country's re-

serve position deviated significantly from its "norm," this could be used as a basis for signaling the need for consultation on whether or not some form of adjustment response might be called for.

While the U.S. proposal was initially viewed by some as a significant departure from the Bretton Woods system, its origin, in fact, can be traced to Keynes' proposal for taxing excess reserve accumulations, and to provisions in the scarce currency clause in the articles of agreement. An approach of this sort has also been advocated in several academic studies. In the mid-1960s, for instance, Modigliani and Kenen outlined a proposal establishing reserve targets for countries, and applying sanctions against countries whose imbalance fell outside a "normal range." The scheme was envisioned primarily as a means of obtaining agreement about the creation and distribution of international liquidity.[3]

Similarly, at the Burgenstock Conference proposals by Cooper, Marsh, and Willett were discussed, calling for limited or full exchange-rate flexibility, in which a country's official reserve position would determine when adjustment response was called for. While these schemes differed according to specific rules that might be applied, each attempted to set some limits on the amounts of reserve accumulation or losses that would be allowed before the disequilibrium was deemed a matter of international concern.[4]

RESERVE INDICATORS AND RULES FOR FLOATING EXCHANGE RATES

In the various proposals for a reserve indicator system mentioned above, it was generally not anticipated that a system of floating rates would be in operation. Hence, one issue that might be raised is whether reserve indicators are still needed under the present situation of managed floating. It may be felt, for instance, that under present circumstances, rules of this sort would merely add unnecessary constraints on the system.

In general, there seem to be no clear reasons for giving floating-rate countries less scope to keep their exchange rates from appreciating than is given to countries maintaining fixed parities. Maintenance of a fixed parity does, however, provide a check on overt competitive depreciation, which would be lacking in a floating-rate system. Thus, to limit this possibility, one might appropriately consider special rules for floating-rate countries.

There would be several possible ways of formulating rules to guard against this problem. If reserve norms have been established, one possible rule would be that a country could not allow its reserves to rise above its norm while its exchange rate was below its initial

parity. This would be analogous to a possible provision under a reserve-indicator system that a country normally would not be allowed
to devalue when its reserves were above the norm nor to revalue when
its reserves were below its norm. This approach also might fairly
easily be adopted to handle transitional problems where it was generally accepted that a country's current reserves were excessive or
deficient.

An alternative to this fairly loose stock approach would be a more
stringent flow approach. This would be based on the idea that reserves
should not rise while a country's exchange rate was falling. The ob-
verse, if one were worried about competitive appreciation, would be
that reserves should not fall while the exchange rate was appreciating.
This would seem to be a less important concern, however.

If it were desired to make such a rule a little less stringent,
threshold limits could be introduced. For instance, the rule could be
that a country's reserves could not rise by more than X percent while
its rate was falling, or was below some initial level, where X was a
much smaller number than the width of the reserve bands. This approach has the advantage that initial reserve norms do not have to be
identified. Thus, it could be introduced during the present "interim"
float, without having to wait for final agreement on a full-fledged reserve-indicator system. On the other hand, however, it would seem
much more difficult to integrate this approach with a recognized need
for particular countries to recoup previous reserve losses or work off
past excessive accumulations of reserves.

STOCK VERSUS FLOW TARGET VARIABLES

The question of whether a stock or a flow formulation is more
appropriate largely depends on the purpose that is envisioned. For
example, Cooper has argued that parity changes should be linked to
changes in reserves, rather than to reserve levels as Willett had suggested.[5] The basis for preferring a flow formulation was that use of
reserve levels as a target could be destabilizing unless responses to
parity changes were very quick. Clearly, this is a critical consideration where one is primarily concerned about day-to-day management
in reserve positions. This would be especially relevant, for instance,
for individual countries that are interested in managing their reserve-
and exchange-rate positions.[6]

If, however, one envisions a reserve-indicator system, not as a
guide to daily reserve positions but rather as a means of achieving international agreement on limits to disequilibrium, a stock formulation has
greater relevance. In this case, the system basically indicates the
range within which an individual country has discretion to pursue

independent policies without regard to its balance-of-payments position.
Where there is a major concern over the structure of the balance of payments, a reserve indicator system may need to be supplemented with codes of good behavior concerning countries' use of various policies to influence the structure of their balance of payments, and/or agreement on consistent structural objectives of the major countries that go beyond rather general codes of good behavior coupled with the moral suasion of international surveillance. While there may be somewhat greater scope for this type of antisocial behavior under floating rates, it is a basic problem under any exchange-rate system.[7]

PERFORMANCE OF A RESERVE INDICATOR
SYSTEM FOR THE DEVELOPING COUNTRIES

Several representatives from developing nations have argued that under a reserve indicator mechanism such as the United States has proposed, developing nations should receive special treatment, on the basis of a contention that developing-country reserves are normally more volatile than those of developed nations, because of the heavy concentration of developing-country exports in primary products and resulting high variability of their export prices and revenues. Hence, it is argued that if indicator points were set at the same positions relative to "base level" for developing as for developed countries, this would lead to excessive and unwarranted adjustment pressures on the former.

The available evidence does not support this contention, however. It is true that the variability of exports is somewhat greater for developing countries than for industrial countries, but studies undertaken by the U.S. Treasury found that over the period 1960-72 the variability of developing-country reserves was actually somewhat less than the variability of reserves for the industrial countries.

There is also more direct evidence on how a reserve-indicator system would have worked for developing countries, on the basis of historical behavior. A recent submission by the International Monetary Fund staff to the Committee of Twenty's Technical Group on Indicators analyzes how various objective indicators would have performed over the period 1961-71 for 10 primary producing and 13 industrial countries. The study indicates that the reserve indicators performed for the primary producers not worse, but actually even somewhat better than they did for the industrial countries. (The ratings were 65 versus 62 for one type of reserve indicator and 73 versus 66 for the other.)

These results should not be taken as definitive, but they do suggest, as do the data on reserve variability, that a reserve indicator system should not, on the whole, present special difficulties for developing countries. (One problem with the measures of reserve instability, for instance, is that deviations from a time trend, rather than deviations from a reserve demand function, are measured. There is some empirical evidence that the latter may differ for developed and developing countries.[8]) There may, of course, be special circumstances influencing particular developing countries (or industrial countries) that will need to be taken into account in applying a reserve indicator system, and the United States is well cognizant of this possibility. It does not appear, however, that the developing countries have cause to believe that a general reserve indicator system such as has been proposed by the United States would work less well for them than it would for the industrial countries.

PREFERENCES OF DEVELOPING COUNTRIES FOR FIXED RATES

In the negotiations on international monetary reform, industrialized countries, for the most part, have favored proposals to allow greater exchange flexibility, either through more frequent exchange rate changes or through wider margins. Many of the developing countries, on the other hand, have viewed these proposals with considerable skepticism. In meetings of both the UN Conference on Trade and Development and CIAP, the prevailing attitude has been that the need for greater flexibility is a problem for developed countries that wish to have a means of countering speculative capital movements. It was feared, however, that increased flexibility among reserve currencies would have adverse effects on developing countries because of their limited ability to adapt to exchange variations, and it was argued that, from the standpoint of developing countries, initiation of capital controls among the developed countries is a more preferable solution.

The basis for these views is examined in this section. It is argued that while the developing countries may experience some inconveniences from day-to-day fluctuations in exchange rates of the key currencies, the tendency on the part of many of the developing countries has been to seriously overstate the costs imposed from greater developed country exchange-rate flexibility, compared with those incurred under the adjustable-peg system.

Reluctance on the part of a number of developing countries to accept greater exchange-rate flexibility among key currencies (and wider exchange bands) stems mainly from a preference for fixed rates for their own domestic currencies. Among others, Cooper has, in his analysis of currency devaluation in the developing countries, examined the theoretical and empirical basis for developing country skepticism about the effectiveness of the exchange rate instrument for correcting balance-of-payments disequilibria. He points out a number of considerations that could make analysis of devaluation in a developing country different from that of a developed country. In particular, he emphasizes that devaluation in an developing country seldom involved a simple adjustment of the exchange rate but often is accompanied by import liberalization. Thus, timing of government policy (both liberalization and macromanagement) may be critical to the success of devaluation in a developing country.[9] However, the question of balance of payments has not surfaced as a major issue in the debate over greater exchange-rate flexibility, where the discussion has focused instead on whether greater flexibility will have a stabilizing or destabilizing effect on international transactions, and on whether it will complicate or simplify the problems of managing the domestic economies.

A number of developing countries are concerned that more flexible rates would lead to increased economic uncertainty and instability in international transactions, and that costs would be imposed on them in the way of forward cover or some other form of insurance against exchange losses. (These arguments generally have not been advanced by countries with some experience with a more flexible exchange-rate regime—for example, Korea, Brazil, Colombia—but by countries that have changed their exchange rate relatively infrequently.) At least in formal statements, however, there has been little recognition that exchange-rate fixity may imply greater volatility of other variables, such as interest rates, prices (measured in foreign currency) and incomes. For instance, under floating rates there is a strong tendency for exchange-rate changes to offset indifferent rates of national price inflation, thus leading to greater stability of foreign currency prices as expressed in domestic currency. Moreover, when one examines the repercussions on the developing countries of fixed exchange rates in the developed countries, the tendency on the part of the developing countries to equate exchange-rate flexibility with instability appears even less warranted. To the extent that maintenance of fixed rates in the developed countries leads to capital controls and restrictions on trade flows, for example, the direct consequence may be instability of imports from and capital flows to the developing countries.

A further problem with the arguments of the developing countries against greater flexibility is that they tend to implicitly assume that the alternative is a system of exchange rates that are forever fixed. This option, however, simply does not exist, given that there will continue to be structural changes that must be accommodated. An ad-

vantage of permitting more frequent exchange-rate changes is that
movements over time may appear more predictable than sudden, discrete changes. In this way, use of more flexible exchange rates can
alleviate much of the disruptive effects associated with the "crisis-
oriented" exchange realignments of 1971 and 1973. To the extent
that developing-country governments are "risk averse," it would appear that they, too, should prefer more frequent, small changes over
infrequent, large changes in which the stakes of the gamble are much
greater.

A related reason for opposing greater flexibility is that it would
create a number of pegging (or currency-bloc) problems for the developing countries. The nature of the problems envisioned depends to
some extent on whether an individual developing country automatically
pegs to its major trading partner in response to a reserve-currency
fluctuation, or on whether there is doubt as to the correct currency
to peg itself to. Hence, it is useful to consider these two cases separately.

Problems Associated with Pegging to the Major Trading Partner

If the trade and financial transactions of an individual developing
country are predominantly restricted to one currency area, it is generally assumed that an individual developing country would continue to
peg its own currency to that of its major trading partner. One of the
main concerns of the developing countries in this case is that greater
flexibility would increase the geographic concentration of their exports
and could lead to formation of inward looking trading blocs. This view
has been especially pronounced among Latin American countries whose
trade is heavily concentrated with the United States. In assessing its
validity, it is important to separate the political and economic factors
involved. Greater exchange rate flexibility will undoubtedly mean that
many of the developing countries will choose to peg to a particular
currency. This will require explicit government action that in some
cases may prove politically embarrassing. *

It does not follow, however, that greater flexibility accompanied
by pegging per se by developing countries would lead to greater geographic concentration of trade or to increased intrabloc trade relative
to trade between blocs. In the case of Latin America, for example, if

---

*It can also be argued, however, that the political trauma asso-
ciated with devaluation in many developing countries should be considerably reduced if a developing country pegged to a depreciating currency

continued depreciation of the dollar as well as continued Latin American pegging to the dollar) took place, one would expect over time the nondollar volume of Latin American imports to decrease relative to the dollar-bloc volume. However, one would also expect the nondollar volume of Latin American exports to increase relative to the dollar-bloc volume. Thus, on the import side, intrabloc trade flows would appear to increase relative to trade flows between blocs, but the opposite would be true on the export side.* To the extent that developing-country trade flows were influenced by factors affecting risk, as well as return, it is possible that trade flows within a currency bloc could be increased relative to trade between blocs. The latter influence, however, is likely to be only marginal.

Which Currency to Peg To?

If a particular developing country has a diversified pattern of trade and/or financing, the decision about which currency to peg to may not be obvious. In this case, moreover, pegging to some currency could result in trade shifts vis-a-vis competitors who pegged to a different currency. Hence, there may be "real" costs associated with making a wrong decision.

There is undoubtedly some merit to the argument that increased flexibility will complicate pegging decisions for some developing countries. However, it is also relevant to point out factors that should serve to mitigate this problem. One factor is that under a regime of more frequent exchange-rate changes the magnitude of any reserve currency realignment is likely to be considerably smaller than was true of the 1971 and 1973 currency realignments. Hence, the cost of making a wrong decision is considerably less than that under a system in which exchange-rate changes are infrequent. (In the case of the 1971 and 1973 currency realignments, many of the developing countries that pegged to the dollar were worried about the increased burden of their outstanding nondollar denominated debt and the decline in the purchasing power of their dollar reserves. These concerns resulted from failure to also consider gains associated with the realignment. The IMF study of the effect of the Smithsonian realignment on the developing countries, for instance, concluded that for 78 developing countries as a group the increase in annual debt service payments resulting from the realignment would not introduce a new significant element in their external debt management.)

---

*Consideration as to whether intrabloc export and import shares would increase (as opposed to volumes) is more complicated and requires knowledge of price elasticities of demand and supply.

From an empirical standpoint the problem is also likely to be
limited to a small number of developing countries. An IMF staff report on the impact of the 1971 currency realignment singled out the
following countries as having experienced the largest effective exchange-rate changes vis-à-vis the developed countries: Thailand,
Indonesia, Zaire, Zambia, Kenya, Iran, Korea, Taiwan, Ceylon, and
Chile. These countries pegged to the dollar but had a sizable portion
of trade with countries that did not peg to the dollar. In terms of regional breakdown, the pegging problem is likely to be less serious for
most of the African countries, which peg to sterling or to the franc,
and for Latin American countries, where trade with the United States
is still predominant. As a group, the Asian and the Middle Eastern
countries exhibit the most diversified trade patterns.

Finally, the arguments of the developing countries assume a
country should peg to some reserve currency. This policy may not be
optimal in all cases, however. Some of the above problems can be
overcome if developing countries are able to allow some degree of
flexibility of their own domestic currency, or they may choose to peg
to a basket of currencies. The latter option is one that has been proposed by the IMF, for instance, to value the Special Drawing Rights,
and provides a means of minimizing the impact of exchange realignments.

CONCLUSION

Successful reform of the international monetary system, by
definition, involves striking a balance between the need for international coordination of economic policies and the desire for national
autonomy. While the Bretton Woods system managed to achieve these
twin objectives throughout much of the postwar period, the bias in the
adjustable-peg system against exchange-rate changes ultimately caused
inappropriate policies to be pursued in a world with high capital mobility. This, in turn, led to a situation in which there was a continuing
dispute over the proper circumstances for balance-of-payments adjustment and whether surplus or deficit countries were responsible
for initiating the adjustment response.

Acceptance of greater exchange-rate flexibility today has helped
to eliminate much of the tension that arose between surplus and deficit
countries, and has permitted a greater degree of autonomy in national
policies. This has been especially important during the period of unusual uncertainty in the international commodity markets. While we
have only had a relatively short period in which to observe the effects
of a more flexible system, the price that has been paid to date (1975)
in the form of increased transactions costs and yield differentials to

date appears modest. Moreover, the U.S. proposal for a system of reserve indicators (originally submitted as a means for indicating when a country should adjust) can be used as a basis for providing rules for floating, thereby providing a guard in the system against competitive depreciations.

Despite the initial opposition of many developing countries both to exchange-rate flexibility and to reserve indicators as an approach to international guidelines for floating rates and balance-of-payments adjustment, it is our view that for the vast majority of developing as well as developed countries, the initial inconveniences caused by exchange-rate flexibility would be more than offset over the longer term by the contribution of exchange-rate flexibility to international economic growth and stability.

NOTES

1. Ronald I. McKinnon, "Exchange Rate Flexibility and Monetary Policy," Journal of Money, Credit, and Banking, May 1971: 339-55.

2. Based on further studies of the performance of the floating-rate system we continue to hold this view. See Richard Sweeney and Thomas Willett, eds., Exchange Rate Flexibility and International Monetary Stability (Washington, D.C.: American Enterprise Institute, forthcoming, 1976).

3. F. Modigliani and P. B. Kenen, "A Suggestion for Solving the International Liquidity Problem," Banca Nazionale del Lavoro Quarterly Review, 1966: 3-17.

4. See George Halm, ed., Approaches to Greater Flexibility of Exchange Rates (Princeton, N.J.: Princeton University Press, 1970).

5. Richard Cooper, "Comment on the Howle-Moore Analysis," Journal of International Economics, November 1971: 437-42.

6. Subsequent simulation work by Kenen has even more strongly indicated that a stock formulation is quite unsatisfactory as an automatic rule for day-to-day exchange-rate management. See P. B. Kenen, "Floats, Glides, and Indicators," Journal of International Economics, May 1975: 107-52.

7. For further commentary on this see the excellent discussion in Paul Wonnacott, The Floating Canadian Dollar (Washington, D.C.: American Enterprise Institute, 1972), chap. 6.

8. See, for example, Jacob A. Frankel, "The Demand for International Reserves by Developed and Less Developed Countries," Economica, February 1974: 14-24.

9. R. N. Cooper, Currency Devaluation in Developing Countries, Princeton Essays in International Finance, no. 86, June 1971.

CHAPTER

14

DOMESTIC MONETARY
POLICY AND THE
EXCHANGE-RATE
SYSTEM
Robert L. Sammons

No one would dispute the statement that the relationship between
monetary policy and the balance of payments (or economic conditions
in the rest of the world in general), so far as the United States is concerned, is different now than it was before August 1971. But how
much it is different, and even the direction of the change, may be in
dispute. The view that we should be especially cautious in executing
monetary policy under the existing flexible exchange-rate system
seems contrary to the received (Keynesian) doctrine that public policy, both monetary and fiscal, should be designed to encourage full
employment and economic growth at home, subject to whatever price
constraints the body politic is willing to accept, with any balance-of-
payments disequilibrium that might result being eliminated by exchange-
rate adjustment. Of course, Keynes did not have in mind the situation
that seems typical of today's world (the threat of unemployment and
inflation at the same time); many of his followers deplore the present
excessive tolerance of inflation.

GOALS OF MONETARY POLICY

There are really two related questions to be discussed. One is
straightforward: Does a country have more freedom under flexible rates
rates or under fixed rates to adapt its monetary policy to (perceived)
national objectives? The second is more subtle: Will the tradeoff between inflation and employment be resolved differently under the two
systems?
One could approach this topic either from an analytic or from a
normative viewpoint: Either what the relationship has been or what
it should be. In either approach, there are two important considera-

tions to be kept in mind as we proceed, in order to keep us on a reasonably manageable track. First, we shall be dealing primarily with the U.S. situation, that of a reserve-currency country. This means that even before the formal suspension of gold convertibility in August 1971 the balance of payments had little or no direct effect on the monetary base—that is, the assets, and hence the liabilities, of the Federal Reserve System, the latter, of course, providing the reserve base of the commercial banking structure. Second, we shall try to distinguish clearly between dilemma and nondilemma situations, the latter being when considerations of both domestic and international policy objectives are pulling on monetary policy in the same direction, although, of course, reasonable men may disagree at any particular point in time about the appropriate domestic goals or about the balance between conflicting goals.

First, I will comment briefly on the analytical aspect: when, in what direction, and to what extent monetary policies in the United States have been affected by international considerations. To put it more bluntly, has the Federal Reserve ever followed policies that were considered less than fully appropriate to meet domestic objectives because of balance of payments or other international considerations? My personal answer, based on the public record and a general knowledge of events over the past 15 years or so, is, "Well, hardly ever." I am, of course, referring to monetary policy in its general thrust and not to the specific measures, or instruments, employed in implementing that policy.

I should interject a point about policy goals. Contrary to oftenheard categorizations of the objectives of public economic policies, I do not put balance-of-payments equilibrium in the same category as full employment, economic growth, price stability, and socially acceptable distribution of income as objectives. Rather, at least under a fixed exchange-rate system, but perhaps under flexible rates as well, balance-of-payments equilibrium is only a constraint or an intermediate objective, one that, unless achieved, may significantly impede the attainment of the fundamental goals.

So far as international considerations are concerned, the measures taken by the Federal Reserve in the decade preceding 1971 were all clearly designed not to temper domestic policy to the international winds but to shelter that policy from storms appearing to originate from abroad. I will cite a few specific examples:

1. Exemption of official foreign deposits from Regulation Q interest-rate ceilings: This was designed to reward foreign central banks for not converting dollars into gold, in spite of the fact that central banks are not supposed to be profit-maximizing institutions.

2. Operation twist: The Federal Reserve abandoned its bills-only (more accurately, bills-preferably) policy in the early 1960s and began providing reserves to the banking system by purchasing long-term securities; the purpose was, of course, to bend the short end of the yield curve upward and thus to deter short-term capital outflows—primarily, but not necessarily only, outflows of private capital.

3. The swap network and Federal Reserve intervention in exchange markets: As it worked out, swaps were employed to give an exchange guarantee to foreign official dollar balances in the event of formal devaluation of the dollar and thus, again, to discourage requests for gold conversion.

4. The voluntary foreign credit restraint program: This was designed to keep U.S. banks from lending to foreigners the funds provided to them for the purpose of encouraging domestic expansion.

5. Reserve requirements against Eurodollar borrowing and other foreign capital inflows: The stated purpose of this measure, first introduced in 1969, was to hinder large banks from adding to inflationary pressures by expanding loans to large businesses, but it must be recognized that much of the pressure came from foreign central banks, many of which were losing reserves rapidly because of extremely high interest rates in the United States. Paradoxically, these requirements were imposed even while the U.S. balance of payments was still in fundamental deficit.

There were, it is true, a couple of occasions when discount-rate increases were officially attributed to international considerations. One was an increase of 0.5 percent (from 4.5 to 5.0) in the discount rate on the day sterling was devalued in 1967. This action was billed as a precautionary move in the face of growing inflationary pressure and uncertainty.

Of course, the directive of the Open Market Committee to the account manager since the early 1960s has referred to balance-of-payments reasons for a particular policy stance. Balance-of-payments considerations were specified as constraints when the directive called for easing or maintaining ease and were cited as an additional reason justifying a restrictive posture, when the latter was the order of the day. But, to the best of my knowledge, no one, either in the Federal Reserve or outside of it, has ever attempted to quantify the influence of that particular clause in the directive on the total thrust of monetary policy.

RESERVE STATUS OF THE DOLLAR

Of course, the ability of the Federal Reserve to take as little account of foreign conditions as it did depended directly on the reserve status of the dollar, which confers two advantages on the U.S. monetary authorities: First, they are not faced with reserve losses when running a balance-of-payments deficit; second, the balance of payments, as already stated, has no direct effect on the monetary base. In those respects, at least, the de facto floating dollar has not made a great deal of difference. But the need for and the use of specific "fences" has, of course, changed. Obviously, swaps are no longer used to give exchange guarantees to foreign reserve holdings of dollars, except for small amounts arising from swaps for foreign currencies used to intervene in exchange markets at times of market disorder. And the expansion of the swap network recently seems clearly to have been in contemplation of its possible use to support currencies other than the dollar. The reserve requirements against Eurodollar borrowing are still in effect, but these were never used for balance-of-payments objectives. And the voluntary foreign capital restraints (VFCR) have been terminated.

Most economists, from Keynes and Friedman on down, have argued that a flexible exchange rate gives more freedom than a fixed rate to follow a monetary policy suited to domestic needs. A corollary to this argument is that fixed rates are per se inflationary, especially for non-reserve currency countries. In times of balance-of-payments surplus, international reserves tend to rise, expanding the monetary base; the rise is followed by an expansion in bank credit and the money supply, obviously inflationary influences. Central banks often find it hard to offset these tendencies, especially where the only tool is increasing reserve requirements, a device particularly disliked by commercial banks. On the other hand, a reduction in reserves, the reserve base, and the money supply consequent on a balance-of-payments deficit are easily offset, and there are always strong pressures to do so, especially from political quarters.

Technically, the flexible-rate people are right: Under flexible rates a country is free to follow any domestic monetary and fiscal policy it chooses, provided it is prepared to accept any exchange rate set for its currency by the market or other monetary authorities. The proviso is important, for the question really boils down to this: Are the chances that U.S. domestic policies will be slanted more toward price stability and less toward full employment (under any given circumstances) greater now than they were before August 1961? Chairman Burns' statement, and some deductive reasoning, seem to answer in the affirmative. An empirical answer is not yet possible—and may never be.

FLEXIBLE RATES AND INFLATION

In earlier debates on the flexible rate issue I used to argue that widespread public support for antiinflationary policies would be more

likely under flexible rates; the public at large could see what inflation
was doing to the international value of its money (as the exchange rate
depreciated) more clearly than when the symptoms were simply a decline in exchange reserves or an increase in the external debt. Recent
events have somewhat weakened my confidence in the validity of that
argument.

Nevertheless, the vicious circle seen by Burns—monetary ease,
leading to declining (or low) interest rates, leading to capital outflow,
leading to exchange depreciation, leading to cost-push inflation (higher
prices on imports and exportable goods)—means that the external sector tends to amplify rather than absorb the price inflationary effects
of domestic policies. At the same time, it also enhances the income-
generating effect of the expansionary policy, because imports are
more expensive (and therefore, in real terms, decline), while exports
become cheaper (in terms of foreign currencies) and/or more profitable (and therefore, in real terms, tend to rise). Thus a flexible-
rate system both encourages and enables the monetary authorities to
lean toward the side of price stability more than does the fixed-rate
system.

On the surface, this would seem to be particularly true for the
United States, in comparison with the situation prevailing before 1971,
when, as maintained above, balance-of-payments considerations appear to have had little net effect on monetary policy. For nonreserve
currencies the outcome is somewhat more ambiguous. I have already
described the inflationary bias of a fixed-rate system, through the
ratchet effect on the monetary base. The fear of running out of reserves will, of course, lend prudence to the policy makers. But
flexible rates will avoid the direct monetary effects of balance-of-
payments surpluses or deficits while, perhaps, inducing well-informed
central bankers to avoid inflation in order to avoid currency depreciation.

But my basic position is that avoiding inflation depends on states-
manship and on an informed public, with both people and government
willing and able to take a long-range view of the national welfare.
There is no magic in the gold standard, Special Drawing Rights,
flexible rates, or even international cooperation (much as the last is
needed). In a world of sovereign states, each country will make its
own choice in the tradeoff between employment and inflation, given
the circumstances of the time. A single world currency (or permanently fixed exchange rates, which amounts to the same thing) might
help to reduce the risk of inflation, though this is far from certain.
But we are far from that point. We have individual currencies whose
value will continue to fluctuate against each other for many reasons,
some good and some bad. And I am enough of a populist to be unwill-
ing to crucify the population of any country on the cross of fixed exchange rates.

15

THE MANAGEMENT OF FLOATING EXCHANGE RATES

Wilfred J. Ethier
Arthur I. Bloomfield

Since March 1973, the world economy has been subjected to a number of major shocks that have radically transformed the international monetary system and the prospective structure of international payments. Early in 1973 a succession of severe foreign-exchange crises led to the collapse of the Bretton Woods system that had prevailed, except for an interruption in the last four months of 1971, since the end of World War II. The system of fixed but occasionally adjustable exchange rates gave way to the widespread floating of the major currencies. Late in 1973 came the oil crisis. The quadrupling of the price of crude oil by the major oil-exporting countries caused an enormous increase in payments to these countries by the oil importing nations. It is estimated that the increased cost of oil imports will convert the 1973 current-account surplus of the industrial countries as a group (some $12 billion) into deficits that may reach as high as $35 billion to $40 billion. The developing countries that are oil importers may face aggregate current-account deficits of some $15 billion to $20 billion. The oil-exporting countries could in turn have a current-account surplus of some $70 billion, as compared with a 1973 surplus of some $7 billion. Deficits and surpluses on this scale could continue for some years ahead, although the estimates are of course subject to a wide margin of error.

Throughout 1974 rates of inflation continued to rise. For the year as a whole the price rise in many countries was the steepest in 20 years, and the inflationary trend become quite general and worldwide. The oil crisis has given further impetus to this trend and has apparently contributed also to the softness in economic activity that has begun to emerge in some industrial countries, even in the face of the unremitting inflationary surge. The resulting disruptions and uncertainties introduced into the world economy led to the postpone-

ment by the Committee of Twenty for the indefinite future of plans for
a return to a more flexible system of "stable but adjustable" par
values and for other closely related reforms of the international monetary system.

THE INEVITABLE FLOAT

The 1973 developments underscore and in part explain the first
of three salient features of the present international monetary outlook:
the inevitability of the widespread floating of exchange rates for a
considerable period into the future. The years since World War II
have witnessed a steady integration of the world economy in an environment that has on the whole been remarkably stable. Events since 1971,
however, have both revealed and generated great uncertainty concerning the basic economic interrelations among the various nations, including, in particular, the equilibrium structure of exchange rates
and its future course. In addition to the developments in 1973 mentioned above, one might cite the cumulative effect of differential growth
rates and other developments not properly reflected in exchange-
rate changes or other price adjustments in the period 1949-71; the
fact that the pattern of relative rates of inflation among the developed
nations seems to be changing and is in any case highly uncertain; the
great tightening in primary-product markets in general; and the fact
that the long-run impact of the 1971-73 exchange-rate changes is
still far from clear. These factors could on balance prove transitory,
or they could signal longer-run changes; the essential point is that we
simply do not know. Furthermore, the great increase in the volume
and volatility of internationally mobile liquid capital, which is itself
one of the facets of international integration, increasingly renders unacceptable to national authorities any obligation to defend exchange
rates that are or threaten quickly to become disequilibrium ones.

Thus, the decision by the Committee of Twenty was not only
inevitable but eminently sensible. It would simply be impossible to
establish a set of exchange-rate parities that could be maintained for
any sustained period of time. That an early return to a system of par
values, no matter now thorough the provisions for flexibility, would
be an exercise in futility is now widely recognized by businessmen,
central bankers, and economists alike.

MANAGED FLOATING

As it happens, the system of widespread floating exchange rates
that came into effect in March 1973 has operated satisfactorily during

a period of economic and political turmoil throughout the world. Despite considerable and perhaps at times exaggerated swings in exchange rates, foreign trade and investment have not been seriously affected by the float. Business for the most part seems to have adjusted itself to the new regime without undue difficulty or inconvenience. The spot and forward exchange markets have in general functioned well, despite some aberrations in the earlier part of the period. Exchange speculation has not been predominantly destabilizing, contrary to what had been feared in some quarters. International monetary crises have been avoided, at least in their conventional form. The initial impact of the oil crisis and the effect of other shocks have been cushioned. Countries have acquired a greater degree of freedom to pursue macroeconomic policies aimed at domestic objectives. There has been no evidence of competitive exchange depreciation, long regarded as a major threat posed by a floating-rate system.

Of course the float has not been entirely free or unmanaged. Monetary authorities have intervened in the exchange market from time to time, and in some cases on a more continuing basis, in order to influence the movements of rates. The system that emerged has in fact been a hybrid one. A declining number of the leading continental European currencies (the "snake" currencies) have been kept within a narrow range of fluctuation of each other by official intervention, while they have been jointly floated against the dollar and other outside currencies with only periodic intervention. Several leading currencies, including the U.S. and Canadian dollars, the pound sterling, the Swiss franc, and the Italian lira, have been floating independently, subject to varying degrees of official exchange operations. Finally, a large number of currencies, including those of Japan, Australia, and many of the developing countries, have, through extensive intervention operations, been kept relatively stable against the dollar, with occasional alterations of the support levels.

These observations suggest a second feature of the current international monetary outlook: The widespread float will in fact be a managed one, in the sense that it will be accompanied by considerable, though probably varying degrees of, intervention by national authorities.

Some supporters of floating rates argue that rates should be completely unmanaged, if the full potential benefits of the system are to be realized. They oppose all official exchange operations—and, indeed, use of payments control—to influence the exchange rates of currencies that are floating against each other. Even if this view is valid in principle, however, it would be quite unrealistic to envisage a perfectly free float.

Many if not most central banks will in fact continue to intervene in the exchange market in order to smooth out highly erratic swings in their exchange rates or to cope with emerging disorderly market conditions. They will also be under strong pressure to intervene when exchange-rate movements threaten domestic goals. They will be tempted deliberately to depreciate their exchange rates or to keep them at unduly undervalued levels in order to gain competitive trade advantages in time of recession or of rapid structural change, or to maintain them at unduly overvalued levels in time of inflation.

THE NEED FOR RULES

Despite the considerable degree of official exchange intervention by most of the leading countries, there appears as yet to have been no major conflicts of policy in the national management of floating exchange rates. In view of the worldwide inflationary conditions prevailing, none of the industrial countries has sought deliberately to depreciate its exchange rate in order to gain competitive trade advantages. The countries participating in the European "snake" scheme did not resist the strong upward pressures on their currencies against the dollar in May to July 1973, at least not until disorderly market conditions had begun to emerge at a time when all central banks agreed that the dollar had become markedly undervalued. Nor did the United States resist the sharp advance in the dollar against all of the other leading currencies in late 1973 and early 1974, although that advance wiped out much of the earlier decline.

Indeed, if there has been any evidence of competitive exchange-rate policies, it has pointed rather in the opposite direction. Many of the major industrial countries, including Japan, the United Kingdom, and Italy, have sold foreign exchange on a large scale throughout much of the period in order to moderate or resist a depreciation of their currencies. A desire to reinforce domestic antiinflationary policies was one of the considerations behind these interventions, but in none of these cases did the primary motive seem to have been to deliberately "export inflation." Indeed, in the case of Japan the marked depreciation that would otherwise have occurred in the yen, long an undervalued currency, would have been more objectionable to other leading industrial countries than the support operations that were actually pursued. Late in 1973 and early in 1974, moreover, the European monetary-bloc countries likewise sold foreign exchange on a significant scale in order to cushion the sharp decline in their currencies against the dollar.

But here again the primary motive does not appear to have been an effort to export inflation; a desire to maintain orderly markets appears to have been dominant. Reference might also be made to the revaluations of the German mark and Dutch guilder in June and Sep-

tember 1973, respectively, against their partner currencies, largely
for reasons internal to the "snake" scheme.

Thus, although many of the leading industrial countries tended
to lean against the wind when their currencies were under downward
(but not upward) pressure, there were no sharp conflicts of policy or
retaliatory behavior in the national management of exchange rates.
Indeed, the United States and many of the countries in the European
monetary bloc coordinated some of the exchange-market operations
that they undertook, both when the dollar was falling and during its
subsequent rise.

In somewhat broader perspective this lack of conflict may be
viewed as part of a general coincidence of national interests that has
more or less characterized the international monetary scene since
1971. There seems to have been a broad consensus among the main
industrial countries as to the "appropriate" levels of—and "acceptable"
range of fluctuations in—their exchange rates against each other. For
example, there was general agreement at the start of this period that
the dollar was overvalued, and on two separate occasions it proved
possible to reach international agreements on new structures of par
values or central rates. During most of this period economic activity
in the major nations has been more in phase than at any other time
since World War II, and there has been a convergence and common acceleration of rates of inflation. Attention can also be called to the
"common bond" created by the recent oil crisis and to the fact that
the worldwide commodity boom has muted the long-running U.S.-EEC
conflict over agriculture. Finally, a natural desire to avoid common
crisis in the face of the disintegration of the old system should be
recognized.

This broad coincidence of interest with regard to the way in
which the international monetary system has been operating is in
sharp contrast to the aggressive U.S. diplomacy characterizing the
early part of this period and, more generally, to the failure of the
major industrial nations to reach agreement on longer-run issues,
such as trade policy and the formal details of a new international
monetary system. Indeed, this combination of a workable consensus
on the short-run management of exchange-rate policy with a fundamental lack of agreement on long-run reform is another potent reason why
continued floating figures prominently in the international economic
outlook.

But it would be a serious mistake to rely upon this consensus
for the indefinite future—or, more specifically, over the period (of
unknown length) of widespread managed floating. For the coincidence
of interests upon which the consensus rests is very fragile, indeed.
Signs of its dissolution have already appeared: Several European governments now appear to be increasingly concerned, relative to the

United States, about indications of slackening activity, as compared
with inflation, and the initial "common bond" created by the oil crisis
is giving way under the gradually developing differential balance-of-
payments effects of that crisis on individual countries. As the commodity boom abates, the agricultural issue will also reintensify. Indeed, the U.S. reluctance to maintain export supplies in the face of
domestic shortage and the supply increases induced by higher prices
could render this issue sharper than ever. The unprecedented common
phasing of activity can hardly be expected to continue indefinitely, and
the interdependence of domestic inflation and exchange-rate policy
could well become a source of increasing irritation. More generally,
that underlying uncertainty concerning basic economic interrelations
that implies the inevitability of widespread floating also mitigates
against any complacency regarding the continued absence of major exchange-rate policy conflicts. This is the third salient feature of the
present international monetary outlook.

In view of our arguments that floating seems to be inevitable
over the foreseeable future, that the floating will in fact be managed,
and that the present freedom from sharp international conflicts over
exchange-rate policy rests upon a fragile basis, we conclude that international rules of conduct of some sort for the management of floating exchanges are necessary. For in the absence of such international
rules or guidelines, national or bloc conflicts of policy could arise
that would pose a serious threat to orderly international trade and financial arrangements in a floating-rate system. No serious conflicts
of this kind, for reasons already noted, have arisen since the inaugura-
tion of the present float. Yet the burden of our argument is that to an
increasing degree the potential for conflict exists and could come out
into the open.

WHAT KIND OF RULES?

The first question to be faced is the very general one, concerning the comprehensiveness of the set of rules. They could potentially
fall anywhere between the extremes of no rules at all and a complete,
detailed specification of a new international monetary system. The
latter would require a degree of international agreement on basic issues of reform that has not been forthcoming. Since rules that would
pertain to a regime of managed floating are needed as soon as possible, we deem it necessary to consider minimal reform programs.

In particular, rules should possess three properties. They
should be sufficiently general and nonrestrictive to be both widely acceptable, at least conditionally, and also entirely free of the necessity
for their implementation of prior agreement on basic outstanding issue

such as asset convertibility, the role of the dollar, and so on; they
should offer some protection against the major dangers from managed
floating; and they should be sufficiently flexible so as not to impede
progress toward agreement on a permanent reform and so as to be
compatible with a broad range of such programs and also with a broad
range of interim arrangements by individual central banks. Flexibility is also required so that the rules could be applied to most nations
and so that the program could have wide appeal; at the least, the participation of most of the leading industrial nations would be desirable.

The next question that arises involves the scope of behavior to
be covered. Rules appropriate to a system of extensive, managed,
exchange-rate floating could conceivably encompass a large number
of areas. These could include rules regarding:

1. Permissible and nonpermissible (and/or mandatory and non-
mandatory) official exchange intervention;
2. The medium and the method of such intervention;
3. The coordination of official intervention so as to avoid the
possibility of countries working at cross purposes in the exchange
market, even when the intervention is permissible;
4. The settlement of currency balances acquired through intervention; and
5. The use of policies other than exchange intervention designed
to affect exchange rates—for example, capital controls, exchange restrictions, monetary policies.

International agreement on area 1 is most important, since it
deals with a matter on which lack of agreement could have the most
serious consequences. For it is this area that is most directly relevant in dealing with the possibility of competitive exchange behavior
or exchange-rate policy conflicts generally—the primary reason for
rules.

Thus, the rules must address themselves to area 1, but what
about the other areas? Area 3, and to some extent area 2, has to do
with the general subject of central-bank cooperation. Now such cooperation has been rather prominent and important thus far in the float,
as it has been throughout the postwar period—in sharp contrast to the
experience of the 1930s. Indeed, it is possible that the steady development of such connections over a quarter-century will be regarded in
the future as the single most significant accomplishment of the Bretton Woods system. But these areas must be left for the most part to
the flexible ad hoc responses of central banks to actual circumstances;
they need not and, indeed, cannot be provided for in advance by specific rules.

In addition, prescriptions calling for specific central-bank cooperation or for prior consultation under certain specific circumstances

180 WORLD MONETARY DISORDER

cannot be relied upon to meet the need for formal rules in other areas, notably area 1, because such cooperation may be least reliable when the need is greatest—that is, in the face of sharply divergent national interests. In such areas there must be some formal code of behavior more concrete than a mechanism of central-bank cooperation and consultation.

With regard to area 4, we might also rely to some extent upon ad hoc arrangements between specific central banks. For example, there are the arrangements made by the "snake" countries in 1972 for Italy's benefit, before that country dropped out of the scheme. Another example is the 1973 agreement between the Federal Reserve and the Bundesbank to "split" the profits or losses resulting from ordinated exchange intervention. Nevertheless, agreement on specific rules would be necessary to deal with this area in anything like a comprehensive way. But such an agreement would obviously require at least a conditional agreement on such issues as asset convertibility. Thus, area 4 cannot really be dealt with in a minimal reform program. There should therefore be no general rules dealing with the settlement of currency balances acquired through intervention, although arrangements between specific central banks can be expected from time to time. A central bank that unilaterally decided to buy foreign exchange would therefore have no assured means of disposing of the balances thus acquired, except through subsequent (permissible) sales on the exchange market. This fact would, of course, be one element in the bank's decision regarding intervention, because of the possibility of exchange losses that intervention might entail.

Area 5 clearly constitutes an area for potential rules, since the interdependence between the exchange markets and other economic policies has been quite marked. Exchange-rate movements during the current float have been influenced in the great majority of countries by controls over capital movements and by changes in such controls. These controls were in fact tightened in the first half of 1973. Early in 1974, however, the United States lifted its controls over capital exports, and many European countries relaxed their controls over capital imports, in both cases the aim was partly at least to check the rise in the dollar against the "snake" currencies. A number of countries have also from time to time adjusted their monetary-policy stances with an eye to influencing the movements in their exchange rates. In addition, trade policies have occasionally been altered with the same end in mind, the recent Italian import controls being a good example. Success in eliminating policy conflicts in the exchange markets might indeed simply shift the scene of such conflict elsewhere, but this is really a quite separate issue, for it is clearly desirable to coordinate national economic policies and to remove such conflicts to as great an extent as possible, regardless of what is happening in

the exchange markets or what rules have been adopted regarding intervention. There will thus be no further discussion of problems relating
to exchange controls, trade measures, monetary policies, and so forth,
it being understood that cooperation in this area is nonetheless of great
importance in its own right.

We are left, then, with area 1, namely, with the nature of the
rules to be adopted regarding official exchange intervention. Three
broad types of rule (not necessarily mutually exclusive) are possible
here. First, the rules could specify circumstances when official intervention by a central bank would be mandatory. The Bretton Woods
system was of this type, as were most of the suggested reforms of
that system, such as wider bands or the crawling peg; any rules of
this type to be considered now would necessarily have to be much
more flexible. Second, the rules could be of the opposite sort and
specify circumstances under which certain types of intervention
would be prohibited. Third, instead of pertaining directly to intervention, the rules could specify circumstances under which prior consultation or international cooperation of some sort would take place.

A scheme based upon rules of the first and third types would,
in our judgment, be impractical and/or inadequate. The latter, for
example, is realistic only in the sense that it is likely to be adopted
by default, and the former is ruled out by that very impossibility of
establishing the fixed equilibrium-exchange-rate structure that we
have argued makes floating inevitable. Any sort of prespecified mandatory intervention, no matter how flexible, would potentially lead to
the sort of crises that repeatedly occurred under, and ultimately top-
pled, the Bretton Woods system. We opt, therefore, for rules of the
second type.

But what kind of intervention should be prohibited? We wish to
prevent competitive exchange-rate policies by central banks, but which
concrete acts are of this kind? Any official intervention designed to
influence the exchanges is by its very nature an attempt to interfere
with market forces. But completely clean floating is just not in the
cards. We should like to rule out attempts to export inflation or unemployment through deliberately induced exchange-rate movements.
But any exchange-rate movement, regardless of its cause, will to
some extent influence domestic and foreign economic performance,
and who is to judge what evil lurks in the hearts of central bankers?
Not that motive need be all that important in any case; the response of
the rest of the world to one central bank's actions will clearly depend
upon economic conditions in the rest of the world. Furthermore, one
must not be concerned only with official intervention to push exchange
rates away from prevailing levels. The continued maintenance through
intervention of palpably overvalued or undervalued exchange rates
could equally be regarded as unneighborly behavior. The Bretton

Woods system in the 1960s offers a number of clear examples of the
latter. It is simply not possible to give an operational definition of
just what central-bank activity constitutes "competitive exchange-rate
behavior." Indeed this is one more potent reason why we need a highly
flexible set of rules. We must cast a coarse net to trap and catch the
big fish. Our rules should be confined to attempting to prevent both
of those visible, overtly aggressive acts that are most likely to induce
retaliation as well as the prolonged maintenance of outdated exchange
rates.

To summarize, a system of rules for dealing with the managed
float should embody the following simple features. It should be a
minimal reform program, at once broadly acceptable and highly flexible. It should consist of rules regarding official exchange intervention. The rules should specify when intervention is not permissible
rather than when it is mandatory, and they should be addressed to preventing the most pronounced sort of central-bank conflict.

THE REFERENCE-RATE PROPOSAL: A
SPECIFIC PROGRAM

We now discuss in detail a specific proposal of rules for a managed float that conforms to the general principles developed thus far.
The proposal involves the establishment of a "reference exchange
rate" for the currency of each participating nation. The following two
rules constitute the scheme.

1. No central bank would ever be allowed to sell its own currency at a price below its reference rate by more than a certain
fixed percentage (possibly zero) or to buy its own currency at a price
exceeding its reference rate by more than the fixed percentage. This
is the sole restriction imposed upon central-bank intervention.

2. The structure of reference rates would be revised at periodic
prespecified intervals through some defined international procedure.

An important feature of rule 1 is that no specific kind of intervention is ever required, although any central bank that wished would
be free to attempt to maintain its exchange rate within some band of
its reference rate. Indeed, completely free and permanent floating
would be perfectly acceptable, and "transitional floating" would require no prior approval or notice.

Rule 1 is of the minimal reform, "thous-shalt-not" type for
which we have argued. It is thus intended to be a source of great flexibility that would make the plan politically more acceptable and also
allow individual central banks or groups of central banks unilaterally

to adopt any of various possible exchange regimes (clean floating, true pegged rates, group floating, wider bands, and so on). In addi-. tion, it will facilitate the formation of reference rates, for the lack of mandatory intervention implies that a nation will sacrifice comparatively little economic sovereignty in agreeing to a specific reference rate— which it is under no obligation to defend—and that regular multilateral revisions will be technically possible without inducing those exchange-rate crises that must develop when the authorities attempt to maintain an exchange-rate structure that is about to be revised.

Rule 1 essentially inverts the basic idea of a par value from a pegged rate that must be maintained to a point of reference away from which the market rate must not be deliberately forced. Under "normal" circumstances one would expect to find exchange rates near their reference-rate values, with central banks intervening at their own dis-cretion to smooth out fluctuations, just as under the Bretton Woods system one found exchange rates in "normal" circumstances well within the band limits where intervention became mandatory. For not only would central banks tend, in varying degrees, to defend the reference rates, but the structure of such rates, formulated via rule 2, would constitute in effect a statement by the central banks as a group of what they regarded the equilibrium structure of exchange rates.

Under "abnormal" circumstances central banks could allow greater deviation from reference rates in response to greater pres-sure. Complete floating or intervention, either to smooth out fluctua-tions or to slow down movement away from reference rates, would be permissible, but rule 1 would prohibit attempts to induce or to accel-erate such movement. For example, if the rates established in Feb-ruary 1973 had been regarded as reference rates, the subsequent cen-tral-bank behavior described above would have been compatible with the present proposal, whereas any attempt to accelerate the decline of the dollar in May to July of 1973 would not have been compatible.

Rule 1 would also in "abnormal" circumstances give the struc-ture of reference rates a stability quite the opposite of what obtained under the Bretton Woods system. For example, it has often been ob-served that upward pressure on a pegged exchange rate presents traders with an opportunity for "one-way gambles" that could cumula-tively induce further inflows of funds. With rule 1, pressure of this degree would cause authorities to allow the exchange rate to rise, with the rise above the reference rate perhaps being slowed by inter-vention. Now as the exchange rate is driven further above its refer-ence-rate value, traders would become aware that the central bank could sell but not buy the currency, thus adding an element of risk to further purchases by traders. The greater the rise in the exchange rate, the more it would have to fall before the central bank would have the option of buying domestic currency. And traders would also know that any subsequent upward revision of the reference rate would not necessarily serve to nail down their profits, as it would not imply the realization or maintenance of a higher exchange rate.

The main purpose of rule 1 is to limit competitive exchange-rate behavior by central banks. This is our coarse net. No set of workable rules could comprehensively eliminate such behavior; even the Bretton Woods system was subject to it. By not allowing central banks to force departures of market rates from reference rates, we attempt to impose a very simple and workable rule that strikes at the most overtly aggressive sort of behavior. By allowing unconditional floating, we provide a country with one means (albeit a partial one) of neutralizing the effects of a reluctance by some central bank to allow its exchange rate to adjust.

Rule 1 is thus intended to serve two purposes. It should facilitate the technical functioning of the exchange-rate system by greatly reducing the likelihood of crises while still furnishing a point of reference for exchange rates. And it attempts to limit aggressive central-bank behavior of the kind just noted. Rule 2 likewise has two functions. It is intended, first, to provide a mechanism for the periodic adjustment of reference rates so that reasonably realistic levels can be approached and maintained, for that very uncertainty that makes floating inevitable would make periodic adjustment in the structure of reference rates necessary. In addition, it is necessary in order to minimize the possibility of countries intervening to maintain overvalued or undervalued exchange rates. An unfortunate characteristic of the operation of the Bretton Woods system during the 1960s was the failure of the par values of several important currencies, notably the dollar, the yen, and the mark, to adjust fully (or even to adjust at all) to changing circumstances. Second, rule 2 is intended to be the means for the injection of a formal international mechanism into the scheme. Such a mechanism can serve as a vehicle for international cooperation, as a lightning rod to draw away international conflicts and tensions from violations of rule 1 and as a cornerstone for the possible future evolution of a reformed international monetary system. Thus, we think it desirable that the scheme have an open door for the entrance of such a mechanism, and this is our door.

The close interdependence between the two rules of our proposal should be emphasized. The success with which rule 1 attains its objectives clearly depends upon the success of rule 2 in ensuring that the structure of reference rates at any time is reasonably realistic. And the ease with which rule 2 can be implemented depends upon rule 1, both in that international agreement on a structure of reference rates can be more easily realized when little loss of economic sovereignty is involved and in that international consultation on such matters need not trigger or accompany an exchange crisis.

The reference rates must, of course, be defined in terms of some standard. This is a point of very little importance for such a minimal program as this, and it can be decided upon at the commencement of the plan. For concreteness we can think of the reference rate for each currency as being defined in terms of SDRs, with the cross rate between a domestic currency and the central bank's chosen intervention currency as the rate thus relevant to rule 1.

The precise mechanism for implementing rule 2 and for the initial establishment of a reference-rate structure is more important, but it would also be decided upon at the commencement of the scheme (the reference rates, of course, need not coincide with present par values or central rates). A wide range of alternatives is possible. For example, it could be agreed that in each quarter (or at some other interval) the finance ministers or heads of central banks of the participating nations would negotiate the new structure of reference rates. This would amount to holding periodic negotiating sessions like those that in 1971 and 1973 successfully achieved agreement on new structures for the (far more binding) values of pegged exchange rates. Alternatively, changes in reference rates could be made by or in conjuction with some international institution, such as the International Monetary Fund (IMF).

Various technical devices, such as automatic "crawling reference rates" on some other uses of objective indicators, could possibly be employed instead of or in addition to negotiation, and they could also be conceivably used by some subgroup of countries. However, we are skeptical of wide agreement being reached to incorporate such a method, and, indeed, we must grant that any provision involving the mandatory adjustment of reference rates may be too much to hope for at the present time. Nevertheless, there should be a strong presumption that adjustments would be made in response to market forces. The latter would be indicated, for example, by pronounced deviations of market rates from reference rates, significant changes in the reserve levels of those central banks undertaking intervention, and perhaps even other developments, such as an oil price rise, that are expected to influence the exchange markets. In any case, it will be easier to achieve progress toward the mandatory adjustment of reference rates than toward the mandatory adjustment of market rates where so much more is at stake.

If all else fails, and if no agreement on an explicitly multilateral procedure can be reached, each central bank could unilaterally stipulate its own reference rate at periodic intervals. Consultation with at least its principal trading partners would then be in each central bank's own self-interest.

ALTERNATIVE PROPOSALS

We shall now discuss some possible alternatives to the reference rate proposal that also embody the same general principles. One can concoct a huge number of such alternatives by focusing on minor differences of detail, but, sticking to more general differences and ignoring the details, one might distinguish two main alternatives. The first would shift the focus of attention from exchange-rate levels to reserve levels, and the second would replace the reference rate by the current (or a recent) market rate. These will be discussed in turn.

Reserve levels could easily be incorporated into our own proposal —for example, as indicators of the way that reference rates should be adjusted. Indeed, we would expect this to be done, at least informally. But we are here interested instead in the possibility of using reserve levels as a basis for differentiating between permissible and nonpermissible exchange intervention. For example, one could stipulate that target reserve levels rather than reference rates be set via rule 2. In that case rule 1 could be altered to read: No central bank shall accumulate reserves when its actual stock of reserves exceeds the target level by more than a certain percentage and the price of its currency is not rising; no central bank shall sell reserves when its reserve stock is below its target level by more than a certain percentage and the price of its currency is not falling. There are obviously a number of alternative methods of utilizing reserve levels for this purpose, but the above proposal can be used as our prototype.

Both this and the reference-rate proposal conform to the general principles developed above and therefore share many properties, but there are some important differences between the two. First, the reserve-level counterpart of rule 1 is more cumbersome because of its twofold nature and would therefore be more difficult to apply in concrete situations. For example, it would be far more difficult to tell whether or not the rule was being violated. Who would know whether exchange rates were rising or falling when reserves were actually sold? This must be counted a definite minus against the reserve-level variant—but perhaps not an important one.

More significant is the fact that in order to decide upon target reserve levels it is obviously necessary to decide first upon what constitutes reserves, what the worldwide level of liquidity should be (and, thus, by implication the "average" amount of flexibility in the system), and how to adjust the target levels when exchange rates change (and, thus, by implication problems such as conversion guarantees). All of this is in addition to those difficulties that are partly analogous to those of implementing rule 2 of the reference-rate proposal. Now since the major reason in the first place for investigating a minimum-reform proposal is that agreement seems remote on such issues, we regard this as a very serious drawback, indeed.

Finally, at a more basic level, the fundamental goal of any proposal is, presumably, maintenance of an approximation to an equilibrium structure of exchange rates. There is no such thing as the equilibrium structure of reserve levels. When they are used to determine whether intervention is permissible, reserves are merely being used as proxies for exchange rates; they contribute no desirable features and merely introduce another possible source of error.

The second class of alternative proposals would replace our suggested reference rates by the current market rates. Again, a great many specific variants are possible. For example, recent proposals that central-bank intervention be limited to "leaning against the wind" fall in some sense into this class. For our prototype we consider the version consisting of the following single rule: No central bank would be allowed to sell its own currency when its price was falling or to buy its own currency when its price was rising. Again, we focus on the differences between this scheme and our proposal, ignoring the considerable similarities.

The main difference between this proposal (which we shall refer to as "leaning against the wind") and our scheme is, of course, the absence of a structure of reference rates. Thus, leaning against the wind lacks the point of reference in the exchange markets and the inherent vehicle for international cooperation, both of which we regard as desirable features of our scheme. Some individuals may prefer to avoid such features, but we do not.

There is a further technical difference between the two proposals. Under leaning against the wind a central bank could in effect engineer a depreciation (or appreciation) by leaning more in one direction than in the other whenever the opportunity would arise. This may also be true under the reference-rate proposal and in fact follows simply from the lack of mandatory intervention. But under leaning against the wind the new rate could then be defended, while under ours it could not. For example, a central bank could "leak" a rumor of an impending trade deficit, easier money, and so on, thus inducing a speculative sale of its currency on the exchanges. Under either scheme the central bank would be allowed to refrain from intervention and thus enable the exchange rate to depreciate until the (deliberately induced) speculative selling ceased. But under the present proposal the central bank could then defend this new lower rate against any tendency to return to equilibrium and justify such intervention as leaning against the wind. Under our plan this would not be possible once the exchange rate fell below its reference rate.

Leaning against the wind could also be used as a justification for preventing adjustment to a new equilibrium exchange rate, similarly to what happened during the 1960s. This is also possible in the short run in our scheme (and probably in any scheme other than pure

floating)—that is, one could conceivably argue that central banks
should be allowed to lean only with the wind rather than against it).
Why should it always be desirable to resist market forces? But rule
2 of the reference-rate proposal is intended to provide a mechanism
to deal with just this problem. By contrast, a resistance to basic market forces is inherent in the very idea of leaning against the wind.

Finally, the leaning-against-the-wind proposal involves measuring central-bank behavior, not against a specific exchange-rate value
but rather against the way the exchange markets are changing. This
would make violations of the rule much less obvious in practice. This
problem can be limited somewhat by a proper formulation of the leaning-against-the-wind rule, but it cannot be eliminated.

In closing, we emphasize two points about the pair of alternative
proposals discussed in this section. First, each proposal is a prototype, chosen for convenience to represent a number of possible variants. Second, although we have discussed the quite substantial differences between these alternatives and the reference-rate proposal,
the similarities are in fact extensive, and we wish to present the
reader with a menu of possible ways of implementing the general
principles for which we have argued.

CONCLUSION

The reference-rate proposal does not pretend to cover or provide for all of the problems that might arise under a regime of widespread managed floating. Many of these problems, as indicated earlier, can and should be handled on an ad hoc basis through central-
bank cooperation and international consultations of the kind so successfully developed and implemented in the past 25 years. But this machinery cannot always be relied upon and may indeed prove inadequate
when most needed. Our proposal is designed to meet such situations
and to minimize the possibility of the more aggressive forms of competitive exchange behavior—and the resulting conflicts of policy—that
could arise in the management of the float. Among other things, our
rule 1 would prevent a country from deliberately pushing its exchange
rate away from its reference rate, while our rule 2 would attempt to
assure that reference rates would not depart too far from true equilibrium exchange rates for long and that countries could not maintain exchange rates at unduly overvalued or undervalued levels through official intervention for any length of time.

Despite the apparent simplicity of our rules, they in fact conceal
many difficulties that will arise in actual practice. First and foremost, reference rates should, of course, bear some approximation
at any time to true equilibrium exchange rates, if the logic of the

scheme is to be fully realized. Unfortunately, the concept of equilibrium rates is at best a fuzzy one and cannot easily be defined in operational terms. Even with the best intentions on the part of the participating countries, there will inevitably be disagreement as to what the
initial reference rates and their subsequent periodic changes should
be. Second, it may well prove difficult to obtain the consent of all
the participating countries to bind themselves to any set of rules, however simple. Third, there is the question of policing the rules, particularly rule 1. How precisely is one to determine whether or not
rule 1 has been violated in any particular case? If a violation is un-
ambiguously established, should sanctions be imposed, and if so, what
kind of sanctions should there be and by whom imposed? Presumably,
the IMF could play a key role in this matter (as well as in advising on
appropriate reference rates), but would participating countries be
willing to subject themselves to surveillance by the IMF? These are
difficulties that must be faced if _any_ meaningful set of rules is to be
adopted. The reference-rate proposal is meant to minimize such
problems.

Since March 1973 the float has operated reasonably well and no
major conflicts in exchange-rate management have as yet been apparent. But this situation, for reasons indicated earlier, may not always
prevail. It seems important, therefore, to put the managed float on a
more systematic basis, as compared with its present unplanned char-
acter, so as to forestall the possibility of such conflicts. This is precisely the major purpose of the rules underlying our proposal.

MONETARY POLICY UNDER
FIXED AND FLOATING
EXCHANGE RATES
Henry N. Goldstein

Both in the United States and abroad there is continuing debate over the most useful approach to take in implementing and measuring the thrust of monetary policy. Some prefer to look at the structure and level of interest rates; another school prefers to look at the general availability of credit measured by indexes other than interest rates; a third faction insists that the most useful index is the rate of change in the nation's money stock. Some 20 years ago, the so-called monetarists who make up this last group were regarded as a simple-minded fringe who had never read their Keynes. But in the last decade the monetarists have won an increasing number of converts, even capturing the ideological allegiance of one of the 12 Federal Reserve Banks.

The case for implementing and measuring monetary policy by the rate of change in the money supply stands or falls on pragmatic grounds. It depends, specifically, on the answers to two questions: First, if it really wants to, can the central bank determine to an acceptable approximation the growth in the money supply? Second, is the relationship between money-supply growth and subsequent movements in real output and prices more stable and predictable than the relationships between alternative policy indicators and output and prices? If the answer to both questions is affirmative, then presumably we should all become monetarists.

Of course, the answers might well be affirmative for some countries but negative for others. A monetarist policy orientation might,

Published in somewhat different form as "Monetary Policy Under Fixed and Floating Exchange Rates," in National Westminster Bank Quarterly Review, November 1974, pp. 15-27.

for example, be preferable for the Federal Reserve, but an interest-rate-oriented policy might be more desirable for the Bank of Canada. In general, we might expect an economy's "relative openness" to outside influences (as conditioned by the ratio of its exports and imports to its GNP and by the ratio of its external credit flows to its total credit flows) to be an important determinant of the "optimal index" for conducting monetary policy. Another factor might be the nature of the economy's exchange-rate system—that is, whether the external price of its currency is pegged or floating.

RECENT EVIDENCE ON THE LINK BETWEEN PRICES AND MONEY

A recent skirmish in the war between the monetarists and non-monetarists has been fought in the pages of the monthly Review of the Federal Reserve Bank of St. Louis. Responding to criticisms of Federal Reserve policy, Arthur Burns has contended in a detailed open letter to Senator William Proxmire that little if any blame for the acceleration of price increases during 1973-74 can be attributed to Federal Reserve actions.[1] In a rebuttal, Milton Friedman has asserted that the Fed is responsible for the greater part of our recent inflation.[2] According to Friedman, there is a well-established link between the annual rate of change in the economy's money supply ($\dot{M}$) over a given two-year period and the annual rate of change in consumer prices ($\dot{P}$) over the subsequent two-year period: An above-average rate of increase in $\dot{M}$ in one biennium leads to an above-average rate of increase in $\dot{P}$ in the subsequent biennium. Friedman argues that the accelerated rise in the U.S. consumer price index during 1973-74 stemmed primarily from an unduly rapid rate of increase in the U.S. money supply during the 1971-72 biennium. To support his position he presents a table showing a statistically significant relationship between growth rates in prices and growth rates in money for lag-matched bienniums over the past 14 years. This relationship remains significant whether one chooses to measure the money supply by M_1, by M_2, or by M_3.

If we are to reduce inflation in the United States, Friedman contends, the Federal Reserve will have to slow the rate of increase in the money supply. Nothing else will do the trick—not bountiful harvests, not a decline in economic activity abroad, not (as Arthur Laffer might recommend[3]) a reversal of the recent devaluation of the dollar.

Friedman further asserts that the lagged relationship between money and prices, which he shows to have existed in recent years in the United States, also holds in other countries:

Studies for the United States and many other countries
reveal highly consistent patterns. A substantial change
in the rate of monetary growth which is sustained for
more than a few months tends to be followed some six
or nine months later by a change in the same direction
in the rate of growth of total dollar spending. To begin
with, most of the change in spending is reflected in
output and employment. Typically, though not always,
it takes another year to 18 months before the change
in monetary growth is reflected in prices. On the
average, therefore, it takes something like two years
for a higher or lower rate of monetary growth to be
reflected in a higher or lower rate of inflation. [4]

Is this assertion really true if we carry Friedman's observations
further back in time for the United States? And does it also hold if
we examine the data for other leading industrial countries? Somewhat
to my surprise, I found that the relationship between money and prices
postulated by Friedman has prevailed both for the United States and
for most other leading countries throughout the 1950s and 1960s.

Table 16.1 summarizes the relationships. It shows the results
of a series of simple linear regressions of price changes against
money-supply changes in the 10 countries for which such data are
available in a publication of the Federal Reserve Bank of St. Louis.
In the regression for each country the dependent variable is the annual
rate of change in the CPI over successive bienniums ($\dot{P}_t$), and the single explanatory variable is the annual rate of change in the money supply, defined as demand deposits plus currency, for the preceding
biennium (M_{t-1}).* I used 17 overlapping biennial observations for
each country (with one exception where 15 observations were used).
Money-supply observations ranged from 1954–56 through 1970–72,
while CPI observations ranged from 1956–58 through 1972–74. (In
estimating $\dot{P}$ for 1972–74, it was first necessary to estimate an average annual price level for 1974 for each country. This was done by
multiplying the available CPI index for February 1974 by 1.06.)

---

*My figures are derived on a slightly different basis from Fried-
man's. He uses annual rate-of-change figures computed from average levels of a given variable in the first quarter of year n and in the
first quarter of year (n + 2). I use annual rate-of-change figures derived from the average level of a variable over the entire course of
year n (actually an average of 12 monthly observations) and its average over the course of year (n + 2).

TABLE 16.1

Association Between Rates of Change in Prices and Money

Country	R^2	Sign of Slope Co-efficient	Slope Coefficient Significant at 5 Percent Level
United States	.75	Positive	Yes
Belgium	.70	Positive	Yes
Canada	.70	Positive	Yes
Italy	.68	Positive	Yes
Netherlands	.70	Positive	Yes
Switzerland	.63	Positive	Yes
United Kingdom	.60	Positive	Yes
Germany	.10 (.74)[a]	Positive	No (Yes)
Japan	.38 (.55)[b]	Positive	Yes (Yes)
France	.02	Negative	No

[a]Association between prices and money since 1965-67 and 1963-65, respectively.
[b]Higher value of R^2 obtained by omitting last observation.

In seven out of ten instances, the coefficient of determination (R^2) is more than 0.5. Significantly weaker associations were found for Japan, Germany, and France. But the coefficient of determination for Japan rises from 0.38 to 0.55 if we drop the very last observation, which includes the price increase for 1972-74. (In Japan this latest biennial price increase was exceptionally influenced by the rise in prices of imported primary products and by an unusual burst of wage increases.) In Germany, the relationship between M_{t-1} and $\dot{P}_t$ is quite weak over the period as a whole. But it turns out to be rather strong if we only include observations since the early 1960s.*

_____

*Germany experienced a relatively high rate of money-supply growth during the 1950s but relatively low rates of price-increase. Part of the explanation probably reflects the exceptional rate of real economic growth experienced during the 1950s, owing to the substantial influx of labor from East Germany. The demand for money balances may also have been growing relatively quickly as inflationary expectations waned with passage of time since the currency reform of

TABLE 16.2

Annual Rates of Increase in Domestic Money Supplies in Leading
Industrial Countries for Recent Bienniums

Country	1964-66	1966-68	1968-70	1970-72
Belgium	7.1	5.3	5.3	10.9
Canada	12.2	12.9	3.5	23.2
France	9.0	5.6	3.1	12.5
Germany	7.0	5.5	8.1	13.1
Italy	14.6	13.0	18.8	20.4
Japan	16.5	14.0	18.4	23.7
Netherlands	9.5	7.7	9.6	17.2
Switzerland	4.2	8.4	9.9	15.9
United Kingdom	1.9	5.8	4.7	14.6
United States	4.4	5.5	5.4	6.8

The third exception is France, where there is simply no significant
relationship between the two variables, either over the entire 20-year
period or over any significant subperiod.

This association between growth rates in national money supplies
and growth rates in consumer prices must be coupled with another interesting finding: Without exception, every one of the 10 countries
included in our study accelerated their rate of domestic money-supply
growth in the 1970-72 period, as compared with the previous biennium
—indeed, with the previous three bienniums (Table 16.2).

As Table 16.2 indicates, particularly striking increases in
money-supply growth rates took place in Belgium, Canada, France,
Germany, the Netherlands, Switzerland, and Britain during the 1970-72
biennium. In contrast, the United States, which is typically accused
of "exporting inflation," appears to have played a rather benign role.
The acceleration in its rate of money-supply growth, comparing 1970-72
with 1968-70, was a mere 26 percent. In Belgium the acceleration
was about 100 percent; in Canada, about 600 percent; in France,
about 300 percent; in Switzerland, about 60 percent; in Britain, about
200 percent.

1948. Both factors would have helped the economy to absorb large
percentage increases in the money supply, without much subsequent
upward pressure on prices.

Was this across-the-board acceleration in the rate of increase
in domestic money supplies in the leading industrial countries the principal immediate cause of the intensified inflation that the world experienced during 1973-74? If so, is there any reason—aside from chance
—why all 10 countries in our sample accelerated their rate of money-
supply growth during the 1970-72 biennium?

Given the evidence from Table 16.1, I find it hard not to accept
its monetarist implications. In my view, world inflation during 1973-74
would probably have been substantially reduced if countries had maintained rates of money-supply growth during 1970-72 at the levels prevailing during 1968-70.

WHY DID MONEY-SUPPLY GROWTH ACCELERATE
IN ALL COUNTRIES SIMULTANEOUSLY?

If we accept this monetarist conclusion, how do we explain the
simultaneous speed-up in money-supply growth in all the leading industrial countries during 1970-72? Sheer chance is an unconvincing
hypothesis. To see just how unconvincing it is, consider the pattern
of accelerations and decelerations in money-supply growth from the
previous bienniums as derived from Table 16.2 and shown in Table
16.3. As a null hypothesis, assume that the probability of any given
element taking a plus (or minus) sign is 1/2 and that the entry for any
given country in a given biennium is independent of the entries for all
other countries for that biennium. Then, according to the binomial

TABLE 16.3

Acceleration (+) or Deceleration (-) in Biennial Money-Supply Growth
from Previous Biennium

	1966-68	1968-70	1970-72
Belgium	–	0	+
Canada	+	–	+
France	–	–	+
Germany	–	+	+
Italy	–	+	+
Japan	–	+	+
Netherlands	–	+	+
Switzerland	+	+	+
United Kingdom	+	–	+
United States	+	–	+

theorem, the odds on experiencing four pluses and six minuses in
any given biennium, as in 1966-68, would be about one in five, while
the odds on experiencing the pattern shown in the column for 1968-70
would be about one in four. Neither result is implausible and the null
hypothesis could not reasonably be rejected for those two bienniums.
But the odds on getting plus entries for all 10 countries, as occurred
in 1970-72, would work out to only one in 1,024—a most unlikely event.
Accordingly, it seems unreasonable to believe that chance was the
main explanation of the across-the-board acceleration in money-supply
growth during these two years.

An alternative explanation of the money-supply developments
shown in Tables 16.2 and 16.3 is that excessively inflationary policies
in the United States were transmitted to other leading countries through
its payments deficit. That is, U.S. deficits under a fixed exchange-
rate regime compelled foreign central banks to buy dollars in the foreign exchange markets, creating in the process balances in their own
currencies that constituted high-powered money for their commercial
banks. These additional domestic bank reserves enabled the commercial banks to expand their domestic plans, bloating the internal money
supplies of the payments-surplus countries.

Of course, central banks have various methods of neutralizing
the domestic monetary effect of foreign-exchange accruals. They can
conduct open-market sales, increase reserve requirements, and
impose direct ceilings on bank-credit expansion. They can also try
to hold down their reserve accruals through controls on capital inflows
from abroad and through exchange-market swap transactions intended
to induce a short-term capital outflow. But when the pressures of a
basic payments surplus are strong and are augmented by speculative
capital inflows, the authorities may be unable to limit the growth of
their commercial banks' reserve base by any means short of currency
up-valuation or by letting the rate float. It seems clear, for example,
that the domestic money-supply impact of massive speculative capital inflows was the main consideration dictating the floating of the
Deutschemark, the guilder, the Swiss franc, the Canadian dollar, and
perhaps the yen on a number of occasions in recent years. The pattern of reserve accruals by foreign central banks lends support to the
theory of exported inflation (or perhaps more accurately of "imported
money-supply increases") for 1970-72. As Table 16.4 indicates, almost all major foreign industrial countries experienced substantially
greater reserve accruals during the 1971-72 biennium than during the
1969-70 biennium.

U.S. DEFICIT NOT "CAUSED BY" U.S. INFLATION

Having conceded that foreign money supplies might well have
grown at a considerably slower pace during the 1971-72 biennium, had

TABLE 16.4

Changes in International Reserves in Leading Foreign Industrial
Countries
($ million)

	1967-68	1969-70	1971-72
Belgium	-163	+660	+1,023
Canada	+342	+1,633	+1,371
France	-2,532	+759	+5,055
Germany	+1,919	+3,662	+10,175
Italy	+429	+11	+727
Japan	+887	1,934	+13,525
Netherlands	+81	771	+1,551
Switzerland	+748	839	+2,356
United Kingdom	-677	405	+2,820

foreign-exchange accruals been less massive, I hasten to make two
related points.

First, it seems misleading to say that the U.S. deficit that produced these accruals was "caused by" a domestic U.S. inflation in any
absolute sense. In fact, the increase in the U.S. CPI during 1971-72
was at an annual rate of only 3.8 percent, as compared with 4.1 percent in the previous biennium. The intensification of the U.S. deficit
in 1971-72 stemmed from several other interacting influences, notably, the differential stages of cyclical recovery in the United States
and Western Europe and the growing loss of U.S. competitiveness—
at the existing exchange rates—both at home and abroad on a variety
of fronts. In brief, the dollar was experiencing a growing secular
overvaluation in terms of a number of leading foreign currencies, but
particularly against the yen.

Second, there is little evidence that U.S. payments deficits
prior to 1971-72 were responsible for sustained periods of excessive
money-supply growth in foreign countries. Suppose that money-supply
growth were primarily due to exchange accruals. We should then expect that periods of above-average foreign-exchange accruals should
be associated with periods of above-average money-supply growth,
and periods of below-average foreign-exchange accruals (or payments
deficit) with periods of below-average money-supply growth. Even
prior to 1971 this relationship was certainly true for very short periods
when massive speculative capital inflows, on occasions, poured into
a given currency. But this relationship is not discernible for periods

as long as three months, as is clear from R^2 values shown in Table
16.5. These values were computed from quarterly data (52 observations) over the period January 1959 through December 1971. Without
exception, they are abysmally low, and only two of the 24 correlations
has both an F statistic significant at the .05 level and a positive slope
coefficient. Prior to 1972 the quarterly rate of money-supply growth
was for all intents and purposes unassociated with quarterly foreign-
exchange accruals in most leading payments-surplus countries.

MORE RECENT MONEY-SUPPLY DEVELOPMENTS

We have suggested that much of the intensified inflation of 1973-74
may be due—in the most immediate sense—to excessive rates of money-
supply growth in all the leading industrial countries. In the United
States this growth was autonomous in the sense that it could have been
readily avoided had policy makers been willing to permit interest
rates—in the short run—to have risen more sharply than they did.
In foreign countries, some significant part of this growth was probably
induced by balance-of-payments surpluses. These surpluses were the
counterpart of the U.S. deficit. But that deficit was not a reflection
of any concurrent burst of inflation in the United States. It stemmed
instead from the maintenance of undervalued foreign currencies, the
par values of which were only abandoned with great reluctance and after intense policy pressure by the Nixon administration.*

The introduction of more realistic exchange rates and the subsequent reduction of foreign official reserve accruals has been accompanied by a marked slowing of money-supply growth rates in almost
all leading foreign countries during 1973 (see Table 16.6). (Until
quite recently, Italy was an exception.) Indeed, in several foreign
countries money-supply growth rates turned negative during 1973 as
the authorities, freed from pegging their currencies in the exchange
market, pressed hard on the money-supply brake.

SOME IMPLICATIONS

Our review of the evidence has a number of implications. First,
much of the recent world inflation would probably never have occurred

---

*Many economists denounced the imposition of the 10 percent
surtax on all merchandise imports from developed countries by the
Nixon administration in August 1971. In retrospect, however, this
action seems to have been well advised. It took "a shot across the
bow" to jolt foreign decision makers into abandoning their mercantilist commitment to undervalued currencies.

TABLE 16.5

Correlation Between Quarterly Changes in External Reserves and Quarterly Changes in Money Supply for Six Countries (Value of R^2 for Four Alternative Equation Forms)

Equation Form	Belgium	Netherlands	Germany	France	Italy	Japan
1. $\Delta M_t = a + b \Delta R_t$	.02	.13*(N)	.02	.00(N)	.05	.11*
2. $\Delta M_t = a + b \Delta R_{t-1}$	.00	.05	.01(N)	.04	.00	.09*
3. $\log \Delta M_t = a + b \log \Delta R_t$	.03	.08*(N)	.02	.00(N)	.12	.02
4. $\log \Delta M_t = a + b \log \Delta R_{t-1}$	.01	.02	.02(N)	.04	.02(N)	.01

Notes: (N) denotes a negative value of b; * denotes an F statistic significant at the .05 level.

Source: IMF, International Financial Statistics.

TABLE 16.6

Annual Rates of Increase in Money Supply, 1971-73

	1st Q 1972 to 1st Q 1973	1st Q 1973 to 4th Q 1973	2d Q 1973 to 3d Q 1973 or 3d Q 1973 to 4th Q 1973
Belgium	14.4	9.3	6.8
Canada	15.8	8.3*	8.5
France	12.2	7.5	4.2
Germany	12.7	-1.9	8.0
Italy	21.6	29.4*	27.2
Japan	27.5	16.8	12.2
Netherlands	8.3	-7.4*	-19.9
Switzerland	0.0	1.4*	-2.1
United Kingdom	9.7	7.1*	-10.8

*From first quarter, 1973 to third quarter, 1973.

if the major foreign currencies had been floating against the U.S. dollar, for then the massive U.S. payments deficits of 1971 and 1972 would never have developed. In the absence of those deficits domestic money-supply expansion in a number of leading foreign countries would presumably have been markedly reduced. Second, if the monetarist thesis has merit, price increases in 1975-76 should be lower than in 1973-74, assuming a continuation of the recent sharp reduction in money-supply growth rates in most major countries. Finally, if central bankers want to continue to have greater scope than they have had in recent years to pursue domestically oriented discretionary policies, they should advocate the maintenance of floating rates. For floating rates eliminates the policy dilemmas that arise when a tighter policy (somehow construed) is desirable for domestic goals but an easier policy is desirable for external balance, and vice versa. They also eliminate the disturbing external impacts on the domestic banking system's reserve base.

SOME THEORETICAL CONSIDERATIONS

Our review of the relationships between money-supply growth rates and rates of increase in consumer prices may perhaps suggest that the authorities would be well advised to follow Milton Friedman's policy advice and eschew an active countercyclical policy. To a considerable extent, of course, this decision should depend on the predictability of monetary policy's short-run impact on real economic activity —an issue that we have not discussed. As is well known, Friedman has advanced some powerful arguments that suggest that attempts to "fine tune" the economy by an active countercyclical monetary policy are likely to exacerbate, rather than reduce, real fluctuations in economic activity.[5]

But perhaps Friedman's policy advice on this important point needs to be modified when the economic environment is characterized by floating exchange rates and by substantial mobility of long-term capital in response to interest-rate differentials. Indeed, in such an environment the central bank of a relatively small country may be better advised to ignore the money-supply growth rate as a policy guide and instead focus on the spread between its long-term rate of interest— and that in the world market.

Take Canada. Assume that the economy is in a recession and that the Canadian dollar is a free-floating currency. If the Canadian authorities respond with a policy of "aggressive ease," Canadian long-term interest rates will decline, as will their margin over corresponding U.S. interest rates. The result will be a curtailment of the normal volume of long-term bond issues floated in the U.S. capital market by Canadian corporations, provinces, and municipalities. With a smaller quantity of U.S. dollars being borrowed and converted into Canadian dollars through the exchange market, the external price of the Canadian dollar will weaken, but as the Canadian dollar depreciates, the demand for Canadian exports and for Canadian import-competing products will strengthen, bolstering output and employment in Canada and moderating the recession. In a relatively open economy this chain of reactions can powerfully augment the ability of monetary policy to strengthen aggregate demand in the face of a domestic recession. And, of course, the same sort of effects, but in reverse, would augment its ability to curb aggregate demand in the face of excess domestic-demand pressures. Accordingly, the case for an activist countercyclical policy seems substantially stronger than when the economy is relatively closed or when external capital flows are relatively small and insensitive to changing interest differentials or when exchange rates are more or less fixed.

One might challenge this contention on grounds that the Canadian current account would respond to a currency depreciation or appreciation only after a considerable lag, or, indeed, that initially it might respond perversely because of the famous "J-curve" phenomenon. But this objection does not withstand examination. The "J-curve" phenomenon applies to the initial perverse effect of the current-account balance in response to a currency depreciation or depreciation

when the current account is measured by the value of current exports
and imports (either in the home currency or in the foreign currency—
the two need not coincide). If this value is measured in the units of
the domestic currency, it may well decline initially, if the short-run
domestic demand for foreign goods is inelastic (or if there are certain combinations of supply elasticities in combination with given demand elasticities). Nonetheless, the flow of new orders to Canadian
exporters and to Canadian firms competing against imports cannot be
perverse. There is bound to be some positive (and presumably fairly
quick) increase in Canadian export orders when the external price of
the Canadian dollar falls, and there is bound to be some positive (and
presumably fairly quick) increase in orders placed with Canadian import-competing producers when non-Canadian goods become more expensive to Canadian buyers because of a depreciation of the Canadian
dollar.

A final qualification of this suggested revised approach to monetary policy under the conditions mentioned might be based on what has
come to be known as the "portfolio approach" to capital movements.
As has been pointed out, a given interest-rate differential may induce
very different amounts of capital inflows or outflows, depending on the
relative stocks of domestic to foreign assets held by domestic investors (or, in the Canadian case, on the relative stock of domestic to
foreign liabilities). But this consideration also fails to vitiate the
case for an activist countercyclical monetary policy on Canada's part.
It merely suggests that the authorities should not gear their policy
rigidly to particular interest-rate differentials. Within considerable
limits, some further widening or narrowing of interest-rate differentials should always succeed in producing a given desired exchange-
rate effect and hence a given desired effect on activity in the export-
and import-competing sectors.

Still, there is one possible rub to this scenario. Suppose that
aggregate demand in the external world is also weak under the conditions assumed. In that event, a policy of aggressive monetary ease
in Canada leading to an expansion of Canadian export orders and a
contraction of Canadian import orders would have an undesired deflationary impact on the outside world. Moreover, if the outside
world counters with a similar policy of aggressive ease, the effectiveness of Canada's activist policy would be blunted.

But such fears seem fine-spun. For one thing, the outside
world is unlikely to have cyclical fluctuations that are precisely in
phase with those in Canada. For another, the difference in economic
size between Canada and the outside world makes any policy-induced
strengthening or weakening of Canada's current-account a relative
pinprick.

In a world of floating exchange rates, then, Friedman's anti-fine-tuning advice would continue to apply to a relatively closed economy such as the United States. But it might be nonoptimal advice for smaller, more open economies.

NOTES

1. Arthur Burns, Federal Reserve Bank of St. Louis Review, November 1973, pp. 15-22.
2. Milton Friedman, Federal Reserve Bank of St. Louis Review, March 1974, pp. 20-23.
3. See A. B. Laffer, "The Bitter Fruits of Devaluation," Wall Street Journal, January 10, 1974.
4. Friedman, Review, p. 21.
5. Milton Friedman, "The Effects of a Full-Employment Policy on Economic Stability: A Formal Analysis," in Essays in Positive Economics (Chicago: University of Chicago Press, 1953), pp. 117-32.

CHAPTER

17

COPING WITH MONEY
MONOPOLY: ISSUES
AND NONISSUES
David G. Tuerck

Recent developments in international finance have had a number
of interesting consequences for the economics profession. One is for
its members to cloister themselves in exotic places, such as Burgenstock, Oyster Bay, and Malibu, where they forgo holiday weekends
for scholarly inquiry. Another may be seen in the fact that certain
pronouncements, once heard for the most part from the cloistered orders of academe, have been heard as well from "practical men": After the suspension of convertibility in 1971 the president of the Federal
Reserve Bank of St. Louis, claimed that "the freely fluctuating exchange rate is far preferable to a fixed one"[1]; the Reuss Subcommittee
on International Economics similarly decried "the yearning for an
early return to fixed rates evidenced at Nairobi" and argued for a
perpetuation of floating rates.[2]

WHAT CENTRAL BANKERS DO

From one perspective these pronouncements from the public
sector are a favorable sign. They suggest a growing awareness of
the inferiority of the pseudo gold standard recently in effect in comparison to the floating-rate standard now in effect. From my own
perspective, however, they err by exaggerating the practical importance of a fixed-rate system. This is for two reasons. First, a
fixed exchange-rate system is at most a costly, legal embellishment
for the underlying economic realities that determine its lifespan.
Second, popular opinion notwithstanding, central bankers do not permanently "fix" and "unfix" exchange rates; rather, they produce nominal money for distribution at home and abroad. In that capacity they
exercise a certain degree of monopoly power, with which, in the

fashion of any monopolist, they distort relative prices for monetary gain. Unlike the ordinary monopolist, however, the money monopolist does not pursue private profits at public expense; rather, we might say, he pursues public profits at public—and private—expense.

As long as central bankers exercise their monopoly power to create money, they will not be able—much less willing—to yield control over exchange rates to market forces. Nor can they distinguish a policy of fixed rates from one of flexible rates according to the way that exchange rates actually behave. As monetary history and the proponents of flexible rates have shown, exchange rates can change when the official policy is to hold them fixed, and they can remain constant when the official policy is to let them change.

This reduces the whole issue to one of what central bankers in-tend to do. We might say that a policy of fixed rates is in effect if central bankers intend to keep exchange rates constant and that a policy of flexible exchange rates is in effect when they do not. That rule would be simple enough if the axioms of revealed preference applied as forcefully to the politics of central banking as they do to the economics of the marketplace. Suppose that the central bank of country A really "intended" to engage in a policy of flexible exchange rates, in the sense that it would not support the exchange value of its currency despite foreigners' unwillingness to accumulate additional claims on it at the existing exchange rate. If the A bank also intended to engage in an expansive monetary policy it might nevertheless arrange with the central bank of country B to engage in a policy of "fixed" exchange rates. Then the A bank could shift part of the cost of its expansive policy to the B bank by inducing that bank to accumulate claims on A. The success of this strategy would depend not on what A really intended to do but on what B thought A intended to do.

The conventional approach to exchange-rate policy views central bank behavior as if it were motivated only by global concerns for internal and external balance. It resolves the issue of fixed versus flexible exchange rates, according to which policy is more likely to stabilize world payments and incomes—as if one country would not be willing to inflict a little instability on another out of its own national interests. In contrast to this approach, I wish to explore a theory of central-bank behavior in which the individual banks of different countries are viewed as monopolists that act out of selfish, nationalistic interests. I will attempt to show that, whether or not central banks intend to maintain fixed or flexible rates, there is a tendency for them to pursue expansive monetary policies at each other's expense. In this theory a system of stable exchange rates is one of equilibrium in mutual exploitation.

Ordinarily, not much importance is attached to the seigniorage or profits that are captured by central banks when they produce fiat

money. Such profits are thought to be small in comparison to the
goals of internal and external balance, with which they might conflict.
However, the small size of the amount of seigniorage collected in
comparison to national income or some other like magnitude does
not necessarily remove any consideration of such profits from the
choice calculus of central bankers.

THE GOAL OF INTERNAL BALANCE

I will consider first the goal of internal balance. From the
overall, social point of view, a fully anticipated deflation is preferred
to either inflation or price stability. Individuals measure the real rate
of interest they earn on an interest-bearing security by adjusting the
money or nominal rate of interest on that security by the anticipated
rate of inflation or deflation. When prices are stable, real and money
rates of interest are the same. When prices are rising, money rates
of interest exceed real rates of interest by the amount of inflation;
when they are falling, real rates of interest exceed money rates of
interest by the amount of deflation.

This has a bearing on the size of individual money holdings. Individuals must count the money rate of interest they receive on interest-bearing securities as a cost of holding a non-interest-bearing security, such as money. As the money rate of interest rises due to
inflation, people will exchange money for other securities, thereby
causing the price level to rise and their real cash balances to fall; as
the money rate of interest falls due to deflation they will exchange
other securities for money, thereby causing the price level to fall and
their real cash balances to rise. People derive benefits from holding
money just as they do from holding any other asset, but they are forced
to economize on their money holdings by virtue of the positive interest
payments they forgo when prices are rising or stable.

All of this means that from the social point of view, the best policy is a deflation that sets the money rate of interest at zero. Because
the cost to the central bank of producing an extra dollar is virtually
zero, the individual should not be forced to economize on his money
holdings, as he must when money rates of interest are positive. Stable
or rising prices are inefficient because they make the cost of holding
money appear higher, from the individual's point of view, than it actually is.

From the point of view of the central bank, however, the appropriate goal is some optimal rate of inflation. In a static (no-real-
growth) economy, the central bank can extract profits from individual
money holders equal to the rate of inflation multiplied by their real
money holdings. These profits are public profits in the sense that

they substitute for tax revenues at given levels of public expenditure and indebtedness, but, as monopoly profits, they impose a social cost greater than the amount of profits captured: The loss to individual money holders is not merely the real money that is captured from them by the central bank but also the resources they use up in economizing on their cash balances, made artificially expensive to hold by artificially high money rates of interest.

This is not to say that central banks attempt to extract profits from the general public for the personal enrichment of their officers and staff or that the profits extracted are the only motive behind a policy of inflation. What is sinister about inflation is that it permits government to levy a hidden tax that is like an overt tax insofar as it imposes a dead loss on society but that is unlike an overt tax insofar as it escapes the normal legislative procedures to which an overt tax is subject. While it may be fruitful to explore a theory in which central banks are assumed to behave like profit-maximizing monopolists, it is not necessary on that account to hold literally that they are profit-maximizing monopolists. Neither is it necessary, on the same account, to attribute purely sinister motives to government or any of its branches. A central bank may adopt a policy of inflation in part to acquiesce in a governmental policy of hidden taxation but in part also to spare society the employment and real output losses that would result from a failure on its part to adopt such a policy.

We have seen that price stability is not a viable measure of internal balance and that a divergence may exist between the viewpoint of society and of the central bank with regard to the optimal rate and direction of price change. Now we will observe that similar considerations apply to the goal of external balance, with an added divergence between national and international points of view.

THE GOAL OF EXTERNAL BALANCE

What is meant by external balance often depends on who is defining it or the circumstances under which it is being defined. In the April 1974 issue of the Federal Reserve Bulletin it was implied that the appropriate measure of external balance varied with whatever exchange-rate policy happened to be in effect at the moment:

> Under a regime of fixed rates, the official settlements balance measured external payments pressure by indicating the extent to which central banks needed to buy or sell foreign exchange to keep exchange rates within their fixed relationships. With freely fluctuating exchange rates, changes in ex-

change rates would be the important indicators of
external balance. However, under the mixed regime
of managed floating rates in operation now, not only
variations in exchange rates but also surpluses or
deficits in reserve transactions must be examined
in appraising the over-all balance of payments position.[3]

If external balance is achieved by keeping "exchange rates within
their fixed relationship," why should central bankers be concerned
per se with the balance-of-payments deficit or surplus? If exchange
rates are stable under a particular exchange-rate "policy" (whether
one of fixed rates, flexible rates, or a managed float), how do we
know that a deficit or surplus in the balance of payments is inconsis-
tent with that stability?

The usual answer to these questions presumes a wholly passive
policy on the part of central banks toward balance-of-payments deficits
and surpluses. According to this argument, the claims that one central bank accumulates on another are destabilizing, because they weaken
the ability of either to maintain the existing rate of exchange between
their currencies. Such claims are temporarily accumulated only to
prevent the exchange rate from changing until such time as "equilibrium" in the balance of payments is restored. The notion of a wholly
passive behavior on the part of central banks in this respect is reflected in the fact that transactions between them are often called
"stopgap" or "accommodating" transactions.

The idea that fixed exchange rates require a passive accumulation of claims by one central bank on another underlies the issue of
fixed versus flexible exchange rates. So interpreted, policies of
fixed and flexible exchange rates have certain advantages or disadvantages, depending on the state of internal balance within individual
countries, the mobility of capital between them, and so forth. What
obviates this issue is a central bank's behavior as a monopolistic
producer of money, whose potential customers include not only its
own citizens but foreign citizens and central banks as well. The con-
ception of a central bank as a money monopolist inverts the conventional interpretation of the balance-of-payments surplus or deficit:
Rather than a measure of probable change in the exchange rate, the
surplus or deficit provides an explanation for its stability.

We have seen why the central bank of an isolated country may
wish to engage in a policy of inflationary finance. In an open economy
the central bank of one country, A, has an even greater incentive to
engage in such a policy, provided it can induce the residents and/or
central bank of another country, B, to absorb some of the additional
A money created. This is because it can exchange the A money ab-

sorbed by B for real goods and services produced in B. By deliberately running a balance-of-payments deficit with B, A can more than
offset the net social harm it would otherwise suffer on account of its
inflationary policy. Because the damage thereby inflicted on B exceeds
the profits captured from B, A's policy will inflict net harm on the
two countries taken together, that is, on the world as a whole. Nevertheless, there are conditions under which B would be likely to comply
in its exploitation by A.

One such condition arises when A money is somehow superior
to B money, that is, when A acquires its monopoly power in B by virtue of an exercise in product differentiation. According to Grubel,
"The U.S. is the World Banker because private American enterprises
are the dominant financial intermediaries of the world business community."[4] Aliber has said:

> The dollar became a reserve currency for several
> reasons—it appeared stable in value and freely con-
> vertible, less subject to exchange depreciation or
> exchange controls than other currencies. . . . The
> U.S. reserve currency role developed in response
> to the ability of U.S. financial facilities to meet
> the needs of other countries for a satisfactory way
> in which to hold their international reserves.[5]

My own preferred interpretation of the long history of U.S.
deficits is not that the dollar has been a weak currency, propped up
by the generous support of foreign central banks: Rather, until the
breakdown of fixed rates, the dollar was a strong currency, strong
enough to make other countries willing to suffer recurrent balance-
of-payments surpluses in order to accumulate additional amounts of
it. These countries acquiesced in their exploitation by the United
States because the alternative, reliance on their own inferior currencies to satisfy growing demands for real cash balances at home,
was even less satisfactory.

CAPTURING SEIGNIORAGE

The superiority of its currency and an expansionist monetary
policy are not the only reasons why one country is able to capture
seigniorage from another. Suppose that country B attempts to reduce
the size of its surplus with A by expanding credit and thereby, in a
sense, reexporting some of its inflation to A. The degree to which
country B is relative to A, the more this defensive policy will increase
inflation in B, leaving it open for A to initiate a new round of mone-

tary expansion. Central banks of individual countries that are small in size relative to the major, money-exporting countries, may regard a submissive policy on their part as a sensible act of self-restraint. One country may be able to capture seigniorage from another because of autonomous growth or a contractive monetary policy. Suppose that country B does experience such growth or, contrary to some of my earlier reasoning, deliberately contracts its money supply. Either action will cause an increase in B's demand for real-cash balances. If prices and wages are not flexible downward in B, country A will be able to satisfy B's excess demand for real balances by expanding its own money supply and by soaking up the resulting unemployment in B. Or if prices and wages are flexible downward in B, A can adopt a neutral monetary policy, permitting B to export deflation to A, and in that fashion capture seigniorage from B. As before, B will run a balance-of-payments surplus with A; A will enjoy a net gain at the expense of B; world welfare will fall. [6]

This concept of external balance eliminates any divergence between public and private (or public and central-bank) points of view with regard to the balance of payments. Suppose capital is not free to move between countries, so that there is no tendency for the real rate of interest of one country to equal that of another. If A expands its money supply, and if B's combined private and central-bank demand for A's money is such that it will absorb additional amounts of A money at the existing exchange rate, then B's surplus with A will expand until the rate of inflation in each country is the same. Forward exchange rates may diverge from spot exchange rates insofar as the combined expectations of private citizens and central bank portend a rise or fall in the spot rate, but there will be no divergence due to interest rate differentials between the two countries.

If capital is mobile, and if B's citizens and central bank are willing to absorb additional amounts of A-money, B's surplus with A will expand until real interest rates are the same in both countries and money interest rates are separated only by the premium or discount on forward exchange. As before, the citizens and central bank of A will mutually gain and the citizens and central bank of B will mutually lose from A's expansionary policy. Also, as before, the exchange rate will be stable, not because either country has adopted a policy of fixed exchange rates but because, for the time being at least, each is willing to acquiesce in A's exploitation of B. An interesting implication of this argument is that total international liquidity will tend to be excessive in nominal terms but deficient in real terms. This follows from the "reserve-currency" country's monopolistic behavior and its propensity to export inflation for national gain.

Finally, I would like to reemphasize the fact that the surplus country's exploitation by the deficit country occurs with the voluntary

compliance of the former. The exploitation that takes place is real
enough but not very sinister by usual standards. It is a little like the
exploitation a man suffers when he allows himself to develop a taste
for Michelob beer and pays a few cents a bottle more for the privilege.
For years the dollar was the Michelob of world currencies. What
caused the most harm is that people kept drinking it long after it went
flat. As Meiselman has shown, one of the worst features of a fixed-
rate system is the agony of getting rid of it.[7]

THE EMPIRICAL EVIDENCE

I should now like to review certain data and institutional developments for the 11-year period 1963-73. The United States had a deficit in official reserve transactions for eight of those 11 years. The
trend toward a worldwide fiduciary money standard was accelerated by
the establishment of the two-tier gold standard in 1968, by the closing
of the U.S. gold window in August 1971, and by the suspension of
U.S. gold purchases in November 1973.

For more than 10 of these 11 years, the world was on a fixed
exchange rate. That particular description of the world monetary
system was firmly abandoned only by mid-March 1973, when most industrial countries "unpegged" their currencies from the dollar. The
transition to a depreciated dollar began more or less with the floating
of the German mark and Dutch guilder in May 1971 and was finalized
by speculative flows from the United States following realignments of
December 1971 and February 1973.

Were central bankers really making serious choices between
widening bands, crawling pegs, and jumping parities, or are these
merely ingenious names that might be given to their actions after the
fact? I would like first to examine certain data pertaining to the period 1963-72 and then to determine how well these dates dovetail
with the more exceptional events of 1973.

According to the theory explored earlier, the amount of seigniorage captured by a central bank should be equal to the deficit in its
balance of payments—somehow defined. (I am ignoring any interest
paid by the United States or foreign-held money.) This deficit, in
turn, should be equal to and determined by the excess of the amount
of money created by that central bank over the amount absorbed by
domestic growth and inflation (that is, by the amount of money created
for export to foreign countries).

In order to test this theory, I computed the percentage change
of M_3 (currency plus demand deposits plus savings and time deposits
at bank and nonbank thrift institutions) and subtracted the percentage
change of real output and of the consumer price index (CIP) for each

year in 1963-72 (see Table 17.1). The result of these computations, multiplied by the size of M_3 for each year, gives a measure of the amount of money created by the Federal Reserve System that year for export to foreign countries. I regressed the official reserve-transactions balance on the amount of this money for export and obtained the following results:*

    1. There was a relatively high positive correlation of B and XM of .812, with B and XM having the same sign in each of the 10 years (1963-72).
    2. Variations in XM explain about 66 percent of the variation in B.
    3. Over this period a $1 increase in XM caused on the average a $2 increase in B. This result is statistically significant.
    4. The average value of B (-$5.3509 billion) was roughly equal to the average value of XM (-$6.6982 billion).

Though not conclusive, these results lend empirical support to the theory under consideration. Indeed, the results would be more conclusive but for certain abrupt changes in the rate of monetary growth over the period under consideration. For example, B (the balance-of-payments surplus) was much too small for XM (the money-import requirements of the United States) in 1966, but that was a year of unusually slow monetary growth, and individual money holders may have allowed their real-cash balance to fall temporarily below equilibrium levels. Similarly, in 1970 the deficit in the balance of payments was too large for the size of XM, but that was a year just following another year of even slower monetary growth; an adjustment lag by money holders remains the most likely explanation.

    My empiricism would suggest that 1973 provides a clear exception to the theory proposed. In that year the balance on official settlements was a negative (deficit), -5.304 billion, while XM was a positive $57.075 billion. However, we might salvage the theory by scrutinizing certain relevant developments. For one thing, the basic balance moved into a surplus for the first time since 1957. For another, the official settlements balance showed a growing surplus, from $0.35

---

*XM, standing for the amount of money created for export or required for import, is given a negative sign for years during which the United States produced money for export and a positive sign for years during which it required money for import, depending on whether monetary growth was greater or less than the combined growth of real output and prices. B will stand for the balance on official settlements, with B negative in years of deficit and positive in years of surplus.

TABLE 17.1

Money for Export to Foreign Countries, 1963–73

Year	M_3	P	λ	π	$P - \lambda - \pi$	XM	B
1963	393.2	.0835	.042	.016	.0255	-10.027	-1.934
1964	426.3	.0843	.057	.012	.0152	-6.480	-1.534
1965	462.7	.0854	.066	.019	.0004	-0.185	-1.290
1966	485.2	.0486	.064	.034	-.0494	23.969	0.219
1967	532.8	.0981	.023	.030	.0451	-24.029	-3.418
1968	577.1	.0831	.048	.047	-.0119	6.867	1.641
1969	593.8	.0289	.028	.061	-.0601	35.687	2.739
1970	641.2	.0798	-.005	.005	.0298	-19.108	-9.839
1971	726.9	.1337	.035	.034	.0647	-47.03	-29.753
1972	822.4	.1314	.065	.034	.0324	-26.646	-10.345
1973	893.2	.0861	.062	.080	-.0639	57.075	-5.304

Note: M_3 = nominal money supply (billions of dollars); P = percentage growth of M_3; λ = percentage growth of real output; π = percentage growth of the CPI; XM = amount of money required for import by the United States (billions of dollars) = $-(P - \lambda - \pi)M_3$; B = U.S. balance-of-payments surplus (billions of dollars) on official-settlements basis.

Source: Economic Report of the President (Washington, D.C.: U.S. Government Printing Office, 1974), Appendix C.

213

billion in the second quarter of 1973 to $2.7 billion in the fourth quar-
ter after a whopping $10.475 billion deficit in the first quarter (at
quarterly rates). Finally, we can view the behavior of central bankers over the last three quarters of 1973 as signifying at least a temporary breakdown in the Federal Reserve's monopoly power over the
production of world money. Pippenger observes:

> The relatively small surplus in the second quarter
> of 1973 . . . suggests that, on balance, central banks
> sold dollars and tended to accentuate the depreciation
> of the dollar. If speculators had followed the same
> policy, their actions would have been described as
> destabilizing.[8]

This parallel between the behavior of foreign central banks and
private speculators is wholly consistent with the theory of central-
bank behavior explained above. Early 1973 was a period of transition
during which central banks and private speculators abandoned their
support of the dollar and caused it to depreciate to a new, more acceptable rate of exchange. Thereafter, the balance of payments moved
temporarily into surplus in order to service the growing demand for
dollars within the United States itself, where the combined rate of inflation and real growth far exceeded the rate of monetary expansion.
    Before closing I would like to note briefly the results of some
earlier studies, particularly those of Grubel and Aliber. Their studies
are similar insofar as they attempt to measure the net cost or benefit
to the United States of its role as a reserve-currency country. Their
methodology is different because they do not attempt to predict the
amount of seigniorage, as measured by the balance-of-payments deficit, but rather to estimate that amount for a given year and for given
data on long- and short-term interest rates, the international investment position of the United States, and so forth. Due to certain intan-
gible items that could not be measured, neither study, in fact, provides a conclusive estimate of the amount of seigniorage captured or
lost by the United States. It is the matter of these "intangibles" to
which I would like to address my final comments.
    Both Grubel and Aliber identify "flexibility" in managing its
balance of payments as an advantage of the U.S. reserve-currency
role and constraints on its ability to devalue the dollar and to maintain
full employment as disadvantages of that role. None of these alleged
advantages or disadvantages is correctly interpreted by them, however.
It is a contradiction to say that the "role" of a country as a source of
international reserves simultaneously increases that country's ability
to manage a deficit and decreases its ability to engage in monetary expansion. When the United States runs a deficit in its balance of pay-

ments, it collects seigniorage from foreigners. When it expands the money supply at home it collects seigniorage from residents and from foreigners. Rather than a consideration that discourages monetary expansion at home, the balance-of-payments deficit is an instrument through which the United States has engaged in monetary expansion to collect seigniorage from foreigners. To that extent, its past (or future) role as a reserve-currency country was an advantage whose exploitation required a certain rate of monetary expansion. The deficit has been a logical and deliberate result of U.S. monetary expansion rather than a deterrent to such expansion.

NOTES

1. Darryl R. Francis, "The Flexible Exchange Rate: Gain or Loss to the United States," Federal Reserve Bank of St. Louis Review 53 (November 1971): 20.
2. United States, Congress, Joint Economics Committee, Subcommittee on International Economics, Making Floating Part of the Fixed Rate System, 93d Cong., 1st sess. (1974), p. 2.
3. "Recent Developments in the U.S. Balance of Payments," Federal Reserve Bulletin 60 (April 1974): 235.
4. Herbert G. Grubel, "The Benefits and Costs of Being the World Banker," National Banking Review 2 (December 1964): 190.
5. Robert Z. Aliber, "The Costs and Benefits of the U.S. Role as a Reserve Currency Country," Quarterly Journal of Economics 78 (August 1964): 443-44.
6. This follows closely the analysis of Robert A. Mundell, Monetary Theory (Pacific Palisades, Calif.: Goodyear, 1971), pp. 147-60.
7. David I. Meiselman, "Worldwide Inflation: A Monetarist View," May 6, 1974. See Chapter 3.
8. John Pippenger, "Balance-of-Payments Deficits: Measurement and Interpretation," Federal Reserve Bank of St. Louis Review 55 (November 1973): 13.

CHAPTER

18

THE USE OF THE
DISCOUNT RATE AND
OPEN-MARKET OPERATIONS
IN AN OPEN ECONOMY
Steven W. Kohlhagen

There has been much written about the relative strengths of
monetary and fiscal policy under alternative exchange-rate regimes.
This chapter extends the previous comparative statics analysis by
dividing "monetary policy" into two components: open-market operations and rediscounting. We specifically analyze under both flexible
and fixed regimes whether open-market operations or changes in the
central-bank discount rate (given an open discount window) have a
greater effect on domestic monetary targets.

This discussion takes the view that activity in the foreign exchange markets is a direct result of disequilibrium in domestic money
and bond markets, along the lines of the monetarist model of the balance of payments summarized by Johnson.[1] For example, with fixed
exchange rates an excess supply of money is satisfied by a trade deficit that soaks up the excess liquidity, while with flexible exchange
rates the adjustment is realized through exchange rate movements and
resulting effects on the price level.

The assumption in many such models of perfectly mobile short-
term capital ties the domestic interest rate to the foreign (or international) rate and implies that the domestic money stock is endogenous
in a world of fixed exchange rates. If domestic authorities attempt to
maintain a domestic interest rate independent of foreign rates (without imposing capital controls), then they must give up control of the
exchange rate or the nominal stock of money. For the purposes of
this chapter, we will assume less than perfectly mobile capital so that
we can analyze more realistically the effectiveness of monetary policies on capital flows, the domestic interest rate, and the supply of
money. This assumption modifies somewhat the now-standard conclusions that monetary authorities have significant control over monetary
variables with flexible exchange rates but are powerless when they peg
the exchange rate.

216

We are not concerned with the long-run questions of the growth rate of the money supply, the level of inflation, or long-run monetary and fiscal policy mixes in a dynamic economy. This analysis is concerned primarily with how monetary authorities can best control monetary variables when faced with exogenous short-run disturbances (for example, shifts in liquidity preference or changes in foreign interest rates). We are addressing the question of which of the tools available to monetary authorities affords them the most control over domestic short-run liquidity conditions under alternative exchange-rate regimes.

We first introduce the alternative monetary policies available to authorities in this analysis, then analyze the factors determining the effectiveness of these policies in a closed economy, after which we discuss the relative powers of open-market operations and discrete changes in the discount rate under fixed- and flexible-exchange-rate regimes, respectively.

MONETARY POLICIES

We assume open-market operations and changes in the discount rate to be the two principal tools of monetary policy. The use of discretionary changes in reserve requirements can be shown to have an identical impact to that of open-market operations in a comparative statics portfolio-balance model of monetary equilibrium. The main difference, of course, being that the smaller are reserve requirements the greater is the leverage of other monetary policies upon economic variables. It will therefore be assumed for purposes of simplification that reserve requirements are unchanged throughout the period of analysis and that whereas the absolute size is less than 100 percent, its actual magnitude will remain unspecified.

We treat discount-rate policy differently from that normally pursued by central bankers. It is assumed that the central bank keeps a completely open discount window to all commercial banks and that the discount rate is used as a policy tool to affect monetary conditions actively, rather than merely as a response to activity at the window. It then follows that the discount rate will lead rather than follow movements in domestic interest rates. Open-market operations are treated as purchases and sales of short-term securities by the central bank. Both policy tools are then viewed as alternative means of affecting domestic short-term monetary conditions.

There are two ways that the central bank can view increased (or decreased) activity at the discount window. It can be seen as a means through which the commercial banks bypass short-run monetary policy, thereby reducing the monetary authority's ability to control the domestic money supply. Alternatively, it can be viewed as a means

through which the commercial banks avoid sudden portfolio shifts imposed upon them by significant changes in central-bank policy (or
changes in private liquidity preference or unexpected flows through
the foreign exchanges), allowing them a temporary escape valve until
they are able to shift their asset holdings permanently in keeping with
changed economic conditions. In the former case the authorities would
most likely discourage discounting as much as possible, whereas a
central bank with the latter viewpoint might well keep a more open discount window.

Note that international flows of short-term capital can also be
viewed as a form of discounting in this context. A commercial bank
in need of reserves can either rediscount a bill at the central-bank discount window or sell some of its holdings of foreign bonds to foreign
residents as a way of building up reserves (analogously, it could borrow from the central bank or from a foreign bank). In either case it
uses the central bank's discount window or the foreign exchange market to change its short-run-asset position in response to changing returns on assets or economic conditions.

MONETARY EQUILIBRIUM IN A CLOSED ECONOMY

Initially, we analyze the differential effects of open-market operations and the discretionary use of the discount rate by the central
bank in a closed economy; later, we will open the analysis to foreign
trade and capital flows.

Increased open market purchases or a reduction in the discount
rate by the central bank induce a fall in the domestic interest rate and
a rise in the domestic money supply. The more responsive the demand
for money to changes in the domestic interest rate, the less effect
these monetary policies will have upon interest rates, and the more
effect they will have upon the money stock. That is, the greater the
public's portfolio shifts between interest-bearing and non-interest-
bearing assets due to interest-rate movements, the smaller the fall
in the interest rate necessary to induce the public to hold a larger
stock of money.

On the other hand, the more responsive commercial-bank borrowings at the discount window to changes in the domestic interest rate,
the smaller the central bank's powers in inducing changes in interest
rates or the money supply through the use of either monetary tool.
In the limiting case, if the commercial banks do not change their position at the discount window in response to changes in the domestic interest rate, then open-market purchases increase the domestic money
supply by the exact amount of the purchases. When this elasticity is
infinite, neither open-market operations nor changes in the discount

rate have any effect on either the domestic interest rate or the money
supply (that is, any change in the interest rate induces increased activity at the discount window until both the money stock and interest
rate return to their previous levels). A central bank that keeps a completely open discount window and encourages its use without limit will
therefore be unable to control domestic monetary conditions through
the use of either open-market operations or changes in the discount
rate.

On the other hand, the more responsive the commercial-bank
discounting to changes in the discount rate, the greater the central-
bank control over the interest rate and money supply through discount-
rate changes.

We have implicitly assumed up to now that there exists no relationship between commercial-bank responsiveness to changes in the
interest rate and changes in the discount rate. Presumably, the more
responsive the commercial banks are to the cost of borrowing from
the central bank, the more responsive they will be to the return they
can receive on the borrowed funds. Therefore, for the remainder of
the analysis we will make the rather restrictive assumption (for the
sake of convenience) that the elasticity of response of discounting to
changes in the interest rate and discount rate are of equal magnitude.
Note, however, that a central bank that can induce highly elastic responses in commercial-bank discounting to changes in the discount
rate, while reducing the impact of interest-rate changes on commercial-bank behavior at the discount window, can significantly increase
the effects of both open-market operations and changes in the discount
rate on the money supply and the domestic interest rate.

Assuming equal responsiveness of commercial banks to changes
in the discount rate or the interest rate, the more elastic the discounting, the less powerful the effects of open-market operations upon either
the interest rate or the nominal stock of money. In the limiting case
with zero elasticity, open-market operations have the maximum impact increasing the money stock by the amount of the open-market purchases; with infinite elasticity, open-market operations have no impact on the money supply or the interest rate.

The more responsive the commercial-bank discounting to
changes in the discount rate (and the domestic interest rate), the
greater the central-bank control over the interest rate and money supply through discount-rate changes. Again looking at the polar cases,
when discounting is completely unresponsive to changes in the discount rate and the domestic interest rate, the effect of a change in the
discount rate on domestic interest rates and the money supply is, of
course, zero. If the responsiveness is infinitely elastic, then a rise
in the discount rate will increase the domestic interest rate until it
is equal to the new discount rate, and the money supply will fall

(through a decrease in discounts and advances) until it is low enough to eliminate the excess supply of money created by the new (higher) domestic interest rate.

The central bank keeping a completely open discount window and not changing the discount rate in response to disturbances will then be faced with a domestic money stock that is determined in part by demand conditions in the market. Except as it can be controlled through changes in the discount rate, the domestic money supply will be endogenous.

The effects of exogenous disturbances, such as changes in liquidity preference, income, wealth, and so on, are also affected by the responsiveness of commercial-bank discounting. As an example, with an increase in liquidity preference the public sells domestic bonds for domestic money, driving up the interest rate and increasing commercial-bank borrowing at the discount window; this increases the money supply and satisfies the increased demand. The more responsive the demand for funds from the discount window by the banks, the greater the effect of the exogenous disturbance upon the domestic money supply, and the less the effect on the domestic interest rate (this could perform a valuable smoothing role in the economy in the event the demand for money was unstable). In the limiting case of infinitely elastic demand for discounts and advances, the interest rate is pegged at the level of the discount rate and the money supply will increase by exactly the amount of the increase in liquidity preference. The monetary authority, when faced with such a disturbance, has a choice among three options:

1. He can do nothing so that discounting operates to allow adjustment in the nominal stock of money and/or the interest rate;
2. He can prevent an increase in the stock of money either by raising the discount rate to discourage the use of the discount window or by decreasing open-market purchases (or increasing sales) by the amount of the increased activity at the discount window;
3. He can prevent an increase in the interest rate (and tight short-run monetary conditions) either by lowering the discount rate to encourage discounting or by increasing open-market purchases.

Thus, in a closed economy a monetary authority faced with an exogenous disturbance must choose between controlling the interest rate and allowing the nominal money stock to be determined by demand conditions, or controlling the money stock while allowing domestic monetary conditions (through the short-term interest rate) to be demand determined. As we shall see, the problem is not as important in an open economy with mobile short-term capital where the domestic interest rate is at least partially tied to the foreign-interest rate.

The use of discount-rate changes versus open-market operations to control short-run domestic liquidity conditions has been discussed in the literature, especially with regard to U.S. monetary policy.[2] Since U.S. policy has been to discourage a completely open discount window and has allowed changes in the discount rate to follow (rather than lead) domestic interest-rate changes, these discussions are not entirely relevant to our analysis. However, it is instructive to briefly review part of their analyses.

Although discounting is responsive to the difference between the rate of interest and the discount rate, there is a great reluctance by the banks to assume greater debt. This historical reluctance on the part of the banks to borrow is in part due to the administration of the discount window and plays a great role in reducing the interest elasticities of discounting. In fact, one opinion holds that commercial banks come to the window only out of need and that, therefore, the response to changes in the discount rate is small.

The fact that open-market operations can just as easily provide liquidity and that discretionary changes in the discount rate can send false signals to the market have been the principal arguments against the use of discounting as a more active policy. The former criticism neglects the fact that the discount window provides an automatic safety valve for banks with liquidity problems that would not be available with a system using only open-market operations. The second argument has two major faults: First, the discount rate in the United States is raised (except in rare cases) only under pressure from rising short-term interest rates, so that few market participants are misled into thinking that the discount rate is a leader rather than a follower, and, second, the discount mechanism suggested in our analysis above would leave no doubt as to its signal, since it would always be an accurate indicator of intended monetary policy.

MONETARY POLICIES IN AN OPEN ECONOMY WITH FIXED EXCHANGE RATES

In an open economy the commercial banks are presented with an additional opportunity to borrow needed reserves or lend excess reserves—namely, the foreign bond markets. In a period of tightening domestic money markets, banks can increase their reserves by borrowing from the central bank (via discounting) or from foreign money markets (through capital inflows realized, for example, by selling domestic bonds to foreign residents and cashing the proceeds into domestic currency). Similarly, when the central bank pursues an easier money policy, commercial banks can reduce excess reserves either by reducing their discounts at the central bank or by increasing their holdings of foreign bonds.

The analysis for an open economy with fixed exchange rates is identical with that for a closed economy, except for the inclusion of the interest elasticity of capital flows. The more responsive the international capital flows to changes in the domestic interest rate, the less the impact of either domestic monetary policy upon domestic interest rates and the domestic money supply. When capital flows are not at all responsive to domestic interest rates, the results are identical to those for the closed economy. On the other hand, when capital flows are infinitely elastic, domestic monetary policies have no impact at all. This latter result is the familiar conclusion that monetary policy has no power with fixed exchange rates and perfectly mobile capital and is a result of the fact that the central bank must interfere in the foreign exchanges to offset the effect of capital flows on the exchange rate.

It is instructive to analyze the size of the short-term capital outflow resulting from an increase in open market purchases by the central bank. If capital is perfectly mobile, then any exogenous change changes in the discount rate when attempting to influence short-run domestic monetary conditions with a fixed exchange rate.

To be sure, the effectiveness of discount-rate changes will be reduced, the more interest elastic the capital flows, but then so will the effectiveness of open-market operations. The primary reason to use discount-rate changes with fixed exchange rates is that this choice at least leaves an option open to the central bank—namely, in times of short-run disturbances, the central bank can wield some power over domestic monetary conditions by restricting the mobility of short-term capital. This is an option not available when open-market operations are the principal tool of monetary policy, because the commercial banks, when faced with restrictions on short-term capital flows, can always increase or decrease their activities at the central bank's discount window.

The effects of an exogenous change in liquidity preferences are analogous to the closed economy case, as an exogenous upward shift in the demand for money induces a rise both in the domestic interest rate and the nominal stock of money. Because of the access to the foreign exchange market, the effect of the liquidity shift upon the interest rate is reduced (as compared to the closed economy case), while there is a greater increase in the money supply. The more responsive the flow of international short-term capital to changes in the domestic interest rate, the less the effect upon the interest rate, and the greater the effect upon the nominal supply of money. The change in the money supply induced by the shift in liquidity preference is the increased quantity demanded as a result of the liquidity shift less the quantity of money no longer demanded as a result of the induced rise in the interest rate. With perfectly mobile capital the domestic interest rate is pegged to the foreign interest rate so that the inflow of capital fully satisfies the shift in demand.

Monetary policy is not so powerful a tool in reacting to exogenous disturbances as it was in the closed economy case. Attempts to achieve an interest rate that is higher than the foreign interest rate will risk capital inflows in the short run and possible exchange crisis in the long run. A monetary authority that reacts to an increase in the money supply that has been induced by an upward shift in liquidity preference by soaking up the increased liquidity through open-market sales will find that its efforts are met by even further capital inflows and continued discounting at the central bank.* In order to control the nominal money stock through open market operations then, the monetary authority must restrict access to the discount window and impose capital controls in the foreign exchanges.

Alternatively, if the monetary authority were to react to the increasing money stock by raising the discount rate, the only leakage from the short-run tight policy would be through the foreign exchanges. If the offsetting capital inflow were felt to be serious enough, then short-run capital controls could be instituted, but no restrictions on the use of the discount window would be necessary, as the bank's access to the window would be the primary source of power available to the monetary authority.

In addition, to the extent that changes in the discount rate are viewed as direct changes in policy, they will have an impact on exchange rate expectations. If changes in the discount rate are taken by speculators to be direct evidence of attempts by the monetary authority to change domestic liquidity conditions, and if it is felt that

---

*It is not clear in this case that the monetary authority would necessarily want to offset the money supply increase. A preferred policy might be to allow the shift in liquidity preference to be satisfied by the market. However, the use of the liquidity-preference-shift variable is merely one example of an exogenous disturbance; other disturbances from which the monetary authority might well wish to insulate the domestic economy's nominal money stock include shifts in foreigners' liquidity preference, shifts in foreign residents' propensity to hold this economy's bonds, shifts in long-term capital flows, and so on. By fixing the exchange rate, the monetary authority surrenders control over the short-term interest rate as long as capital is free to move across international borders. The question addressed here is, given an exogenous disturbance, of the monetary policies available with fixed exchange rates, which gives authorities the best control over the short-run nominal money stock?

the monetary authority has the power to make its policies effective, then speculative expectations will reflect confidence in the monetary authorities' policy, and speculative capital flows will not reduce the affects of the policy. To the extent a monetary authority feels it can make a positive impact on exchange-rate expectations by instilling confidence in its policies, discount-rate changes as a direct signal to market participants will be that much more effective in a fixed-exchange-rate regime. Since the use of open-market operations has a less direct impact as a market indicator, it will not have this property. This provides one additional reason for using discount-rate changes rather than open-market operations in determining domestic short-run monetary conditions with fixed exchange rates.

This use of changes in the discount rate for "psychological effect" has been discussed at length by R. G. Hawtrey, specifically in reference to the English experience with Bank Rate from 1844 to 1914, and was recently analyzed by Hicks.[3] Hicks notes that discount-rate policy provides the possibility of decisive action by the monetary authority, where such policies, when perceived as being decisive by market participants, affect expectations so as to induce the intended effects upon capital markets. This decisiveness is surrendered by authorities when the discount rate is changed merely in response to changing market conditions. Their discussions of the effects on expectations were specifically in reference to domestic markets, but the effects of decisive discount-rate policy would be expected to have similar effects on those market participants analyzing the expected relative rates of return on both foreign and domestic liquid assets.

In short, with fixed exchange rates, in order to exercise effective power through the use of changes in the discount rate, the monetary authority can restrict the mobility of short-term capital, but to use open-market operations effectively, the monetary authority must restrict not only short-term capital mobility but also the activities of commercial banks at the discount window. With fixed exchange rates then, monetary authorities should use changes in the discount rate rather than open-market operations to affect domestic short-run liquidity conditions.* This choice enables monetary authorities to

---

*The use of discount-rate changes to offset short-run liquidity conditions does not preclude the use of open-market operations for longer-run goals. Since the discount window is only available to the banks as a source of short-run funds, it can only serve to offset policies in the short run. For example, if a longer-run tight monetary policy is being pursued through open-market sales during a fixed-exchange-rate regime, our conclusions tell us that if this policy is being temporarily thwarted through increased activities in the foreign

have as much power over the domestic money supply and interest rates as is possible with fixed exchange rates, while minimizing the artificial restraints it must impose to exercise its control over domestic monetary conditions.

MONETARY POLICIES WITH FLEXIBLE EXCHANGE RATES

With flexible exchange rates authorities do not intervene as before in the foreign exchanges, and capital flows do not effect the domestic money supply. As before, the central bank has less control over domestic interest rates, the more elastic the international capital flows, but domestic interest rates are not so rigidly tied to foreign rates as they were in a fixed-exchange-rate regime. However, with flexible rates the more interest-elastic the capital flows, the greater the control of the domestic monetary authority over the domestic money supply through the use of either monetary tool.

An expansionary monetary policy (either through an increase in open-market purchases or through a decrease in the discount rate) induces a fall in the domestic interest rate, which in turn induces a fall in discounting both at the central bank and in the foreign exchanges (through a short-term capital outflow). With fixed exchange rates the monetary authority was forced to intervene in the foreign exchange market and reduce somewhat the intended increase in the domestic money supply. With flexible exchange rates not only does the induced capital outflow not reduce the money supply, but it depreciates the exchange rate and has an expansionary effect on the domestic economy through the current account. This effect is entirely consistent with the expansionary monetary policy being pursued by the central bank. The more interest-elastic the discounting, the lower the capital outflow will be, and the lower the expansionary effect will be through the current account.

To the extent that there is a reduction in the domestic interest rate, there will still be some leakage of the increased money stock (from, say, open-market purchases) out of the system through reduced discounting at the open discount window. However, the greater the induced capital outflows, the less the fall in the domestic interest rate will be, and the less the reduction in discounting from the central bank will be. Consequently, the increase in the money stock as a re-

exchanges and at the discount window, the correct short-run complementary policy is to raise the discount rate (and possibly restrict capital outflows) rather than to increase open-market sales.

sult of a given amount of open-market purchases will be greater, the more responsive the capital flows to changes in the domestic interest rate. This is a small increase to be sure, but it is significant that with a flexible-exchange-rate regime, the greater the capital flows, the greater the impact of monetary policy upon the domestic economy and on the domestic money supply.

Under a flexible-exchange-rate regime then, the central bank would increase the effectiveness of open-market operations by encouraging discounting in the foreign exchanges and discouraging the use of discounting at the discount window. If capital markets are well-integrated, the monetary authority might even consider severely restricting the use of the discount window, since discounting is easily obtained in the foreign exchange markets where it reinforces central bank policy. Since all activity at the domestic discount window merely offsets central bank policy, it serves no purpose to allow it to continue in a flexible-exchange-rate regime especially if there is easy access to foreign financial markets for commercial banks during short-term liquidity crises.

With flexible exchange rates, an upward shift in liquidity preference induces a rise in the interest rate, capital inflows, increased discounting at the central bank, and the nominal money stock. The capital inflow induces an exchange appreciation that has a deflationary impact on domestic economic activity. Since the monetary authority does not interfere in the foreign exchange market, the capital inflow has no direct effect on the domestic money stock. That is, the interest induced purchases by foreign residents of domestic interest-bearing assets induces a current-account deficit as the exchange appreciation makes foreign goods more attractive to domestic consumers and domestic goods less attractive to foreigners. Whereas with fixed exchange rates domestic residents could exchange domestic interest-bearing assets for high-powered money (due to the monetary authority's interference in the foreign exchange markets), with flexible exchange rates the public as a whole can only exchange domestic interest-bearing assets for foreign goods. The only source for more non-interest-bearing assets (that is, money) is through the discount window, where some of the increased demand will be satisfied when the interest rate rises.

The monetary authority could take either of two policy steps to eliminate or at least reduce the pressures resulting from such a disturbance (of which the liquidity shift is merely an example). They could lower the discount rate, thereby making discounting cheaper, or they could purchase securities in the open market to ease credit conditions. Given the effects of the disturbance, the monetary authority should purchase securities in the open market in order to relieve the domestic deflationary pressures. As discussed above, the

use of changes in the discount rate for such purposes would merely encourage discounting and reduce the effectiveness of open-market operations as a monetary tool.

Thus, whereas with fixed exchange rates the central bank should
use changes in the discount rate (while, if necessary, reducing short-
term capital mobility) to control short-run monetary conditions, with
flexible exchange rates the central bank should rely on open-market
operations, encourage short-term capital mobility, and discourage
commercial-bank activities at the discount window (perhaps keeping
the window open for emergency liquidity needs).

The Canadian experience with fixed and flexible exchange rates
has been interesting in light of this discussion. The Bank of Canada
used the discount window differently in the fixed- as opposed to the
flexible-rate period. The bank has not approached discounting as it
is assumed to exist in our analysis. It has traditionally not offered a
completely open discount window and has used the discount rate essentially as a penalty rate, discouraging excessive use of the discounting
privilege. During the flexible-exchange-rate regime from 1954 until
1962 it pursued an unusual discount-rate policy. The discount rate
was pegged at one-quarter of one percentage point above the average
rate of tender for 90-day Treasury bills in an effort to restrict further
the openness of the discount window. This flexible bank rate completely
eliminated the bank's power to use the discount rate as a tool of monetary policy or as a signal to the markets—a signal that presumably
could have been misleading. [4] In 1962, when the exchange rate was
fixed as a result of the crisis in the foreign exchange markets, the
Bank of Canada also decided to release the discount rate from its ties
to the Treasury-bill rate, so as to once again be able to use discretionary changes in the bank rate as a monetary tool and as a signal to
the market. This policy—one that could be considered more normal—
has continued up to the present time.

Our analysis concluded that open-market operations have a comparative advantage during a flexible regime (and that access to the
discount window should therefore be restricted), and that discretionary changes in the discount rate have a potentially greater impact than
open-market operations with a fixed exchange rate. The Bank of Canada therefore would be acting to maximize the impact of short-run
domestic monetary policies by restricting the use of discounting with
flexible exchange rates and reopening the window with a fixed rate,
which is precisely what it did in May 1962.

CONCLUSIONS

In analyzing the effectiveness of changes in the discount rate
versus open-market operations in controlling short-run monetary con-

ditions under alternative exchange-rate regimes, we have viewed the
effects of changes of exogenous variables upon monetary equilibrium
within a comparative statics framework. In regard to the assignment
problem we conclude that domestic monetary policies (either open-
market operations or discount-rate changes) have a much greater impact upon domestic liquidity conditions with flexible rather than with
fixed exchange rates. With flexible exchange rates, short-term capital flows generated by domestic monetary policies do not reduce the
effectiveness of the policies through interference by exchange authorities into the foreign exchange markets but in fact reinforce the policies
through their effect upon the exchange rate and therefore the trade
balance. Since capital flows reinforce domestic monetary policies, the
monetary authority will always prefer that commercial banks respond
to, say, tightening monetary policy by borrowing through the foreign
exchanges, as opposed to fulfilling their liquidity needs at the discount
window and thereby reducing the effects of the tight monetary policies.
Therefore, to maximize its power over domestic monetary conditions,
the monetary authority should encourage international capital flows and
discourage activity at the discount window during a flexible-exchange-
rate regime. It therefore should use open-market purchases as its
principal monetary tool and discourage the use of the discount mechanism.

On the other hand, with fixed exchange rates, the international
mobility of capital reduces the power of either monetary instrument
over domestic liquidity. Assuming the central bank to be indifferent
about the composition of its assets (as between domestic and foreign
assets), it will have greater control over domestic monetary conditions
by using discretionary changes in the discount rate. There are two
reasons for this. First of all, the power of open-market operations
can be reduced through either induced international capital flows or
activity at the discount window. To regain power over domestic conditions the central monetary authority who uses open-market operations must restrict the uses of both sources of credit; he finds that
the more interest elastic capital flows or discounting are, the less
his powers. If the central bank uses changes in the discount rate as
its principal tool, it finds that its powers are greater, the more interest elastic discounting is, whereas they are less, the more interest elastic capital flows are. It therefore only needs to restrict short-
term capital flows to regain some power over domestic liquidity conditions. In addition, changes in the discount rate may be used to signal
the market directly about changes in policy. In the case where this
can generate confidence in the monetary authority, exchange-rate expectations can act to reduce (or even reverse) capital flows that might
have weakened the impact of the monetary policy. Open-market operations can at best provide indirect signals to the market in this way.

In a world of fixed exchange rates, monetary authorities found it increasingly difficult to successfully pursue independent monetary policies. These attempts to achieve monetary autonomy were incompatible with fixed rates and eventually contributed to the instability and collapse of the adjustable-peg system. The recent experience with exchange-rate flexibility can give those central bankers desiring autonomy (especially those attempting to insulate their domestic economies from worldwide inflation) a greater sense of control over domestic monetary conditions. Other central bankers may prefer to return to a fixed exchange rate, at least with their principal trading partners. In either case, our analysis can serve as a preliminary answer to the question of which available policy tools give them the most power over domestic monetary conditions.

NOTES

1. H. G. Johnson, "The Monetary Approach to Balance of Payments Theory," Journal of Quantitative and Financial Analysis, March 1972.

2. See, for example, Joseph Ascheim, Techniques of Monetary Control (Baltimore, Md.: The Johns Hopkins University Press, 1961); Milton Friedman, A Program for Monetary Stability (New York: Fordham University Press, 1959); Alan R. Holms, "Operational Constraints on the Stabilization of Money Supply Growth," in Controlling Monetary Aggregates (Boston: Federal Reserve Bank of Boston, 1969), pp. 63-77; M. E. Polakoff, "Federal Reserve Discount Policy and Its Critics," in Banking and Monetary Studies, edited by Diane Carson (Homewood, Ill.: Irwin, 1963); Warren L. Smith, "The Instruments of General Monetary Control," The National Banking Review 1 (September 1963): 47-76; J. Tobin, "A General Equilibrium Approach to Monetary Theory," Journal of Money, Credit, and Banking, vol. 1, no. 1 (February 1969).

3. John R. Hicks, "Automatists, Hawtreyans, and Keynesians," Journal of Money, Credit, and Banking 1, no. 3 (August 1969): 307-18.

4. J. W. O'Brien and G. Lermer, Canadian Money and Banking (Toronto: McGraw-Hill, 1969), pp. 120-21.

CHAPTER

19

A RECONCILIATION
OF ARGUMENTS FOR
AND AGAINST LARGE
MONETARY BLOCS
Leland B. Yeager

My ideal is a single worldwide money, stable in purchasing power and compatible with full employment. Perhaps private enterprise, perhaps a world authority, could furnish such a monetary system; I do not know how to devise one, however, so my wish for one is empty. Many national monetary systems will exist for the foreseeable future. The question remains of how extensively they should be consolidated into fewer systems (or, conceivably, be fragmented into a larger number). Theorizing about how to redraw currency boundaries might seem irrelevant to live issues, yet the discussion provides a way of organizing important theoretical points concerning the functions of money and prices. It is relevant to the choice of monetary and exchange-rate policies within common markets, to a country's choice of a fixed or floating rate, and to international monetary reform.

This chapter reviews the arguments for monetary consolidation and monetary fragmentation and seeks to clear up apparent contradictions among them. In tackling this job of reconciliation, we must distinguish among several distinct questions on which apparently contradictory arguments may bear. We must also distinguish between how certain economic characteristics of territories are related logically and how those characteristics are related empirically.

ARGUMENTS FOR AND AGAINST LARGE
CURRENCY AREAS

A currency area is the domain of a single currency or of two or more currencies linked together closely enough to be equivalent to a single currency. The links involve fixed exchange rates, unrestricted convertibility, and unified or tightly coordinated monetary management. This definition of currency area is unavoidably a bit fuzzy, since policy coordination may be more or less complete and, like exchange-rate fixity, may sooner or later break down. The term "currency union" or "monetary union," incidentally, implies the merger of formerly separate currency areas into a larger area, of which they become mere "regions." Territory is a neutral term here, implying nothing about monetary arrangements.

The literature of "optimum-currency areas"[1] weighs the arguments for having only a few large currency areas—at the extreme, a single currency for the entire world—against the arguments for a great many independent currencies each circulating in a small area. What weights are deserved by arguments pulling toward opposite conclusions depends on the economic characteristics of the currency areas supposed to exist initially, of the currency unions that might be formed, and of the smaller areas into which existing areas might conceivably be split. The relevant characteristics (defined below) include degree of wage and price flexibility, size, openness or closedness, homogeneity or diversity, factor mobility, and political circumstances.

The general economic principle of diminishing marginal returns and increasing marginal costs yields an enlightening presumption: The further we have already moved toward either extreme of monetary unification or monetary fragmentation, the slighter are the incremental advantages and the greater the incremental disadvantages of moving still further in the same direction. The optimum lies between the two extremes. Just where to draw currency boundaries depends, furthermore, on the characteristics of the territories contemplated.

We will first review the arguments for extreme monetary unification and those for extreme fragmentation and the rebuttals to each case; then we will examine the territorial characteristics governing the amount of weight each of the arguments and counterarguments deserves.

Arguments for Extreme Unification

As a medium of exchange money saves the costs of barter transactions. The larger the area in which a single currency circulates, the more fully it performs this function—for example, it saves the costs of otherwise necessary foreign-exchange transactions. A single currency also economizes on the expense of printing and coining many separate currencies and administering many central banks. At the opposite extreme, with each person having his own currency, money loses its very meaning as purchasing power routinely acceptable by most of the other economic units to which the holder might wish to make payments.

As a unit of account, money economizes on acquiring and using knowledge. It simplifies keeping aware of the exchange ratios among various goods and services. It simplifies accounting. It facilitates quantifying and comparing the costs and benefits of contemplated activities, such as producing incremental amounts of particular goods and services. It facilitates economic calculation. Quoting prices in money facilitates comparing the terms offered by rival sellers and rival buyers and so presumably enhances competition. Having to keep track of a great multiplicity of currencies, of prices quoted in them, and of changing exchange rates would undermine money's performance of its unit-of-account function.

A medium of exchange must to some extent be a store of value. Holding money or claims fixed in money can serve as a hedge against fluctuations in the relative values of other goods and services. As explained elsewhere, money would perform this function poorly in a very small currency area whose external exchange rate dominated local wages and prices. But once a currency's domain is of a certain size, a still larger domain would improve its store-of-value function relatively little. Furthermore, linkage to political units more likely than one's own to pursue inflationary policies would undermine the store-of-value function.

A multiplicity of currencies would complicate money's function as a standard of deferred payments. Perhaps more important than the stability or instability of the exchange rate between a debtor's and a creditor's currency, however, is the stability or instability of the purchasing power of whichever currency the loan is denominated in.

In the ways mentioned, money, as compared with barter, facilitates the functioning of markets and the balancing of supply and demand Increased monetary unification improves the unity of markets and the integration of the economic system and so facilitates reaping the gains of trade and specialization—except as it impairs the effective flexibility of wages and prices, a point considered under the next heading. The additional net benefits of these kinds presumably become smaller as complete monetary unification is more and more closely approached

Arguments for Many Small Currency Areas

Exchange-rate flexibility can provide what we may call "quasi-flexibility" of prices and wages. For familiar reasons (not all of which hinge on money illusion), prices and wages quoted in a country's home currency are unlikely to be flexible enough to keep all markets continuously cleared as supply and demand schedules reflect changes in wants, resources, and technology. A large currency area, accordingly, might well suffer the problems of depressed regions and of hav-

ing to balance interregional payments in the unpleasant way described
by the theory of the income mechanism. (An area-wide monetary
policy expansionary enough to inflate away all localized unemployment
would entail price inflation and probably could not accomplish its purpose over the long run anyway.) Suppose, however, that countries
refrained from forming a currency union and, instead, allowed the
exchange rates among their separate currencies to float. The prices
of each country's labor, other productive resources, and products
would be flexible, after all, as translated at flexible rates into the
currencies of other countries. If, for example, demand for a country's
export products should fall off, exchange depreciation would partly
absorb the impact by lowering their prices in foreign currency and
so helping to sustain foreign purchases. Depreciation would also benefit the country's import-competing industries and ease some transfer
of resources out of the damaged export industries.

    An initial drop in foreign demand for the country's products and
so in the derived demand for its factors of production could conceivably
have either of two extreme impacts: unemployment, with wages and
other factor prices rigid, or factor price cuts sufficient to maintain
purchases and avoid unemployment. Rendering local labor and other
factors price-flexible in terms of foreign currencies and internationally
traded goods enables the impact of the drop in demand to approach the
latter extreme form more closely than it otherwise would. A fluctuating currency permits productive factors to absorb the impact of reduced
demand more fully in the form of worsened terms of trade and less in
the form of unemployment.

    Quasi-flexibility through exchange rates would have the further
though minor advantage of promoting price competition.[2] The producer
of each particular product would find that the prices quoted by outside
competitors, as translated at fluctuating rates, were undergoing continual (though usually slight) changes relative to his own price. It
would be difficult to maintain a rigid price not only in terms of all currencies but perhaps even in terms of the local currency. The more
nearly standardized a product, the less feasible quasi-oligopolistic
price inflexibility would be. Continual slight fluctuations in the prices
of rival producers, as translated at flexible rates, would pose some
slight obstacle to collusion or a live-and-let-live policy of rigid prices.
Even "pattern" wage bargaining could be impeded somewhat.

    Let us not overstate the case. Exchange-rate flexibility is,
after all, only a crude and unselective substitute for flexibility of
each individual wage and price. (That is why we speak of quasi-flexibility.) The more individually flexible wages and prices were, the
less a free exchange rate would have to move when world-market conditions for some particular product changed. This is no reason for
rejecting quasi-flexibility, however, when detailed flexibility is defi-

WORLD MONETARY DISORDER

cient. The two types of flexibility are by no means rivals: Fixed exchange rates do not necessarily promote, and flexible rates do not necessarily impair detailed flexibility.

Quasi-flexibility through exchange rates would help prices and wages perform their functions of conveying information and incentives, facilitating decentralized decision making, balanceing supply and demand on individual markets, balancing the aggregates of transactions that appear in a country's or a region's balance of payments, linking individual markets together, coordinating different sectors of the economy, and facilitating economic calculation. In short, flexibility improves the functioning of the price system. Money itself could thus perform its functions better by <u>not</u> being everywhere the same. If prices and wages are sticky, while too wide a currency area rules out quasi-flexibility, prices and money fail to perform their functions well. A price that, because of changed conditions, no longer clears its market is conveying misinformation and wrong incentives and causing wider disruptions.[3] It is a mistake to suppose that monetary unification necessarily promotes economic integration in the ways that count for human welfare.[4]

Separate currencies tend to compartmentalize macroeconomic disturbances and policy blunders, lessening the contagion of inflation and depression. (Compare the advantage of having several watertight compartments in the hold of a ship.) Separate currencies make it easier for a country's authorities to pursue domestic stability (or the best compromise between unemployment and inflation, if such a tradeoff really exists), despite instability in the outside world. On the other hand, one could argue that monetary linkage to the outside world at a fixed exchange rate tends to dilute an individual country's disturbances and blunders, giving time for their correction before they have irreversible consequences, such as, in particular, price and wage inflation. (This argument for linkage ties in with the familiar argument that fixed exchange rates impose a healthy "discipline" on monetary-fiscal and wage-price policies.)

Reply to the Arguments for Unification

The benefits of unification are derived at the sacrifice of the advantages of quasi-flexibility and compartmentalization. Little can be saved from the expense and nuisance of foreign-exchange transactions, anyway, if countries retain their own currencies, even though exchange rates among them are fixed. Currencies tightly tied together are not fully equivalent to a single currency. The necessary coordination among the operations of national central banks or monetary authorities also has costs and may involve difficult negotiations. As for the political unification necessary for genuine financial and monetary unification, an extreme degree of it would probably not be desirable for reasons of political philosophy, even if it were realistically attainable.

Reply to the Arguments for Fragmentation

The quasi-flexibility offered by fragmentation is only a crude substitute for flexibility in each individual price wage. (On the other hand, a crude substitute may be better than nothing when the genuine article is unavailable.)

Beyond some admittedly indefinable point, multiplying independent currencies and shrinking the domain of each would begin to negate the very concept of money. Already-mentioned expenses and nuisances count against fragmentation. Having a great many independent currencies would leave each one with a thin market on the foreign exchanges, lacking "breadth, depth, and resiliency." Individual transactions might be large enough relative to total supply or demand to cause sharp random exchange-rate fluctuations. Speculation would be inadequately stabilizing, and groups of speculators might even be able to dominate the market for individual currencies and manipulate rates to their own advantage.

TERRITORIAL CHARACTERISTICS AND THE
WEIGHTS OF THE ARGUMENTS

What weights the foregoing arguments and replies deserve depends on the characteristics of the territories considered.

The more flexible wages and prices are in local currency, the less the advantage of quasi-flexibility through exchange rates. The degree of flexibility depends on the prevalence monopolies, cartels, labor unions, and long-term contracts, on the characteristics of products and production processes, on the organization of markets, on the nature of taxation and government regulation, and on innumerable other technological and institutional factors. Flexibility does not mean that prices and wages oscillate wildly. It means, rather, that they are free from impediments to the changes necessary to keep markets cleared. Though flexible, prices would be stable when their fundamental determinants remained unchanged. Flexible prices and wages would keep balances of payments equilibrated in the face of underlying disturbances, even under fixed exchange rates, without large fluctuations in output and employment.

Extreme flexibility is not unequivocally desirable. Inertia or friction has some merit in economic as well as mechanical affairs.

Excessively frequent price changes, including small and reversible ones, would raise the costs of acquiring and using knowledge. Would-be sellers and buyers who experience frustration in finding trading partners can rationally keep the prices they are asking and offering unchanged for a time while canvasing the market to see whether change market conditions really do call for price changes. It may well be beneficial if exchange-rate fluctuations reduce the need for fluctuations in individual prices and wages, particularly in view of the greater sim-plicity, described by the chair-and-piano analogy, of changing one price rather than a great many.

Still, a high degree of price and wage flexibility in the territorie considered does add weight to the arguments for monetary unification and lessens the weight due the opposing arguments.

The economic size of a territory means the volume of its re-sources, population, and economic activity. If one needed a single indicator, total real GNP would be a plausible candidate. The smaller a currency area, the less fully money performs its standard functions (except as independent currencies are needed for quasi-flexibility). Smallness makes for a thin foreign-exchange market. These consid-erations lend weight to the reasons why small territories should form a monetary union. Others may, of course, pull the other way. A small territory is by that token likely to be a "drop in the bucket" on world markets and therefore to face highly elastic demands for its exports and supplies of its imports. High elasticities contribute to the exchange-market stability and therefore to the viability of an indepen-dently fluctuating currency. [5]

The Degree of Openness

A territory's openness is its degree of involvement in transac-tions with the rest of the world relative to internal transactions. In-dicators would be such figures as the share of total output of goods and services exported, share of imports in total domestic absorption of goods and services, and ratio of imports plus exports to GNP. Other considerations being equal, great openness lends weight to sev-eral arguments against monetary independence and for monetary union among regions highly open to each other. The more open a territory, the more (though perhaps not very) significant the nuisance and ex-pense of the correspondingly many foreign-exchange transactions, and the greater the danger, furthermore, that exchange-rate fluctuations might dominate the internal price and wage levels, impairing the quasi-flexibility of prices and wages otherwise to be expected from an inde-pendent currency. Practically by the definition of an extremely open territory, the cost of living in it is composed largely of the prices of

imported and readily exportable goods; other things (such as local
services and the local labor component of shelter and of goods sold at
retail) account for only a small part of the cost of living. People
would be highly aware of the exchange rate and alert to adjust local-
currency prices in line with it. Labor contracts gearing wages to the
cost of living would in effect gear wages to the exchange rate. Currency depreciation would then be ineffective as a way of reducing real
wages in response to some adverse development in economic fundamen-
tals. (More generally, economic policy faces a dilemma when powerful interests resist adjustment of their selling prices to adverse sup-
ply-and-demand changes.) In a highly open economy people would be
effectively inclined to use outside currency not only as a unit of account, as just suggested, but also as a liquid reserve of purchasing
power, undermining the viability of the local currency. All these
difficulties are compounded if the open economy is also small, as it
is empirically likely to be.

The foregoing argument tacitly takes it for granted, however,
that the flexible exchange rate of an open currency area would be highly
unstable; for otherwise, it is unlikely that people would be pathologi-
cally alert to fluctuations. But why should the exchange rate be so
unstable, given stability of the local money supply and reasonable stability in the outside world? The argument tacitly envisages disturbances of a micro nature—changes in "wants, resources, or technology." Suppose, however, that the disturbances are macro—general
price-and-income inflation or deflation. Suppose, further, that these
macro disturbances originate abroad. Appropriate exchange-rate
changes would then tend to insulate the home economy from foreign
instability, preserve the liquidity value of the home currency, and reduce risk in foreign trade. Openness, furthermore, tends to increase
the proportion of disturbances to internal and external balance that
originate abroad (or in the territory's foreign-trade sector) rather
than at home. (A completely closed economy would fell no disturbances
from outside.) Price policy, which includes exchange-rate variation,
is more appropriate than expenditure policy for coping with outside
disturbances.* While a flexible exchange rate would be useful for
warding off the external disturbances characteristic of an open economy, the smallness likely to be associated with openness does pose
difficulties for the working of a flexible rate. The clash between these
considerations is a feature of hard reality, not a sign of logical flaw
in the analysis.

*Compare my International Monetary Relations, pp. 90-96, Cor-
den, Monetary Integration, pp. 18-19, and Herbert Giersch in Burgenstock Papers, p. 149.

   Another suggested reason why a highly open territory should
shun monetary independence is that expenditure policy can serve the
requirements of balance-of-payments equilibrium rather well. (Basically, it would be a policy of keeping in step with other regions of
the monetary union.) Since a large part of total expenditure goes
for imports and exportable goods, expenditure restraint corrects a
payments deficit with relatively little deflation of internal output and
employment. A substantially closed economy, by contrast, would
have to endure widespread domestic deflation to obtain the desired deflation of expenditure on imports and exportables; the foreign-trade
tail would be wagging the domestic dog. A closed economy needs the
monetary independence allowed by a flexible exchange rate.

   A rather abstract and unimportant reason for monetary union
to avoid openness concerns elasticities. In a very open economy,
competing domestic production and consumption are slight, relative
to imports and exports, respectively. These circumstances hold down
the degree to which the elasticity of demand for imports in particular
exceeds the elasticity of total demand for import-type goods and to
which the elasticity of supply of exports in particular exceeds the elasticity of total supply of export-type goods. In holding down the import-
demand and export-supply elasticities, openness tends to detract from
the exchange-market stability of an independent currency. Smallness,
on the other hand, as we have seen, tends to raise the other two of the
four key elasticities. Since a small economy tends to be open and a
large economy to be relatively closed, we might seem to have run into
a contradiction regarding whether smallness-and-openness contributes
to or detracts from the elasticity conditions conducive to a stable foreign-exchange market. The contradiction is not genuine, however,
for smallness and openness are logically distinct though empirically
associated concepts. Smallness contributes to the elasticity conditions
for a stable foreign-exchange market, and what pulls the other way is
not smallness as such but the openness likely to be associated with it.

   This distinction between logical and empirical association is
easier to understand in connection with the possibility of an awkwardly
thin foreign-exchange market: Smallness pulls that way, while openness pulls for "breadth, depth, and resiliency." For a monetary area
of a given degree of openness, smallness makes for a thin market,
but for a monetary area of a given size openness makes for breadth.

   Financial openness may be distinguished from openness to trade
in goods and services. Indicators of its degree might be ratios of debt
to and claims on outsiders to debts to and claims on fellow residents
and ratios of flows of loan and investment transactions with outsiders
to such transactions with fellow residents.

   One might distinguish between the actual openness of a territory
and the potential openness that a monetary union would bring into ef-

fect. One might also conjecture that the distinction is more relevant
for financial than for commercial openness, on the grounds that monetary fragmentation impedes financial transactions more seriously than
it impedes trade. In either case, if the impediment is serious, that
fact strengthens the case for monetary unification. On the other hand,
if underlying characteristics are such that there both actually is and
still would be relatively little financial intercourse (as well as little
goods-and-services trade) among the regions, the convenience and freedom from exchange risk provided by monetary unification would be
correspondingly unimportant.

The last point bears on the question of what monetary arrangements are desirable in view of the degree of financial openness or integration promoted by conditions more basic than policy. A different
question concerns whether a high or low degree of financial openness
or integration would be more conducive to the smooth working of a
specified monetary arrangement. The conjecture seems plausible
that great financial openness is more conducive to the smooth working
of either extreme monetary independence or extreme monetary unification than to some intermediate monetary arrangement. At the one
extreme, a large volume of actual and potential capital movements, free
of controls, would link the foreign-exchange market and the money and
capital markets in different territories together, lending "breadth,
depth, and resiliency" to each, lessening the likelihood that random
imbalances of supply and demand arising from commercial transactions would cause sharp exchange-rate fluctuations, and facilitating
stabilizing speculation. At the other extreme of monetary unification,
highly interest-sensitive capital movements would readily finance interregional balance-of-payments imbalances while the corrective processes characteristic of unification were at work. These corrective
processes would themselves be enhanced by ready marketability of
important categories of financial assets throughout all regions of the
currency union. Changes in the ratios of assets to income and of in-
terregionally marketable to local assets in portfolios would motivate
persons and firms to make readjustments tending to restore interregional equilibirum on current account. This asset-transfer adjustment
process would work better if investors were wealthy enough to hold
large portfolios relative to income, and if wealth, tastes, economic
organization, and the like were similar throughout the monetary union.
Under such circumstances, tight monetary unification would itself
lessen the danger that unification would break down.

That danger is relatively great, however, under the intermediate
arrangement of distinct currencies pegged together at "irrevocably"
fixed exchange rates. Capital movements become highly sensitive to
interest and profit incentives. But as long as the member regions of
the union have separate currency reserves with which to carry out the

exchange-rate pegging and have the potential for balance-of-payments problems, one currency will occasionally come to be regarded as stronger or weaker than the others, and one-way-option speculation may become massive as "everybody begins to expect the irrevocable to be revoked."[6]

Homogeneity and Diversity

Homogeneity and diversity are opposites. A territory is homogeneous if its component parts are similar in their resource endowments and economic activities. In some contexts it might be useful to distinguish between potential and actual diversity. Two territories possessing similar patterns of economic activity might become diverse if an economic union between them fostered regional specialization that their separate economic policies had previously inhibited. It seems empirically likely, however, that the dismantling of trade barriers would contribute more toward specialization and diversity than would the abolition of regional monetary independence.

All other considerations being equal, a currency area should be homogeneous in its resources and economic activities so that quasi-flexibility of wages and prices through the exchange rate is effective rather than crude. Other considerations being equal, a diverse area should be split into internally homogeneous monetary areas. An independent currency would be helpful for a "depressed area" suffering from demand or production conditions not typical of the country as a whole. (On the other hand, a central government sophisticated in using a wide range of policy tools would make regional monetary independence less important than otherwise.) The fact that a given area is homogeneous is no argument against its joining with other areas economically the same as itself, so that their union would still be homogeneous.

Empirically, of course, large size and diversity (and closedness) tend to go together, as do small size and homogeneity (and openness). This fact poses perhaps the most prominent tradeoff discussed in the optimum-currency-area literature: Large size is desirable for the functions-of-money, transactions-economy, and broad-exchange-market reasons already explained; small size is desirable, not for its own sake, but for the greater homogeneity likely to prevail in a small area.

Peter B. Kenen has argued that diversity is desirable in a currency area.[7] More precisely, he seems to have meant that diversity is desirable for a region somehow inexorably fated to belong to a larger currency union. With an independent currency ruled out of consideration, the homogeneity that would argue for independence loses

most of its attractiveness. Diversity, on the other hand, provides insurance against big terms-of-trade or balance-of-payments changes.
Because of the law of large numbers, the independent microeconomic
disturbances influencing each sector of a diversified economy will
tend to have mutually canceling effects on the territory's aggregate
trade balance at a fixed exchange rate and on its terms of trade.
Diversity increases the probability that an adverse shift of demand or
a poor harvest affecting one industry or locality is offset in another,
thus avoiding the balance-of-payments imbalance that would have occurred if the industries and localities had belonged to different countries. Extreme benefits of diversification of this kind accrue to the
world as a whole, which can never have any balance-of-payments
deficits.[8] A single-product economy, by contrast, has all of its eggs
in one basket, so that its trade balance would be subject to wide variations at a fixed exchange rate and so that a flexible exchange rate, as
well as the terms of trade, would be subject to wide fluctuations.

Kenen further argues that when a diversified economy does face
a drop in demand for its exports, unemployment will rise less than
in a specialized economy. Variations in investment at home will be
slighter and will magnify the employment impact of export variations
to a lesser degree. Diversification presumably spells opportunities
to replace lost foreign trade with expanded domestic trade. It not
only diminishes the likelihood of major external shocks but also mitigates the damage caused by such shocks and eases the burden to be
borne by internal policies.

It should be noted that the foregoing arguments refer to external
shocks (or to internal production shocks, such as those that bad weather
might cause) of a _microeconomic_ nature; the shocks considered are
essentially independent of each other rather than pervasive along a
broad front. Kenen does not intend his arguments to give reassurance
about the workability of a fixed exchange rate in the face of serious
business-cycle fluctuations or irresponsible monetary policies in the
outside world.

In stressing the advantages of diversity, Kenen seems to be
contradicting Mundell, who described the advantages of internally
homogeneous monetary areas.[9] The contradiction is merely apparent, however, for the two writers are asking different questions.
Mundell is taking the characteristics of territories as given and is
asking how to draw boundaries. He is not ruling out the possibility
of achieving internally homogeneous monetary areas. Kenen, by contrast, is doing one or both of the following: (a) contemplating a territory yoked with others in a monetary union and asking whether homogeneity or diversity within the region would be better for the working
of this assumedly irrevocable arrangement; (b) contemplating a diverse territory, assumed unsplittable, and asking whether its diversity

recommends its joining a still wider currency union. His answer to
a, as we have seen, finds diversity desirable. His answer to b is in
effect as follows: Since both the prospective member and the contemplated wider union would in any case each be diverse within itself,
and since forming the union could therefore not cost the loss of a non-
existent homogeneity, the standard arguments for a currency area's
being both large and closed would argue for the union. These arguments are buttressed by the reasons already noted for the benefits of
internal diversity for a region within a union. Mundell says that the
first step toward yoking mutually diverse territories together is very
disadvantageous, other considerations being the same. Kenen, in
answering question b, assumes that this first step has already been
irrevocably taken and notes that the incremental disadvantages of
further unification are relatively slight, perhaps slight enough to be
outweighed by the advantages of greater size and closedness. *

Factor Mobility

Mobility of factors concerns how readily labor, capital, and
business enterprise can shift among localities and occupations. Obstacles to mobility might be termed either "sociological" or "occupational." Examples of the former would be people's slavishness to
tradition and lack of adaptability, strong family and other local ties,
language barriers, nonportability of pensions and social-insurance
benefits, labor-union restrictions, and the like. Occupational barriers would be differences between lines of production in the mixes
and qualifications of the factors they employ such that factors displaced from one economic sector have little usefulness in another.
Poor factor mobility enhances the importance of wage and price
flexibility so that adjustment to adverse changes in "wants, resources,
and technology" can occur through wage and price decreases rather
than through unemployment. Poor mobility of factors between areas
argues against sacrificing quasi-flexibility by yoking those areas together in a monetary union. Conversely, the more readily factors
can move between occupations and between localities specialized in
particular occupations, the more easily can an area adjust to changed
conditions, including changes in outside supplies and demands, by
changes in its pattern of production and resource allocation. [10] Its
authorities are less embarrassed than they would be in the case of

---

*This paragraph is not guaranteed as a faithful account of what
Mundell and Kenen actually said. Instead, it suggests an interpretation that reconciles their positions.

immobility by the question of whether to try to inflate away pockets of unemployment at the cost of areawide price inflation.

In this respect, mobility and homogeneity are substitutes; either condition reduces the weight of arguments for carving an area up into monetarily independent parts. Unfortunately, the two conditions and their opposites tend to be associated. In particular, great similarity among a territory's economic activities and in the characteristics required of the factors they employ promotes mobility. While actual homogeneity of occupations would promote mobility, it would also make mobility pointless, since factors displaced from some jobs would find their other potential employers facing the same drop in demand for their output. If the automobile industry falls into depression, what good does it do if labor is highly mobile among automobile firms? Mobility due to homogeneity would be empty and would not reduce the need for price and wage flexibility or quasi-flexibility. The kind of mobility that would reduce this need is perhaps empirically rather unlikely: mobility compatible with diversity of occupations.

The Discipline Argument

A country's degree of policy prudence—its likelihood of avoiding deflationary or inflationary blunders—is a consideration in deciding whether to join prospective partners in a monetary union. If it were less prudent, it would find some advantage in the "discipline" of being yoked to more prudent partners. This "discipline" argument seems most relevant for countries that have an intermediate propensity to inflate. The most inflationary governments are hardly restrained by fixed exchange rates; in fact, they cannot keep their rates fixed for long. Their currencies are pegged at disequilibrium rates most of the time; they are undervalued for awhile after each devaluation but become increasingly overvalued again as inflation proceeds and makes another devaluation necessary. Wrongly pegged rates simply disrupt business without exerting effective discipline. At the other extreme stand the most prudent countries. Their resistance to inflation gains nothing from monetary linkage to foreigners. On the contrary, impulses of imported inflation may sometimes inconvenience them. [11] In between stand the countries whose inflations are not fast enough to require frequent devaluations. Their pegged exchange rates do not become quickly and seriously wrong again after each (infrequent) adjustment. Such countries can benefit from external restraint on inflation. Unfortunately, their benefit is probably matched by the weakening of restraint that their partners experience from being linked to them.

Political Unification

Prospects for political unification form one of the most decisive
and obvious considerations in weighing the arguments for monetary
fragmentation and monetary unification against each other. Monetary
union or the firm fixing of exchange rates requires a high degree of
coordination of money-supply policies, which would hardly be possible
unless member countries sacrificed their fiscal and budgetary independence to a considerable degree. Fiscal and monetary policies
best go hand in hand and, for an "optimum policy mix," should have
the same domains. It might be a bit awkward, partly for political
reasons, if the domain of fiscal policy spanned the domains of several
independent currencies. Kenen notes that "a major difference between
the currency composition of government receipts and the currency
composition of government spending would force the treasury into the
exchange market where, willfully or otherwise, it might well become
the single speculator capable of altering regional exchange rates."[12]
The opposite noncoincidence of monetary and fiscal domains would
pose a more serious difficulty; what a regional government could do
with fiscal policy for macroeconomic purposes would be constrained
by its inability to pursue a monetary policy of its own.* Not only
monetary, fiscal, and budgetary policies but also policies toward trade
union aggressiveness and toward the choice of tradeoff between unemployment and inflation would have to be coordinated. And such extensive policy coordination would require a corresponding degree of political unification. Possibilities of it depend on geographical contiguity
(a minor matter in these days of rapid communication and transportation), ethnic factors, national traditions, and the like. If political
unification is not feasible or desirable, the prospective partners might
as well forget about tight monetary unification also.
        Reasons of political philosophy tell against a centralized world
government (with powers extending beyond those necessary to prevent
armed aggression) and against a world of a few Leviathans only. It
is probably realistic, moreover, to take as given the existing nation-
states and the general degree of independence that each desires. The
live issue is not how to carve the world from scratch into currency
areas but whether each country should have an independent currency

---

*Among minor reasons for the relative feasibility of currency
area's coinciding with a fiscal area is the fact that the fiscal system
helps accomplish palliative transfers of income or wealth from regions
with surpluses to those with deficits in their balances of payments.
Also relevant are other reasons for the particularly easy adjustment
of balance of payments among regions of a well-unified country.

and flexible exchange rate or join with other countries in some sort of monetary union.

RESOLVING APPARENT CONTRADICTIONS

Before summarizing, I will discuss three sources of apparent contradiction between different strands of the currency-area literature. One is the blurring of distinctions between certain economic characteristics of a territory because of our empirical knowledge that certain of them tend to go together while others tend not to. For example, it is desirable that a currency area be both large and homogeneous, yet it is empirically unlikely that an area would in fact be both. Closedness and homogeneity would argue for an area's having an independent currency with a fluctuating exchange rate against the rest of the world, yet homogeneity is likely to go with an area's being open, not closed, to trade. And closedness, while arguing against the fixed-exchange-rate, payments-adjustment mechanism, also argues (for an area of a given size) against the fluctuating rate because of the corresponding thinness of the exchange market.

A second and closely related source of apparent contradiction results from the fact that a particular economic characteristic, or it together with another empirically associated with it, may favor monetary unification in some respects and fragmentation in other respects. Diversity, as we have seen, provides an example. Smallness tends to favor the smooth working of a territory's foreign-exchange market by promoting high elasticities of demand for its exports and supply of its imports in the outside world. On the other hand, smallness makes for a thin market, and the openness associated with smallness detracts from the elasticities of the territory's demand for imports and supply of exports.

Both of these observations remind us of the banal point that not all considerations bearing on a policy choice always pull in the same direction; decisions in the real world can be tough.

A third source of apparent contradiction—as between Mundell and Kenen in regard to diversity—is the ambiguity about just what the question is, to which stated conclusion comes as an answer. Consider the following questions:

1. What economic characteristics of its own territory make a country a good or a poor candidate for joining with others in a monetary union?

2. What characteristics of countries in relation to each other make them good or poor prospects for forming a union? In other words, what are the characteristics of a union (if formed) that would

246   WORLD MONETARY DISORDER

argue for or against its being formed?

3. Given that a territory is monetarily unified within itself and
has a fluctuating exchange rate against outside currencies, what characteristics of the territory and its component regions would most facilitate the smooth functioning of these arrangements?

4. If currency boundaries were to be redrawn from scratch,
how should they be drawn?*

                              SUMMARY AND CONCLUSION

     What characteristics would lend weight to the arguments for
monetary union? It is impossible to answer both briefly and precisely,
since, as we have seen, some characteristics cut one way in some
respects and the other way in others. On the whole, though, we can
say that the following characteristics of the individual country would
count in favor of its joining a union: flexible prices and wages, smallness, openness, diversity, factor mobility, policy imprudence, and
willingness to sacrifice political sovereignty. The opposite characteristics would argue for monetary independence. The following
characteristics of the proposed union would argue for its formation:
flexible prices, large size, openness of its members to each other
but closedness to the outside world, homogeneity, factor mobility,
policy prudence, and acceptability of a unionwide government.

     Realistically, of course, there is much to be said for treating
at least the sovereign industrial states as separate currency areas.[13]
The live question for each of them is whether to retain monetary independence or to join with others in fixing exchange rates or adopting
a common currency.

     Monetary independence and floating exchange rates afford scope
for diverse experiments in trying to reconcile full employment with
money of stable purchasing power. Countries blessed with better
tradeoffs between unemployment and inflation or with more favorable
political, sociological, or ideological conditions have a better chance
to succeed independently than they would have if fixed exchange rates
transmitted to them the inflations of less prudent or less fortunate
countries.

_____

     *This question presupposes that territories have given charac-
teristics and investigates reasons for grouping some into a currency
union and for keeping other separate from each other. It leaves open
the possibility, as some other questions do not, of splitting a country
and perhaps of allotting the split parts to different currency unions.

By yoking countries together monetarily, the Bretton Woods system was a powerful international transmitter (and even a generator) of inflation. The relevant theories are hardly new. (Wilhelm Ropke, for example, was already explaining the process of imported inflation back in the mid-1950s.) Experience of the last few years has afforded massive examples of the processes that those theories describe. We should understand clearly that the Bretton Woods system did not collapse all at once in 1971. Last-ditch efforts to patch up and defend the system stretched from 1969, or perhaps even from 1967, until March 1973. During this period, speculators against the pegged exchange rates enjoyed one-way options on a mammoth scale. Speculative funds surged across boundaries and oceans, inflating the countries of destination without deflating the countries of origin. During the single year 1971, foreign monetary authorities added more dollars to their official reserves than in all of human history up to that time.

Some are inclined to blame the speeding up of worldwide inflation in 1973-74 on the floating of exchange rates from March 1973 on. This is a serious misinterpretation that threatens to keep us from salvaging even a lesson from past policy blunders; it is just another example of something drearily familiar in monetary history: Floating exchange rates, left on the scene after fixed rates have broken down, are quite routinely blamed for the economic disorders that had caused the fixed rates to break down and to which the fixed rates had themselves contributed. In truth, belated abandonment of the Bretton Woods system amounted to locking the barn door after the horse had been stolen.

As Meiselman documents in Chapter 3, the last-ditch defense of the Bretton Woods system contributed to a worldwide money-supply explosion. That explosion did not affect prices all at once. On the contrary, its effects are stretching out over time. What is happening is quite in accordance with monetarist theory, which all along has emphasized lags in the consequences of monetary changes. Once a rapid inflation is under way, furthermore, stopping it is painful, no matter what exchange-rate system currently prevails.

There is no necessary contradiction between the monetarist interpretation of recent and current U.S. inflation and the interpretation that emphasizes the devaluations of the dollar. Monetary expansion did not affect the prices of goods and services in a direct way only. It also helped cause, with a lag, a rise in the dollar price of foreign exchange (until the floating of March 1973 this was a notable example of an administered or quasi-rigid price). When that price did belatedly change, the dollar prices of U.S. imports and exports rose accordingly, and these price increases radiated further throughout the U.S. economy. It is an old familiar theory that monetary expansion works its ultimate effects with lags and through complicated interdependencies among various prices and costs. An emphasis on the role of the exchange rate in these interdependencies need not spell denial of the ultimate money-supply basis of the price inflation.

Since the topic is monetary blocs, it should be remembered that exchange rates have not been floating cleanly since March 1973. In particular, the European "snake" has been in operation. Within the "snake," Germany, the Netherlands, and Norway have revalued their currencies, and typical examples have occurred of one-way-option speculation on prospects of currency revaluation or devaluation. Experience within the "snake" underlines an old point: As long as currencies are in fact distinct, efforts to peg them together will not work well.

It is useless to seek stability of currencies in terms of each other as long as they are unstable in purchasing power—and unstable in different degrees. The issue of pegged versus floating exchange rates is subsidiary to the question of how currencies can be protected against loss of purchasing power over goods and services.

Not pegging currencies together will improve the prospects of protecting their purchasing powers. This, in fact, is a leading argument for the monetary independence of the major countries and for floating exchange rates among their currencies. Under these conditions the countries most able to avoid inflation have a chance to do so. They need not follow along in the inflations of the others. They can provide healthy examples and lessons. This argument for diversity of monetary authorities bears an obvious analogy to the political arguments for federalism as opposed to highly centralized national governments.

NOTES

1. Notable contributions include Robert A. Mundell, "A Theory of Optimum Currency Areas," American Economic Review 51 (September 1961): 657-65; Bela Balassa, The Theory of Economic Integration (Homewood, Ill.: Irwin, 1961), pp. 263-68; Ronald I. McKinnon, "Optimum Currency Areas," American Economic Review 53 (September 1963): 717-25; Ronald I. McKinnon, "Optimum World Monetary Arrangements and the Dual Currency System," Banca Nazionale del Lavoro Quarterly Review 16 (December 1963): 366-96; Delbert A. Snider, Optimum Adjustment Processes and Currency Areas, Princeton Essays in International Finance No. 62 (October 1967); Peter B. Kenen, "The Theory of Optimum Currency Areas: An Eclectic View," in Monetary Problems of the International Economy, edited by Robert Mundell and Alexander Swoboda (Chicago: University of Chicago Press, 1969), pp. 41-60; Thomas D. Willett and Edward Tower, "Currency Areas and Exchange-Rate Flexibility," Weltwirtschaftliches Archiv 105, no. 1 (1970): 48-65. Though too belatedly to take adequate ac-

count of it, I have also consulted Tower's and Willett's manuscript on "The Theory of Optimum Currency Areas and Exchange Rate Flexibility."

2. Wolfgang Kasper argues that flexible exchange rates, by facilitating changes in international prices, would tend to promote competition across borders and impede international collusion among sellers. See his article in Approaches to Greater Flexibility of Exchange Rates, edited by George N. Halm (Princeton, N.J.: Princeton University Press, 1970), p. 386n (hereafter cited as Burgenstock Papers).

3. The contagion of market imbalances is a leading theme of the disequilibrium economics inspired by the work of Clower and Leijonhufvud. See, for example, Robert W. Clower, "The Keynesian Counterrevolution: A Theoretical Appraisal," in The Theory of Interest Rates, edited by F. H. Hahn and F. P. R. Brechling (London: Macmillan, 1965), pp. 103-25; Axel Leijonhufvud, On Keynesian Economics and the Economics of Keynes (New York: Oxford University Press, 1968).

4. As Wolfgang Kasper says (Burgenstock Papers, p. 385), the view of "professional Europeans" that economic integration requires monetary unification is too much centered around an institutional, organizational, and legalistic—not to say bureaucratic—notion of what international integration means. Rather, international integration should first of all aim at the welding together of national markets, so that potential buyers have an undiscriminated choice between home-made and imported goods—with the organizational and legal superstructure to come later.

If functional integration (in the sense of larger markets with equal competitive opportunities throughout) is the prime concern, the fixity of exchange rates may, rather, be seen, in the light of past experience, as a disintegrating factor.

It is instructive to compare the views of the "monetarists" and the "economists" on the sequence of steps to be taken in the economic unification of Europe. The monetarists would fix exchange rates early, even using controls over capital movements if necessary, to prod policy makers into other aspects of unification. The economists call for economic unification first, including freedom of capital movements, with exchange rates helping take care of balance-of-payments problems until finally the rates could be permanently fixed. Compare John R. Presley and P. Coffey, "On Exchange Rate Unification—A Comment in Relation to the European Economic Community," Economic Journal 83 (December 1972): 1380-82. W. M. Corden warns that a "pseudo-exchange-rate union" may create balance-of-payments stresses leading to imposition or tightening of controls over current or capital account transaction. "[The] movement toward one aspect of monetary integration (the exchange-rate union) may well set back the movement to the other (capital market integration)." Corden, Monetary Integration, Princeton Essays in International Finance, no. 93 (April 1972), pp. 29-30.

5. Another point about elasticities, only superficially seeming to contradict this one, appears under the heading of "openness" in this chapter. Both are discussed in Willett and Tower, "Currency Areas and Exchange-Rate Flexibility," pp. 54-55. For a general treatment of the question of elasticities and market stability, see Leland B. Yeager, International Monetary Relations (New York: Harper & Row, 1966), Ch. 8.

6. Marshall Hall and Dhiru Tanna, "On Exchange-Rate Unification: A Comment," Economic Journal 82 (December 1972): 1378. Corden also argues (Monetary Integration, p. 29) that "an attempt to maintain fixed rates without absolute assurance that they can be maintained . . . is an invitation to increased destabilizing capital movements."

7. Kenen, "The Theory of Optimum Currency Areas."

8. Herbert G. Grubel, The International Monetary System (Baltimore, Md.: Penguin Books, 1970), pp. 54-55.

9. Mundell, "A Theory of Optimum Currency Areas."

10. Even so, high labor mobility is a poor substitute for wage- and price flexibility or for quasi-flexibility through the exchange rate, especially when mobility takes the form of outward migration of unemployed labor. The costs of adjustment are concentrated on the unfortunate emigrants rather than being spread more thinly and evenly through reduction of real wage rates. Compare Corden, Monetary Integration, pp. 15-16.

11. Samuel Brittan has suggested that it would make little sense to treat a country either like France, with a record of inflation and devaluation, or like Germany, with a record of more nearly stable prices and of revaluations, as an optimum currency area. See his The Price of Economic Freedom (New York: St. Martin's Press, 1970), p. 173.

12. Kenen, "The Theory of Optimum Currency Areas," pp. 45-46, 46n.

13. Brittan, The Price of Economic Freedom, p. 73.

20

SCENARIOS
FOR DISASTER
AND SURVIVAL
Leonard Silk

Never in the entire postwar period has there been such anxiety among responsible people—government officials, bankers, business executives, economists—about the dangers facing the United States and the world economy. Worldwide inflation has broken loose, with price increases ranging in 1974 from 7 percent in West Germany to more than 30 percent in Greece. In the United States the consumer price index (CPI) rose at an annual rate of 14.5 percent in the first quarter of 1974. Chairman Arthur F. Burns of the Federal Reserve Board has warned that "if long continued, inflation at anything like the present rate would threaten the very foundations of our society."[1]

A COMING CRASH?

There are fears that the inflation will end in a crash. Ashby Bladen says that, given the current rate of inflation and the enormous accumulation of debts already built up in the process of financing it, "a return to either price stability or financial stability without an intervening crash appears to me to be practically impossible. . . . And the longer the crash is postponed by continuing the inflationary process of excessive credit expansion, the worse it will be when it does come."[2]

The threat is worldwide, exacerbated by the enormous deficits being incurred by oil-importing nations as a result of the quadrupling of oil prices in the wake of the Arab-Israeli war of the fall of 1973. David Rockefeller, chairman of the Chase Manhattan Bank, has said privately that he cannot see how the existing financial system can possibly stand the strain of oil-importing nations' inability to transfer tens of billions of dollars a year to the oil-exporting nations. The In-

ternational Institute for Strategic Studies in London says the Arabs'
successful use of the oil weapon is the greatest threat to world stability; it is the first time a group of largely nonindustrial states, using
an economic weapon, have in their grasp a means of bringing a collection of rich, developed nations to their knees—and playing havoc with
the developing countries as well. Harold Lever, economic adviser
to Britain's Prime Minister, thinks a major monetary disaster will
occur within 18 months if oil prices are not reduced.

Avoiding a disaster is a far more complex problem than simply
trying to coax or force the international oil cartel to lower its prices.
"It is no exaggeration to say that the world presently faces the most
difficult combination of economic policy decisions since the reconstruction period following World War II," says H. Johannes Witteveen,
managing director of the International Monetary Fund.[3] And if the
right decisions and actions are not taken, the worst economic disaster
that the world has experienced since the Great Depression of the 1930s
could now happen. To decide what must be done, we must understand
where we are and how we got here.

BACKGROUND OF THE PRESENT CRISIS

The monetary system that emerged after World War II was based
on fixed exchange rates between the dollar and all other currencies
and on the convertibility of the dollar into gold at $35 an ounce. That
system was founded on the economic strength of the United States.
The U.S. economy was not only unscarred by the war but was greatly
augmented by the United States' having served as the "arsenal of
democracy" and the safe haven for foreign assets. Immediately after
the war the United States held almost three-fourths of the monetary
reserves—primarily gold—of the capitalist world.

In the decades following the war the world economy and world
trade experienced the greatest period of growth in all history. But
the monetary system that underpinned that growth gradually weakened
as the dollar lost its strength as a result of continuous deficits in the
U.S. balance of payments. At first those deficits were deliberately
incurred, to pump out dollars and gold as an aid to world reconstruction. But it proved far more difficult than expected to end the chronic
U.S. payments deficits when, starting in the late 1950s, the United
States decided it wanted to get back into equilibrium. Part of the
problem was that the United States was carrying the heaviest share
of the Western world's aid and military burdens. At least as important was the fact that the dollar had become an "overvalued" currency:
At the official price of $35 to an ounce of gold, and in relation to other
currencies under the fixed exchange-rate system, the dollar was

really worth less than its official price. This hurt U.S. exports,
caused too great a volume of imports to be sucked in, and caused U.S.
investors, with their overvalued dollars, to buy foreign assets at bargain prices. And to cover its net foreign deficits the United States
paid with dollars. Foreigners screamed about dollar imperialism—
and about U.S. military imperialism, too. In fact, it was the Vietnam
war that signaled the doom of the world monetary system built on the
dollar and fixed exchange rates. It did this by accelerating the outflow
of dollars to pay for the war in Southeast Asia and, even more seriously, by unleashing U.S. inflation. It had been hard enough to get other
nations to hold tens of billions of dollars as reserves as the chronic
deficits went on year after year, but when governments and businesses
abroad began to lose faith in the dollar as a stable currency, the end
was near.

It came during the Nixon administration as a result of economic
mismanagement. The Nixon economic policy started out cautiously,
depending on slow monetary growth to bring down the rate of inflation
without causing a recession. But when the recession that was not supposed to happen did happen in 1969-70 and the economy continued to
drag along well into 1971, Nixon decided to go for broke with the con-
gressional election of 1972 looming up ahead. Nixon was eager to
win big to secure the foundations of what in those days was called his
"New American Revolution."

Both fiscal and monetary policy were too expansive, and the inflationary spiral received a severe twist that the price controls adopted
as part of Nixon's New Economic Policy (NEP) could not hold. Indeed,
domestic U.S. inflation received a major push from the successive
devaluations of the U.S. dollar, starting in December 1971. Many
U.S. economists have tended to underestimate the inflationary impact
of dollar devaluation, since they have believed that only import prices
would be affected, and U.S. imports constitute only about 5 percent
of the GNP.

EFFECTS OF DEVALUATION

But dollar devaluation raises the dollar prices of all internationally traded (exportable as well as importable) goods. This increase comes immediately in the case of food and raw materials,
more gradually in the case of manufactured products. "Here," says
Randall Hinshaw, "one must distinguish between purely momentary
and lasting price effects." He points out that in the case of dollar
devaluation, the price of U.S. beef, for example, for a short time
is reduced for foreign purchasers (converting their yen or marks into
dollars) below the prices for beef prevailing elsewhere: "This means

that U.S. beef is selling at a terrific bargain. And of course what happens is that meat brokers immediately come in and buy all their beef from the United States until the price of U.S. beef is in line with beef prices elsewhere. Thus the dollar price of beef rapidly goes up. We could see that happening before our eyes early last year [1973], and the same thing happened in the case of soybeans and other primary products."[4] An even more dramatic example might be the incursion of Japanese buyers into the U.S. art market, bidding up prices to levels that wiped out (and more than wiped out, since speculative buying often overshoots the mark) the effect of the devaluation on prices. In the case of manufactured goods, the lagged effect of the devaluation on price may be longer; but in 1974 General Motors, Ford, and Chrysler boosted car prices, attributing it to big increases in raw-material costs.

Nevertheless, the devaluation of the dollar was inevitable after the U.S. balance of payments really got out of control in the early 1970s. In the 1950s and 1960s, U.S. payments deficits had averaged less than $2 billion annually, but in 1970 the deficit soared to $10 billion, and in 1971 to $30 billion. That wrecked the world monetary system put together at Bretton Woods in 1944, based on fixed exchange rates between the dollar and other currencies, with the dollar itself yoked to gold. The United States formally ended convertibility of the dollar into gold on August 15, 1971, as another crucial element in Nixon's NEP.

The United States and other major countries tried to hang on to the fixed-rate system, however, for many months after Nixon slammed the gold window shut. The first devaluation of the dollar at the Smithsonian Institution in Washington in December 1971 (the "greatest monetary agreement in the history of the world,"[5] Nixon termed it) was supposed to be a one-shot realignment of exchange rates that would let the fixed-rate system survive.

"BENIGN NEGLECT"

Nixon and his economic chiefs made no real attempt to defend those Smithsonian rates, however; U.S. policy was still dominated by the concept of "benign neglect." The United States continued to pump billions of dollars out to the rest of the world to settle its deficits, and other countries, struggling to maintain fixed exchange rates with the dollar and among themselves, took those dollars into their monetary reserves, paying out national currencies to those private businesses and bankers that were accumulating the excess dollars. The result was worsening inflation in Europe and Japan.

Yet nations clung to the fixed-rate system until they were literally drowned in a hemorrhage of dollars. In January 1973 what had begun as a barely noticed flow of funds from Italian lire into Swiss francs (as rich Italians, fearful of Communist strikes, moved funds out of the country) suddenly became a raging dollar crisis when the Swiss, worrying about inflation resulting from the influx of funds, floated their franc. Billions of dollars in the hands of speculators, oil sheikhs, multinational corporations, and some foreign central banks then went pouring into West Germany.

The German central bank paid out billions of marks in exchange for dollars in a vain effort to prevent the mark's exchange rate from rising, until fears of inflation from flooding their economy with marks at last caused German officials to yield. The mark floated up. And the dollar floated down. The whole world monetary system was afloat, and the Bretton Woods system was dead.

But did the end of the fixed-rate system, so important a culprit in the propagation of world inflation, mean the end of inflation? Certainly not in the short run. Indeed, its immediate effect was to heighten inflation and inflationary fears. The further depreciation of the dollar accelerated price inflation in the United States, worsened the lack of confidence in the dollar (still the world's key currency in the absence of any other to take on that function), and hastened the flight from all paper currencies into gold and other commodities.

The free-market gold price, at $65 an ounce before the world currency float, soared as high as $190 an ounce. But the price of gold itself was anything but stable in highly speculative trading, and Johnny-come-latelies have been hurt as the gold price has plunged below various theoretical support levels.

In the rush away from currencies and paper securities of all kinds, prices of many other commodities—cocoa, cotton, wheat, lead, copper, rubber, sisal, sugar, soybeans—have soared. In some instances, particular events—such as the huge U.S. wheat deal with the Soviet Union, poor weather, and the celebrated disappearance of the anchovies off the west coast of South America—worsened the commodity inflation. But the overall trend was no fluke: The overall index of commodity prices doubled from January to October 1973.

And then came the Yom Kippur war, and the first use of the oil weapon.

THE OIL WEAPON

The use of the oil weapon was obviously motivated partly by military and political factors—it was a means of bringing pressure on the United States, Western Europe, and Japan to support the Arab cause against Israel. But it was also economic, and the fact that Iran, an ally of the United States, took the lead in pushing for the highest possible oil prices emphasizes its economic motivation. All the oil producers sincerely want to be rich.

Was the use of the oil weapon, then, essentially a consequence of the unleashing of worldwide inflation? It seems clear, on chronological grounds alone, that it was. Without the skyrocketing of other commodity prices, bringing pressure on the oil producers to raise their prices to protect their terms of trade, and without the worldwide inflationary boom that was putting pressure on supplies of fuel and raw materials, there might have been no oil weapon.

However, the initial oil embargo, cuttingthe world supply of oil by nearly one-fourth at its height, opened the way to a greater and more devastating increase in oil prices than would otherwise have occurred. The price of a barrel of oil in the Persian Gulf before the Arab-Israeli war averaged $2.10; after the war it averaged nearly $8.00. This translates into an increase of approximately $70 billion in the oil bills of the importing countries in 1974 alone. In 1975, if the price holds, these extra payments for oil will rise to about $90 billion, and by 1980 they may be as high as $150 billion. Cumulatively, the extra revenues flowing to the oil-producing countries could exceed three-quarters of a trillion dollars by 1980.

The impact of these higher oil bills creates an enormous shock to the world economy—a shock that is both inflationary and contractionary. As Richard Cooper of Yale has noted in another part of this book, [6] oil producers had levied a $70 billion excise tax on the rest of the world. On one side, this tax, paid to foreigners, has a contractionary effect, since it forces the oil-importing countries to reduce their demand for other goods (and incidentally reduces their real living standards to pay for more expensive oil). The cut in total demand for other goods will not be made up by higher demands on the part of the Arabs and other oil-exporting countries, which have too little population and too little absorptive capacity to make up the difference by raising their imports in equal amount from the oil-consuming countries. Simultaneously, the oil price increase is inflationary in increasing production costs in the West. In addition, the huge oil bills and payments deficits are likely to constitute a powerful pressure, open or concealed, upon the oil importers to increase their own prices to cover their deficits. This phenomenon is what some economists call "the thousand-dollar cat for the thousand-dollar dog."

The drain of oil money to the Arabs and others may also choke off much productive investment in the West. There is a feeling in the banking community, for instance, that there is a major danger ahead, because the unspent balances of OPEC countries are different from the big holdings of the Germans or the Japanese. The OPEC holdings, it is believed, will be largely removed from the productive, long-term investment process. Because OPEC nations lack domestic economies large enough to absorb more than a minor fraction of their investable funds, the world will be thrown into a state of monetary and economic disequilibrium. The system can simply break down. Those nations with the most serious balance-of-payments deficits will be incapable of paying their bills, and will have to block off imports or default on their foreign debts. Private financial and nonfinancial institutions can be caught in a severe squeeze, unable to pay their obligations. If two or more countries now find themselves in credit trouble simultaneously, says Charles Kindleberger, a "liquidity crisis of the 1890, 1907, 1921 or 1929 type could reappear."[7]

What outcomes are possible? The futurologists have taught us to write various "scenarios" as a way of clarifying the possibilities, so some scenarios follow.

HYPERINFLATION

World inflation can worsen, as every group in different societies —labor, businesses, landlords, farmers—races to catch up with inflation and governments run the printing presses faster in order to retain for themselves the same (or a larger) share of national resources. But the "double-digit" inflation in the United States, Europe, and Japan is very far from true hyperinflation. A hyperinflation is one in which prices increase at a rate in excess of 50 percent per month—or 41 percent per month, compounded continuously. Cagan has calculated the average monthly rate of seven past hyperinflations as follows:[8]

		Percent
Austria	October 1921 to August 1922	47.1
Germany	August 1922 to November 1923	322.0
Greece	November 1943 to November 1944	365.0
Hungary	March 1923 to February 1924	46.0
Hungary	August 1945 to July 1946	19,800.0
Poland	January 1923 to January 1924	81.4
USSR	December 1921 to January 1924	57.0

Clearly, the most famous hyperinflation, Germany's in 1922-23, was not the worst. That dubious honor goes to Hungary, after World War II, with a 19,800 percent monthly rise. Fortunately, Hungary is known for its great mathematicians.

However, what strikes one about all the past hyperinflations is that they came in the wake of wars and revolutions. The social upheaval (with the breakdown in the supply of goods attendant on past hy-

perinflations) seems unlikely at present in major countries of the
West.

BOOM AND BUST

Inflation may boil on a while longer, but, finally, the pile of
credit will fall down, as in 1929. Government and the monetary author
ities of the Federal Reserve System could cause it by cracking down
too hard.

Alan Greenspan suggests that "one danger is a world financial
crisis following the failures of one or more of the major Eurocurrency
banks as a result of borrowers in oil importing countries defaulting on
their loans." A second danger, he warns, is that oil-importing countries "will attempt to avert the consequences of the shift in real income implied by the dramatic change in oil prices and in the process
exacerbate their already very difficult inflation problems."[9] If such
a situation were not to lead to hyperinflation, however, eventually a
credit crunch and severe recession would be highly probable.

Such recessions could spread from country to country, as nations moved from free-trade policies to protectionism. Some nations
would band together into tight regional blocs to cut themselves off
from outside disturbances, but the net effect of this would be to reduce
economic efficiency, reduce world income and growth, and probably
breed both political and economic conflicts among nations and in the
process expose the Western nations to risks of expansion or hegemony
from the Communist powers. The three most likely blocs outside the
Communist bipolar world of the Soviet Union and the PRC would be
ones centered on the United States, Western Europe, and Japan. Presumably each would bid for special relationships with various developing countries.

The above scenario might also be called "The 1930s Revisited,"
although, one hopes, in somewhat milder form, and without World
War II as its crowning glory.

BUMPY BUT SAFE LANDING

This scenario sees the world economy working itself back into
reasonable equilibrium by a combination of jarring adjustments. One
of the most crucial of these would be lower oil prices (if not in absolute terms, then in "real terms")—that is, in relation to other prices.
The latter course implies that world inflation still has a way to go,
until the industrialized countries of the West and the oil-poor developing countries have adequate time to raise their own prices more or

less up to the level of oil prices. To be sure, the oil producers are not going to like this, and the adjustment process may instead become an ongoing world inflationary spiral.

A second element in the struggle toward equilibrium must be a recycling of oil money to the oil-importing countries. To some extent this will happen through the natural workings of the private capital markets. But it will have to be facilitated by governments and international agencies, especially to be sure that the weakest countries, such as India, Pakistan, Bangladesh, and others on the verge of starvation, do not collapse economically or are not driven to desperate military actions. The problem arises because the Arabs and other oil producers seem certain to lend or invest their surplus capital in some countries and not in others. So there will have to be secondary flows of capital among the oil-consuming countries, either privately or publicly, although it is far from sure yet that those secondary flows will take place, at least in adequate volume.

The third element required for a return to equilibrium would be a slowdown of inflation. But this could mean a slowing of world development and trade, and probably a plunging of many world commodity prices, carried to excesses by wild speculation. Most countries may prefer to follow a more inflationary course, rather than see their commodity prices collapse. Even a cautious optimist, Robert Solomon, warns that understanding how a gradual adjustment might take place "should not blind us to the serious disruptions caused by the higher oil price: these include impacts on prices in an inflation-ridden world, on aggregate demand, and on the structure of production and investment."[10]

How much cooperation there will be among the oil-importing nations remains in doubt. Relations among the United States, Europe, and Japan have been badly strained. The European Common Market itself is in disarray, its plans for monetary union all but wrecked. The developing nations, far from unified among themselves, are bitter toward the industrial nations and eager to imitate the oil-producing countries in forming price-boosting cartels.

A "new nationalism" is loose in the world. In the United States, Congress seems in no mood to "make sacrifices" for the rest of the world, and many other countries appear to be turning inward. However, Harold van Cleveland, a senior vice-president of the First National City Bank of New York, sees this new nationalism as passive and defensive, rather than demonic like the dangerous German and Japanese nationalism of the 1930s: The dependence of both Western Europe and Japan on U.S. military strength is a major source of his belief that the "new nationalism" will remain essentially passive rather than aggressive, according to this scenario.

WORLD WAR III?

If there should be a real breakdown in the world economy, the
new nationalism might be transformed into something like the old nationalism, with the present generation of leaders giving way to a new
generation of unimaginable Hitlers, who would arise to establish "order" over economic and political chaos and who would see utility in
foreign adventures.

After all, the nationalism of the 1920s was relatively passive.
It was out of the ruins of depression that the lizards of National Social-
ism, Fascism, and Co-Prosperity Spheres emerged. In what countries—rich or poor, capitalist or socialist—demonic nationalism may
yet develop this scenario does not say. But it is not beyond probability
to imagine some of the above scenarios leading to World War III. Is
the buildup of armaments in the Soviet Union and the United States,
the testing of a nuclear device in India, the heavy use of oil money by
Iran and the Arab states, and similar military preparations elsewhere
a recognition, conscious or unconscious, of where the world is heading?

There is a possible scenario that says that somehow everything
will work out. Is there a case for this view, apart from the familiar,
wishful interpretation of weekly or monthly economic indicators?
Some feel that crises usually find solutions: "It is always a mistake,"
says Greenspan, "to construct a hypothetical set of relationships and
project them to a point of irrevocable disaster. Such deterministic
forecasts invariably preclude countervailing forces which arise as a
crisis begins to unfold." For this reason he thinks "a solution will
develop," although he admits that it is difficult "not to view the future
with some trepidation."[11]

David I. Meiselman is optimistic about a coming slowdown in
world inflation. A monetarist—that is, a proponent of the doctrine
that inflation is a direct consequence of changes in the money supply—
Meiselman elsewhere in this book[12] blames the blowing up of the world
money supply via the mechanism of the old fixed-exchange rate monetary system for worldwide inflation.*

The abandonment of fixed exchange rates and shift to floating
rates in early 1973 made it unnecessary for central banks to go on
pouring masses of marks or yen or francs or other national currencies
into their economies to keep their exchange rates from rising against
the dollar. Thus inflation was made worldwide, rather than restricted
to particular countries. Now, he argues, the major countries can follow independent and less expansionary monetary policies, and have be-

*See Chapter 3 of this work.

gun to do so. In the nine principal members of the Organization for
Economic Cooperation and Development (OECD) other than the United
States, the average increase in the money supply has slowed down
from an annual rate of 25.9 percent in the fourth quarter of 1972 to
5.1 percent in the fourth quarter of 1973. However, there is about a
two-year time lag from changes in monetary growth to changes in the
price level. In the case of the United States, the money supply slowed
from an annual 7.3 percent in the fourth quarter of 1972 to 4 percent
in the fourth quarter of 1973 to rates approaching zero in the second
half of 1974. Nevertheless, as Meiselman says, his note of potential
optimism for the world inflation may have to be qualified for the
United States, since it may still not be "clear that the Federal Reserve
System has basically altered its highly expansionary policy" of recent
years."[13] However, Burns insists that the Federal Reserve will follow a firm and noninflationary policy, even though some increase in
unemployment would inevitably result; he would rather have an increase in public-service employment programs than substantially ease
money.

This all sounds solid and sensible, but the problem is not so
easily resolved. A restrictive monetary policy, in the midst of the
worst inflation the United States has experienced since World War I,
has put interest rates through the roof. The Stock Market has been
clobbered. Funds have been draining out of savings banks and savings
and loan institutions, and the housing industry has been badly hurt.
Electric utilities have been hit both by the high cost of oil and the high
cost of money. (Consolidated Edison, the largest electric utility in
the country, has passed a dividend and virtually cut itself off from
the equity market as a source of funds; New York State is rushing to
its rescue at a cost that may run to hundreds of millions.)

Many commercial banks are hard pressed to meet their obligations, having borrowed short and lent long. The Franklin National
Bank of New York, like Con Ed, passed its quarterly dividend, something no major bank had done since the Great Depression. The Franklin has been rescued by the Federal Reserve Bank of New York by an
infusion of over $1 billion.

Some economists fear that not just the Franklin but much of the
commercial banking system is in a fragile and potentially illiquid position. As recently as 1965 only 13 percent of the banks' total liabilities
were borrowed from the money markets and 62 percent came from demand and savings deposits; now those proportions are about 35 percent
and 45 percent, respectively. It has been getting more and more expensive, and riskier and riskier, for the commercial banks to go on borrowing short-term money to finance the loans and investments of their
customers—many of whom are also tightly strained for funds, thanks
to the inflation.

If the Federal Reserve keeps money too tight to check the inflation, it could send many institutions and companies to the wall. If
it eases money too much to prevent a widening disaster, it will keep
the inflation going. As Hyman Minsky puts it, the Fed must decide
whether to go on riding the tiger or jump off. Even the relative optimists do not find this a pleasant choice. In the attempt at a soft land-
ing one could be eaten by the tiger.

AVOIDING DISASTERS

Of course, the outcome is not preordained. All these scenarios—
and others as well—are possible. What actually happens will depend
on policies and actions still to be taken.

In my view, there is indeed the potentiality of a crash. Capitalism has a history of great instability; it is inherent in its structure
and functioning. After so long a period of expansion and inflation, a
major decline and depression would be a normal resolution of the
dangerous expansion of money and credit, and the serious imbalances
within and among nations.

But I also think that both runaway inflation and a crash can be
avoided. The elements essential to a reasonably successful resolution
of the crisis, in my view, are the following:

● A significant reduction in the price of oil, whether in absolute or
real terms—that is, relative to other prices. This would reduce to
more manageable proportions the payments deficits of the oil-importing countries. It would be far better if the price reductions were absolute and not only relative, since this would reduce the inflationary
pressures on oil-importing countries and the temptation to resort to
countervailing inflation as a means of getting back into equilibrium.
● Assistance from nations in balance or in surplus in their balance of
payments to those in heavy deficit (as from the United States after
World War II to the rest of the Western world). To a degree, private
capital markets can recycle oil producers' funds deposited, for instance, in New York, London, Frankfurt, or Tokyo, to deficit countries. But national governments and international bodies—not only the
International Monetary Fund (IMF) or the International Development
Association of the World Bank but new funds set up by the Arabs or
the Iranians—will have to help support those deficit countries in greatest need and for that reason least credit worthy. If the Arabs and
Iranians hesitate to lend their money long term in the West, this will
create serious problems, since the recipient countries and financial
institutions would then have to go on borrowing short—from the Arabs
and Iranians—and lending long to nations with huge balance-of-payments

deficits. In the past, such practices would have been regarded as too risky. But in the future, financial institutions and governments in the West may have to take such risks, on the assumption that the oil-exporting countries will have to leave much of their capital somewhere in the West (invested at short term, but continuously turning over) and that it may be riskier to the world economy not to lend to the poor, deficit-ridden countries than to help finance them.

● The assurance of long-term stable markets for the oil-poor developing countries at fair prices. This is likely to involve negotiating commodity agreements. It may also be desirable to link foreign aid to new issues of Special Drawing Rights (SDRs), which would become the principal monetary reserve medium of the new world monetary system. World monetary order cannot be achieved without special measures to help the poor. And world political order can certainly not be attained without efforts to rescue them from stagnation and starvation.

● A set of rules for the world monetary system, which is in process of evolving. Currencies should continue to float (an effort to return to fixed rates now would be an inflationary disaster), but there must be rules for floating so that exchange rates will not be driven up or down to unrealistic levels by market forces or prevented from moving into balance by unwarranted government intervention. One specific proposal for new rules would be to set or permit each nation itself to announce a new structure of exchange rates, which would be periodically adjusted in response to market forces, but during each period of time, no national central bank would be allowed to sell its currency when it should fall below its "reference rate," and no central bank would be allowed to buy its own currency when it should rise above its "reference rate." In other words, central banks could stabilize against market forces but not reverse them.

Recognition of the fact that, at its roots, inflation is a national problem—to an alarming degree a problem originating in the United States, which is still the most important economy in the world. It is difficult to envision a stable world economy without a stable U.S. economy.

The U.S. government has been irresponsible in its conduct of economic policy, running excessively large deficits in periods of high employment, flooding its own economy with money—and that of the rest of the world, too, through the huge deficits and outflows of dollars under the old fixed-rate exchange system. The avoidance of a repetition of the frightful events that led to depression in the 1930s will require an act of political will and economic creativity in the United States and in conjunction with its allies. If it is not forthcoming, the consequences could be a splitting up into regional economic blocs, economic stagnation, worse inflation, and, finally, a financial breakdown, followed in all probability by some as yet unimaginable political disaster. Never has the need been greater for enlightened and energetic U.S. leadership, close cooperation with other nations, and the united action that was so lacking in the 1920s and 1930s.

NOTES

1. Arthur F. Burns, in a speech given at the 141st Commencement Exercise, Illinois College, Jacsonville, Illinois, May 26, 1974.
2. Ashby Bladen, in a speech, "Management of Funds: The Middle 1970's," for the National Industrial Conference Board Seminar, June 6, 1974.
3. H. Johannes Witteveen, in a speech, "Recycling the Oil Billions," at the Economic Club of Detroit, May 6, 1974.
4. See Chapter 5 by Randall Hinshaw.
5. Richard M. Nixon, in a speech given for the International Monetary Conference at the Smithsonian Institution, Washington, D.C., December 17, 1971.
6. See Chapter 12 by Richard Cooper.
7. Charles Kindleberger, "Why World Bankers Are Worried," in Challenge, November 1974.
8. "Monetary Dynamics of Hyperinflations," in Studies in the Quantity Theory of Money, by Milton Fredman, ed., University of Chicago Press, 1957.
9. Alan Greenspan, Business Outlook, published by Greenspan and Co., New York, 1974.
10. Robert Solomon, in a speech, "The Oil Price Impact on the International Monetary System," at the 1974 International Accounting Conference, New York, May 13, 1974.
11. Greenspan, Business Outlook.
12. See Chapter 3 by David Meiselman.
13. See Meiselman, op. cit.

ABOUT THE EDITORS
AND CONTRIBUTORS

PATRICK M. BOARMAN, Executive Director, Institute for Economic and Legal Analysis, New York. He previously served as Director of Research and Senior Economist of the Center for International Business, Pepperdine University. Dr. Boarman was Professor of Economics on the faculties of the University of Wisconsin, Long Island University, Bucknell University, and the University of Geneva (Switzerland). Other experience includes economic consultantships with the Office of the Secretary of the Treasury, the World Trade Institute (New York), the General Electric Company, the American Telephone and Telegraph Company, and the U.S. House of Representatives.

Dr. Boarman is the author of numerous books and articles in the field of international economics, including Germany's Economic Dilemma—Inflation and the Balance of Payments (New Haven, Conn.: Yale University Press, 1964) and The World's Money (Lewisburg, Pa.: Bucknell University, 1965). He is the recipient of many awards in the United States and abroad for his scholarly contributions, including the Distinguished Service Cross of the Order of Merit of the Federal Republic of Germany. He holds undergraduate and graduate degrees from Fordham University and Columbia University, and the Ph.D. in economics from the Graduate Institute of International Economics of the University of Geneva.

DAVID G. TUERCK is Director, Center for Research on Advertising, American Enterprise Institute for Public Policy Research. He was previously Director of Research, Center for International Business, Pepperdine University, where he served at the time of his work on this volume. He is co-author (with Leland Yeager) of Trade Policy and the Price System (New York: Intext Publishers, 1966).

ARTHUR I. BLOOMFIELD has been Professor of Economics at the University of Pennsylvania since 1958. Previously, he served as economist with the Federal Reserve Bank of New York, and as visiting Professor of Economics at Johns Hopkins University, Princeton University, the City University of New York, and the University of Melbourne. Dr. Bloomfield received his Ph.D. from the University of Chicago. He has served as a consultant to a number of U.S. government agencies and commissions and international organizations and is the author of numerous books, monographs, and articles on international finance and monetary policy, including Monetary Policy Under the International Gold Standard, 1880-1914 (New York: Federal Reserve Bank of New York, 1959).

RICHARD N. COOPER is Professor of International Economics at Yale University. He has served as Senior Staff Economist to the Council of Economic Advisers, as Deputy Assistant Secretary of State for International Monetary Affairs, and is consultant to the National Security Council. He is the author of several major works, including The Economics of Interdependence (New York: McGraw Hill, 1968) and Currency Devaluation in Developing Countries (Princeton, N.J.: Princeton University Press, 1971).

WILFRED J. ETHIER is Professor of Economics, University of Pennsylvania. He received his Ph.D. in economics from the University of Rochester and is the author of numerous articles dealing with international economics.

HENRY N. GOLDSTEIN is Professor of Economics, University of Oregon. He has served as Staff Economist with the Board of Governors, Federal Reserve System, and has published many articles on balance-of-payment questions and forward exchange operations.

RANDALL HINSHAW is Professor of Economics at the Claremont Graduate School. He has served as Economist with the Division of International Finance, the Federal Reserve Board, and also as adviser on trade and international monetary problems with the U.S. Mission to NATO. He serves as the Director of the well-known Bologna-Claremont series of biennial international monetary conferences, and is the author of distinguished works in the field of international economics including The European Community and American Trade: A Study in Atlantic Economics and Policy and Monetary Reform and the Price of Gold.

DONALD L. KEMMERER is Professor of Economics (emeritus) at the University of Illinois, Urbana. He is President of the Committee for Monetary Research and Education, Inc. He has served as a consultant with the Organization for Economic Cooperation and Development and has lectured on international finance and American economic history at the University of Montpellier, at Munich University, and at the University of Melbourne. Dr. Kemmerer has written a number of books in his field, including (with C. Clyde Jones) American Economic History (New York: McGraw Hill Co., 1959).

STEVEN W. KOHLHAGEN did his undergraduate work at the College of William and Mary and received his Ph.D. in economics from Stanford University in 1974. He is currently Associate Professor of International Business and Applied Economics in the Schools of Business at the University of California, Berkeley. His publications in various journals deal with direct foreign investment in the Pacific Basin, the effect of exchange-rate changes on direct investment, and the performance of the foreign exchange markets in the current floating regime.

MIROSLAV A. KRIZ is a retired Vice-President of the First National City Bank of New York (1958 to 1973). Previously, he served on the staff of the Federal Reserve Bank of New York and was a member of the Economic and Financial Department of the Secretariat of the League of Nations. Born in Czechoslovakia, he was educated in France and has a Ph.D. from the University of Paris. Mr. Kriz is a regular contributor to the Britannica Book of the Year and to the Encyclopedia Americana of articles on the gold standard, international finance, and so on. He is the author of numerous articles in scholarly and popular journals on international monetary problems.

ARTHUR B. LAFFER is Associate Professor at the Graduate School of Business, University of Chicago. He is a consultant to the Secretary of the Treasury and to a number of leading business organizations. Previously, Dr. Laffer was an economist with the U.S. Office of Management and Budget, and a research associate at the Brookings Institution. He is the author of many articles on monetary policy and balance-of-payments issues in leading journals. More recently, he has attracted considerable attention in both academic and government circles as the result of his advocacy of fixed exchange rates, based on his findings that flexible rates contribute to the aggravation of worldwide inflation.

ALFRED MATTER is Senior Vice-President and head of the Economics Department of the Swiss Bank Corporation, Basel. Mr. Matter studied law and economics in Switzerland, then entered diplomatic service, specializing in commercial financial questions. He is recognized as an authority on the role of gold.

DAVID I. MEISELMAN is Professor of Economics at Virginia Polytechnic Institute and the State University at Reston. He was previously Professor of Economics at Macalester College and Associate Editor of the National Banking Review. His publications include The Term Structure of Interest Rates and The Measurement of Corporate Sources and Uses of Funds.

YOON S. PARK is with the International Bank for Reconstruction and Development (The World Bank), in charge of capital market research. He has written widely in the areas of capital markets and international finance. Dr. Park was educated in Korea and in the United States and holds the D.B.A. in international finance from the Graduate School of Business Administration, Harvard University. He is the author of many publications in his special fields of interest including The Euro-Bond Market (New York: Praeger Publishers, 1974).

ROBERT L. SAMMONS is an economic consultant who previously served as Associate Director of International Finance of the Federal Reserve Board of Governors, and as Director of the Balance of Payments Division of the Department of Commerce.

NICHOLAS P. SARGEN holds graduate degrees in economics from the University of California, Berkeley, and Stanford University. Currently, he is acting Assistant Director for Policy Research with the U.S. Treasury; previously, he taught at the University of Santa Clara, among other institutions, and was a consultant at Stanford Research Institute.

WILSON E. SCHMIDT is Professor and head of the Department of Economics, Virginia Polytechnic Institute and State University. Previously, he served as Deputy Assistant Secretary for Research, U.S. Treasury, as Professor at the Johns Hopkins University Bologna Center, and at the George Washington University, where he held the rank of Professor and Chairman. He holds a Ph.D. in economics from the University of Virginia and has served as a consultant to numerous government agencies, private foundations, and international organizations. Dr. Schmidt is a prolific writer on international economic questions for scholarly journals, as well as for the popular press, and he has served in editorial capacities with several leading economic journals.

LEONARD SILK is a Member of the Editorial Board of the New York Times, and a specialist in economics reporting for that newspaper. Formerly, he was Chairman of the Editorial Board of Business Week magazine. He has been a Senior Fellow at the Brookings Institution and is the author of Contemporary Economics (New York: McGraw Hill, 1970), and Capitalism: The Moving Target (New York: Quadrangle Books, 1974).

PAUL A. VOLCKER was appointed President of the Federal Reserve Bank of New York in 1975, having previously served as Undersecretary of the Treasury for Monetary Affairs since January

1969. Mr. Volcker has degrees from Princeton and Harvard universities. Following his graduation from Harvard, Mr. Volcker spent a number of years as an economist with the Federal Reserve Bank of New York. In 1957, he accepted a position as Financial Economist of the Chase Manhattan Bank. In 1962, Mr. Volcker was appointed Director of Financial Analysis of the U.S. Treasury, and in 1963 as Deputy Undersecretary for Monetary Affairs by Secretary C. Douglas Dillon. In late 1965, he returned to Chase Manhattan Bank, where he was Vice-President and Director of Forward Planning at the time he was appointed Undersecretary.

THOMAS D. WILLETT is Deputy Assistant Secretary for International Affairs, U.S. Treasury. Previously, he was Professor of Economics and Public Affairs at the Graduate School of Business, Cornell University. He has also served on the faculties of Harvard University, the University of Virginia, and the Fletcher School of Law and Diplomacy, Tufts University. He holds a Ph.D. in economics from the University of Virginia and is the author of many books and articles concerned with international and economic issues. Dr. Willett has served as editor and/or member of the editorial board of Public Policy, The Quarterly Journal of Economics, The Review of Economics and Statistics, and The Journal of Economics and Business. He was a member of the Burgenstock Group, studying greater flexibility of exchange rates, 1969-70.

LELAND B. YEAGER holds a Ph.D. from Columbia University and is Paul Goodloe McIntire Professor of Economics, University of Virginia. He is author and/or editor of numerous works in the field of international economics, including International Monetary Relations (New York: Harper & Row, 1966). Dr. Yeager is currently President of the Southern Economic Association.

JACK ZWICK is Professor of Business and Director of International Business Programs, the George Washington University. Previously, Dr. Zwick was Vice-President and Partner, E. M. Warburg, Pincus and Co., Director of the World Trade Institute, World Trade Center (New York), and Professor of International Business, Columbia University. He is the author (with David Zinoff) of International Financial Management (New Jersey: Prentice-Hall, 1969).

ENERGY, INFLATION, AND INTERNATIONAL
ECONOMIC RELATIONS (Atlantic Institute
Studies—II)
                    Curt Gasteyger, Louis Camu,
                    and Jack N. Behrman

INTERNATIONAL FINANCIAL MARKETS: Development of the Present System and Future Prospects
                    Francis A. Lees and
                    Maximo Eng

INFLATION: Long-Term Problems
                    edited by Lowell C. Harriss

MONEY AND FINANCE IN CONTEMPORARY
YUGOSLAVIA
                    Dimitrije Dimitrijevic
                    and George Macesich